Annie's War

Annie's War

A New Zealand woman and her family
in England 1916–19

The Diaries of Annie Montgomerie

Edited by
Susanna Montgomerie Norris
with Anna Rogers

OTAGO

DEDICATION

This book is dedicated to Annie and Roger's great-grandchildren,
Hew, Jane, Belinda, Edward, Debbie, David, Richard, Meredith
and Hayden.

Published by Otago University Press
P.O. Box 56 / Level 1, 398 Cumberland Street
Dunedin, New Zealand
university.press@otago.ac.nz
www.otago.ac.nz

First published in 2014
Text © 2014 Susanna Montgomerie Norris

The moral rights of the author have been asserted.

ISBN 978-1-877578-75-5

A catalogue record for this book is available from the
National Library of New Zealand.

This book is copyright. Except for the purpose of fair review, no part
may be stored or transmitted in any form or by any means, electronic or
mechanical, including recording or storage in any information retrieval
system, without permission in writing from the publishers.

Front cover: Brothers Seton (left) and Os, with mother Annie

Publisher: Rachel Scott
Editor: Anna Rogers
Page design and page layout: Quentin Wilson
Index: Robin Briggs
Printed in China through Asia Pacific Offset

CONTENTS

Acknowledgements		6
Foreword		8
Preface		10
Editor's Note		12
Chapter One:	The Voyage	13
Chapter Two:	Arrival in England	21
Chapter Three:	Seton in Uniform	29
Chapter Four:	The Move to '40'	44
Chapter Five:	Another Year of War	59
Chapter Six:	Death from the Sky	98
Chapter Seven:	Seton Goes to France	129
Chapter Eight:	1918	137
Chapter Nine:	Seton Gets a 'Blighty'	163
Chapter Ten:	Holiday in Devon	169
Chapter Eleven:	Armistice	189
Chapter Twelve:	1919	202
Chapter Thirteen:	Last Days	228
Chapter Fourteen:	Going Home	236
Epilogue		245
Index		247

ACKNOWLEDGEMENTS

My first thanks must go to my grandmother, Annie, without whom this book would not have happened, and to my Aunts Winifred, Alex and Beryl, who kept her diaries and memorabilia. My very great thanks to my cousin, John Montgomerie, who first showed me the diaries 13 years ago, and has provided such wonderful background material and photos. I am delighted that we have been able to talk over and share so much of this family story.

This book would never have come to fruition without the enthusiasm and invaluable help of Glyn Harper, Professor of War Studies at Massey University, whom my husband Mike and I first visited in 2012. Glyn has really been part of the team.

Anna Rogers is a wonderful editor, who has assisted me through many ups and downs. Her footnotes add so much interest to the book and she knows how to edit and yet keep the essence of the text. My heartfelt thanks, Anna. *Annie's War* owes so much to you.

I am grateful to Rachel Scott, the publisher at Otago University Press, whose guidance and help have brought the book to print. My thanks, also, to all her team.

I thank my son Hew and sister Egidia for their ongoing support, and Joan Rosier Jones, who gave me so much guidance and backing in the early years. Anita Miller helped to type out the diaries over four years of deciphering spidery writing. Scott Flutey helped me to see how the computer made all this possible, and when the computer appeared to have lost it, Jordan Rees came to the rescue. Thank you all.

Hinemoa and Ed Boyd and the staff at H & A Print were most helpful in dealing with the manuscript pages as they came through from Anna and did the binding for me. Lesley and Rochelle at Paige's Book Gallery in Wanganui have always shown great enthusiasm for this book, and the staff at Aramaho

Acknowledgements

Books and Lotto organised the safe couriering of 100-year-old photos and documents to Dunedin.

Thanks, also, to my friend, chemist Sue Gardener, who spent hours checking the drastic-sounding medications Annie used to treat her family and herself, to Lloyd Hook in Temuka, who made great efforts to check out the family of Fergie, who features so much in the diaries, and to Geof Elston at Timaru Boys' High, where Fergie went to school.

Patrick Jones in the United Kingdom, who had two grandfathers who were First World War pilots, very kindly organised a website for my father Seton's diaries and letters. My husband and I really appreciated meeting him in London on two occasions. Felicity Campbell, a local historian, gave support. Evelyn Williames supplied the photo of her grandfather, John Tilley, a second cousin who gave Annie so much support and comfort in terrible times. Friends who have always taken an interest in the project include Val Cowan, Michelle Watson and Cynthia and Ken Henderson. Thank you all.

Finally, I give many, many thanks to my ever supportive and computer literate husband, Mike. He helped me to decipher and type out the diaries, and together we visited so many of the places mentioned in this book. Without Mike this book would have never been completed.

Susanna Montgomerie Norris
June 2014

FOREWORD

Annie's War is a special book. It presents the reader with not only the forthright views of an articulate and intelligent woman during the First World War, but the history of a New Zealand family in those hard years. This unique volume is a tribute to Susanna Norris's dedication in preserving her family records and to her determination to have her grandmother's remarkable diaries published. Otago University Press is also to be congratulated for producing a very different type of publication on New Zealand and the First World War.

When Roger and Annie Montgomerie leave New Zealand with their four children in June 1916, bound for London, they have no idea what is ahead of them. The intention is that the two boys, Oswald and Seton, will enlist and that possibly 50-year-old Roger may take the King's shilling too. Many trials and tribulations lie ahead but the family soon finds itself at the centre of world events. The Montgomeries are in Britain during the frequent nightly Zeppelin raids and witness two 'Zepps' being shot down. They are caught up in the spy mania sweeping the land. Annie observes, with sharp criticism, the numerous London prostitutes targeting the well-heeled Anzac soldiers. She records the daylight bombing raids on the city. The Montgomeries not only witness the deadly influenza virus of 1918 sweep the land but members of the family soon fall victim to it. And Annie's diary records it all.

At the heart of Annie's war, though, is her overwhelming concern for two sons on active service. Both Oswald and Seton eventually join the Royal Flying Corps as pilots. This was a dangerous occupation, especially the actual process of obtaining one's 'wings'. More RFC pilots were killed in training accidents than through enemy action. Both boys have some narrow scrapes and one is wounded while serving on the Western Front with his squadron.

Several themes emerge from Annie's writings but three are especially evident. The first is her hatred of the war, which is taking the lives of so many fine young men and women. After watching a film about tanks on 6 February 1917, she writes in her diary: 'The pictures were very good but sad and depressing to me anyhow. I hate war with all its cruelties and injustices.' In December 1917, when her youngest son Seton is about to depart for the Western Front, at only 19 years of age, Annie echoes what many mothers must have felt: 'My precious baby boy going to France tomorrow. I'm just stupid and headachy and stunned.'

A second powerful theme is Annie's, and the rest of the family's, growing sense of national identity. They are proud to be New Zealanders and soon realise that they are different from the English. As Annie states, shortly after her arrival in Britain: 'Little NZ doesn't need to stand aside for anything.' She complains bitterly about English arrogance, muddle and incompetence, and is very vocal about the many fine qualities of people from New Zealand, Australia and the other colonies. On 12 July 1917 Annie writes:

> One can't help compare this English leisure-loving life with our more earnest one. These people don't know what discomfort is; they don't dream of such lives of grind as ours are. But our race is a finer one than theirs – looks, brains, physique and, I believe, self-respect.

At the end of the war she is sick of Britain and cannot wait to return home. It is now a 'rotten country' and the people there 'grabbing wasters'.

The overriding theme of this book, though, is the importance of family. For Annie the family is her world and she will do anything to keep it together. Early in her diary, she records that most women on board the ship taking the Montgomeries to Britain are on their way to join soldier husbands and that this 'magnet seems universally potent' (3 July 1916). A month later she notes during a lifeboat drill: 'Families are not to be separated so I am happier.' War is usually the great destroyer of families but, for the Montgomeries from Wanganui, this terrible conflict brings them closer together.

Annie's War and the story of the Montgomerie family is a small part of the diverse experience of New Zealand and the First World War, but it details an unusual and critical time. This is history as lived at the heart of world events during the years 1916–19. It makes compelling reading and reveals much of what it was like to be so far from home and facing great risks almost every day.

Glyn Harper
Professor of War Studies, Massey University,
Palmerston North
2014

PREFACE

Waitaki Boys' High School,
August 9th, 1914

Dear Mother and Dad,

You seem very perturbed about the war. I tell you I don't care a scrap for the Germans and all their battleships. You need not entertain the slightest fears as to the result of the war, and trouble that might come off out in the Pacific.

To take the ecclesiastical view of the matter as you ought to see for yourself; the Germans are in the wrong and do you believe the wrong will win? And has it ever won? …

Surely you put your trust in the British Empire and what it stands for, and worry your head off…

These words were written by 16-year-old Seton Montgomerie from his boarding school in Oamaru. Two years later he and his older brother Oswald were on their way to England to join the armed forces. But they would not be far from loved ones. Their mother Annie, my grandmother, had decided that if her boys were going to fight, then the whole family would go to support them.

Both she and her husband, Roger Arnulph Montgomerie, were the children of Scots immigrants who sailed into Dunedin's Port Chalmers late in 1862. Annie's people, the Masons, came from the Glasgow region, Roger's from near Irvine in Ayrshire. Annie was born in 1867, Roger in 1866. The couple did not meet until the 1880s, and then in the North Island, because the Mason family settled up the Mangawhero River, out of Wanganui, and Roger's family in the Makirikiri Valley near the town. From 1871 the Masons carved a farm out of remote, dense bush towards the central mountainous plateau; my great-grandmother, also Annie, did not go into town for nine years. In 1887 Roger Montgomerie was given the lease of a farm named Taukoro, from a stream that runs through it, which lay even further inland, in this region of steep, rugged bush-clad hills.

A family of four was born after Roger and Annie married on 27 April 1893: Annie Hylda Winifred, known as Winifred (or Wid or Tiny), in 1894, Roger Oswald (known as Oswald or Os) in 1896, Hew Seton (known as Seton) in 1898 and Sybil Alexandra (known as Alex or Al) in 1902. When the Montgomeries set off for the other side of the world in June 1916, a manager, A.E. Barron, known as Ernest, was engaged to care for Taukoro.

For four years from the beginning of the voyage, Annie Montgomerie kept a diary that gives a unique day-to-day insight into those years of war for one New Zealand family.

Susanna Montgomerie Norris

EDITOR'S NOTE

Not all the entries in Annie's very comprehensive diaries have been used; a selection has been made to tell the family's story and to convey the atmosphere of their life in wartime London. Annie's spelling and punctuation have been left as they are in the original diaries, with occasional emendations for the sake of clarity. From August 1916 letters from Annie's son, Seton, also form part of the narrative. Where prices appear in square brackets, Annie wrote them in the margin of the diary.

The footnotes help to fill in the gaps for modern readers. For these a variety of sources was used. Among the most useful were the National Library's Papers Past site (www.paperspast.natlib.govt.nz), the Auckland Museum's Cenotaph database (muse.aucklandmuseum.com), Archives New Zealand's Archway site (www.archway.archives.govt.nz),the multimedia website www.firstworldwar.com, 'Lost Hospitals of London' on www.ezitis.myzen.co.uk, and The National Archives (www.nationalarchives.gov.uk). For Roger Montgomerie's wartime forestry work, nomads.awardspace.co.uk/ross.html was helpful. Seton Montgomerie's story and diary entries can be found on www.airwar1.org.uk. Professor Glyn Harper was invaluable in answering military queries.

Books consulted included Paul Baker, *King and Country Call: New Zealanders, conscription and the Great War* (Auckland University Press, 1988); John Crawford and Ian McGibbon (eds), *New Zealand's Great War: New Zealanders, their allies & the First World War* (Exisle Publishing, 2007); Martin Gilbert, *The First World War: A complete history* (2nd edn, Weidenfeld & Nicolson, 1994); Glyn Harper, *Spring Offensive: New Zealand and the Second Battle of the Somme* (HarperCollins, 2003); Philip J. Haythornthwaite, *The World War One Source Book* (Arms and Armour Press, 1992); Gavin McLean, *Captain's Log: New Zealand's maritime history* (Hodder Moa Beckett, 2001); Anna Rogers, *While You're Away: New Zealand nurses at war 1899–1948* (Auckland University Press, 2003); Hew Strachan, *The First World War* (Simon & Schuster, 2003); Ian Westwell, *World War I Day by Day* (Zenith, 2004).

THE VOYAGE

CHAPTER ONE

When the Montgomerie family embarks on the RMS Remuera, *12,500 tons, which leaves Wellington on Thursday, 22 June 1916 under the command of Captain H.E. Greenstreet, Roger is 50, Annie is 49, Winifred 22, Os 20, Seton 18 and Alexandra 14. There are 35 passengers in the first saloon, 62 in the second, including the Montgomeries, and a third saloon of 159.*

As Annie indicates in her entry for 3 July, the ages of those on board range from three months to a 74-year-old woman who has lost a son and is going to England to be near her other son, who is in the trenches in France. 'Most of the women on board are going home to join soldier husbands, some with children, some without. The same magnet seems universally potent.'

Friday 23 June 1916

Left harbour about 9 o'clock last night and had a peaceful night. This morning Wid was the only one absent at breakfast but I had to hurry away from mine and lose it. Wid got up at 11 and she and I had a glass of stout. I went to sleep on our chairs on deck. Lunch was a repetition of breakfast: I lost mine and Wid went without. Al, boys and Dad [Roger] are getting on famously. Sea is pretty rough with high wind and rain. Fairly cold on deck. Wid and I had to leave about five o'clock and have dinner in bed.

Antipodes Friday

Alex and Dad sole representatives of family at breakfast. Just our luck, a whale seen within a few chains of ship and blew off steam. Alex is best sailor of all, even Dad lost his breakfast this morning. Wid and I sat on deck all day but couldn't go down for any meals, just had a glass of stout for lunch and an apple for afternoon tea. Then dinner in bed for me, but Wid stayed on deck. The ship's chart has got us down for Friday again (Antipodes Friday) and they say we have to get an extra day. Ship tea is abominable.

The man who invented dried milk wants hanging or else made to live on it himself for a solid month.

Saturday 24 June 1916
Today the sky is a little blue and there was no wind, just a heavy swell with the ship seesawing up and down in the most alarming fashion. Roger thinks she's a clinker of a seaboat perhaps! We had quite a convoy of birds round our stern all day. Yesterday only half a dozen shared the desolate-looking ocean with us.

Sunday 25 June 1916
Wid and I had breakfast in bed, and I had all other meals in saloon … Nothing eventful happened all day, just the same sullen grey sea, not even an albatross to cheer us up. Yesterday evening they had choir practice in first saloon and this morning had church service. As I couldn't go none of the others would. We are now 1,063 miles from old NZ. Our party has resolved itself into ourselves with Miss Clere, Mrs Wood and Mr Fergusson as auxiliaries. The captain had lunch at our saloon at one of the long tables.

Monday 26 June 1916 1,356 miles
Got my sea legs at last, up first this morning. Had my first sea water bath. Wid in bed all day, Mrs [Ina] Stephens came to see her in morning. Washed 3 doz handkerchiefs this morning at hung them in bibby to dry.[1] Sea is calmer today and we have our porthole open for the second time this trip. The first mate sat at head of our table today for lunch. Sunshine this afternoon. All but Wid stayed up to supper. Dad, Al and boys great on quoits and deck billiards.

Tuesday 27 June 1916 1,646 miles
Windy and choppy sea. Both decks wet, had to change to other side which we don't like. Foghorn was blowing at intervals all night because of the fog. Sounded very eerie. Saw the captain on his rounds for the first time. He is quite a dear, reminds one of [Wanganui's] Dr Innes. Mrs Stephens came along to our drawing room, but inside is very muggy. One albatross only on view today. Supposed to be a dance tonight but too rough to hold it.

---

1   A bibby was a stateroom on the passageway of a ship. Named after the Bibby Line, on whose vessels, travelling between England and India, the rooms were first used.

Wednesday 28 June 1916

Still windy and choppy, and plenty of white horses on view. Captain Greenstreet came on deck just as I got there. He has a cheery word for everyone. Tried our own side of deck again but found it very wet and windy. A number of people have gone down again today. One albatross on view today. We all think the sea very rough. The deck steward couldn't carry cups of beef tea round the corner of the deck without having it whipped out of cups.

Friday 30 June 1916

Glorious day, blue sea and sunshine … All and sundry are up on deck today, even Wid, who also came to lunch in saloon for the first time since we started. Three petrels following today. This life is a very lazy one, talking, eating, sleeping. Our routine is – early tea, then soon afterwards stewardess announces bath is ready. On going to bathroom one finds water is run (salt) and basin with hot fresh water also ready. Then dress leisurely for 8.30 breakfast. After that lying in deckchair talking, reading or sleeping whiles the hours away or an occasional walk thrown in.

Saturday 1 July 1916

Another fine morning but not so good an afternoon. One albatross and two petrels today. Wid and Miss Clere had first game of quoits. This afternoon had our first 'thrill': the ship's foghorn blew, the engine stopped and from both ends of ship the sailors flocked, lifebelts in hand. It was only boat drill which they have every Saturday afternoon if possible. But it was enough of an insight to be emotional. Some mothers ran for their chicks, all looked a bit alarmed. Had singsong in evening in saloon.

From Sunday 2 July, when Annie writes 'Sunny blue Pacific', shipboard life becomes more pleasant as the Remuera *takes advantage of the trade winds. There are porpoises to admire, a dance and a play. Annie is proposed for a sports committee 'but I declined, said brain not brawn was my strong point'. The family discovers, on 5 July, that 'our friend Mr Fergusson', Robert Arthur Fergusson from Timaru, also on his way to enlist, is a relation. Like Roger, he is a cousin of Sir James Fergusson, who was governor of New Zealand 1873–74. On 8 July Annie's entry ends 'Battle of Jutland'. In this naval clash in the North Sea near Jutland,*

Denmark on 31 May and 1 June, 14 British ships and 11 German vessels were sunk and there were more than 8500 deaths. Both sides claimed to have won. After the crossing of the equator on 11 July Annie reports much warmer temperatures and ice cream rather than beef tea at 11 o'clock.

Thursday 13 July 1916

All feeling the heat, very little wind, had a fruit sundae today. The third class have invited second saloon to a concert tonight. Got some very exciting war news, through by wireless today, about German attempted invasion of England and 30 transports sunk. Also 40 naval boats to our 14; we are a bit worried to hear about the submarines hiding in American harbours. Tonight we waited on deck to see first lights of Panama. Saw tropical lightning and thought it was flashlights at first. Then saw the lighthouse light shining for us. Girls slept on deck again. I felt the heat dreadfully.

Friday 14 July 1916

Panama, a glorious harbour 10 miles wide, dotted with little islands which are beautifully green. The health officer came out to pass us and we took our pilot on board before breakfast. Roger waked me at 5.30 and I dressed and came up on deck at once. The official brought American papers which say our dreaded submarine is at Newport News [in Virginia], just where we are going, but all the news of yesterday is otherwise rubbish. American stretching, just as I said at the time. After breakfast we moved to Balboa and anchored at wharf. It was just crowded with interest all the way, the train running along breakwater to fort at entrance, even a Ford car running along it. Two lighthouses close together looking like white clear Cleopatra's Needles. The huge machinery plants and dredges, glimpses of a town beyond, then the wharves with boats lying anchored. (Even a Japanese which Roger saluted in Maori.) A Negro woman standing on wharf with a tray of fruit on her head was one of our first artistic sensations, a real old Aunt Chloe; crowds of black men with a sprinkling of whites. When we tied up at the wharf we were the 'thing of the moment'. Crowds of blacks and whites were staring at us and we at them.

We can't go through the canal today because we draw 25 feet of water and it is only every other day that they flush the locks for that depth; it is usually for 23 feet draught. Some men came on board after we tied up at the wharf and distributed booklets on Panama. A lot of passengers went off almost at once to see the sights. We had a two hours spin in a car in afternoon … The darkies, men and women, were a huge interest to us and the scantily clad sometimes naked nigger children amused the family muchly. The funny little fruit stalls, the queer foreign tropical look everywhere caught our eyes, funny little donkey carts with black men driving, plenty of motor cars, buses and vehicles of all descriptions with mules in harness, steam rollers even, all in a conglomeration on every narrow street … Some darkies came on board today with goods of all kinds to sell. We got some PCs [postcards] and a Panama hat. The absolute blackness, pitch blackness, of most of the Negroes was a complete surprise to us. Some of the first class took a special train to Colon and back, captain too.

Annie gives a long and detailed description of the next part of the journey – from Balboa, to Miraflore to the Pedro Miguel lock and then through the Culebra (or Gaillard) Cut, the artificial valley that forms part of the Panama Canal, 'the biggest ditch in the world', which links the Pacific and Atlantic oceans. The cut emerges at Gatun, which Annie calls 'just a tropical picture, every outlook is beautiful. I hated having to go down for my dinner. The sunset tints on township and on foliage of hills around will remain a memory for all time, just beautiful.' Then 'three locks one after the other and we are 85 feet lower than the Gatum Lake and out into the Atlantic'. Soon after they anchor in Colon.

Sunday 16 July 1916
Woke in morning to see the rosy tints of dawn flushing a blue blue sky, huge butterflies fluttered about. Our cabins were almost uninhabitable when we went down, we were all at melting point. We left Colon just after breakfast, a large artificial harbour with stone breakwater. An American warship with three submarines at its side adorned the harbour. Also were joyful to see four interned German merchant ships who had the cheek to flaunt their ensign as we passed.

Monday 17 July 1916
Man overboard before breakfast; crowds on deck in no time. Boat launched and after him. He is a religious maniac from the third and wonders what all the fuss was about. He was 'Only having a swim before breakfast' he

said, when the captain remonstrated with him about risking other men's lives trying to save him. One big shark and four small ones followed boat to ship's side. The maniac is locked up now. The 'Mrs. Meddlesome' of the ship said to a passenger, 'Anyhow, he was ready to visit his maker.' To which the passenger replied, 'His maker was evidently not ready to meet him and sent him back.'

After passing Jamaica and Cuba, they are in sight of the American coast before breakfast on 22 July.

Monday 24 July
Several people wished us a safe voyage and one man suggested leaving Alex here to go to one of their wonderful! American schools to be turned into an American! lady. We were polite and didn't tell him we didn't admire Americans sufficiently. Newport News is not much of a place at all. The shops here have some bargains and American quarters are very nice but the general effect is shoddy and the humid heat is awful … Earning one's bread in the sweat of one's brow is no good here, it makes the sweat pour to raise a finger.

Their next stop is Halifax in Nova Scotia.

Friday 28 July 1916
Poor old Os had violent earache through the night, came in to me three times to have hot oil put in. Had doctor to him this morning, as both ears were discharging blood. Doctor ordered syringing and keeping them warm, so he came on deck well wrapped up with flannel and wraps. Then Mrs Standish lent him John's balaclava. We reached Halifax this morning, have moored at wharf to put on naval gun. The town looks very inviting, the best we have seen so far, and it's British, with British flags flying. An auxiliary and a cruiser of ours are in harbour and some smart-looking sailor boys put our gun on. We saw our first policemen in blue since leaving New Zealand.

The town is hilly like Wellington, the land as one approaches the town is covered with Canadian pine. No niggers messing around, just nice English-looking blue jackets. Heard that the *Bremen* submarine has been sunk by the cruiser *Sydney*. If true, it has been pretty close to us, the horrible thing.² We left Halifax at 4.30 p.m. Wid and I were lying down when the engines started. I got up and watched, through the porthole, the town and shores of Nova Scotia recede from sight. Our next sight of land should be England.

Monday 31 July 1916

Have tidied up my belongings and put a few necessaries together in case of submarine scare, which may come later on but I hope sincerely that it won't. One woman is sleeping fully dressed each night already and heaps are feeling pretty scared. Last night when the foghorn started suddenly one woman rushed to side of ship ready to jump into boat and several flew to their lifebelts.

Heard two shots out of one naval gun, soon after breakfast this morning. Threw out boxes and fired at them, shooting not very wonderful. A lot of rifle shooting at boxes too, but no Bisley marksmen distinguished themselves.³ A gunship looked us up about breakfast time this morning, didn't come very close, just identified us I suspect.

Tuesday 1 August 1916

Still a bit foggy. Just settled down to my darning when Alex came up on deck and said Seton wanted me. Arrived in my cabin and found Seton there covered with rash, which we believed to be prickly heat. Kept him well dusted with boracic until about lunchtime. Stewardess got liquid menthol and rubbed him, which gave great relief. In afternoon it came on very badly and I tried whisky, sulphur and picric acid, then in desperation asked two of our nurses about it, and they prescribed sal volatile inwardly and bicarbonate of soda in solution to dab on.⁴ It was very successful. Tonight the stewardess has rubbed in menthol again. Os is much better. Slept in pyjamas for the first time, in case of being submarined, but one doesn't feel exactly certain that this peace will not be suddenly invaded. We are not travelling on the usual route, and all the authorities say we are not in real danger until the last 10 or 14 hours, but all the same – the chance is there – mines or submarines.

Friday 4 August 1916

The captain's 50th anniversary, so second saloon presented him with cup

---

2 The *Bremen* was one of seven merchant submarines that took cargo between the United States and Germany in 1916, through the Allies' naval blockade. Its disappearance is still a mystery.

3 Since 1890 Bisley in Surrey has been the home of the British National Rifle Association, founded in 1859, under royal charter, to promote marksmanship. The annual shooting competition is still held at what is regarded as the world's most famous shooting centre.

4 Boracic powder was widely used. Sulphur was, and still is, used for a variety of skin disorders. Disturbingly most widely used in munitions and explosives, picric acid was available at chemists in these years for treating burns, herpes, malaria and smallpox. Sal volatile was a scented solution of ammonium carbonate in alcohol, used as smelling salts.

and autograph book. He is one of the very best. Rough seas today, which is just what the captain wished for. Several fishing smacks about today – quartermaster said they are Scottish ones. It seems we are off the coast of Scotland now; we certainly are doing plenty of moving around. In afternoon had boat drill, which consisted in putting on lifebelts and going up on deck to be told our appointed boats in case of trouble. Families are not to be separated so I am happier.

Saturday 5 August 1916
Sea not quite so rough. But still choppy with white horses. Making for Cape Ushant light on coast of France, should be there about two am tomorrow. Then a few hours – and England.

ARRIVAL IN ENGLAND

CHAPTER TWO

While the Montgomeries were at sea a fierce battle was being waged along the Somme River in France. The British attacked the German lines on 1 July 1916 and by nightfall they had suffered over 57,000 casualties; more than 19,000 men had died, the biggest loss by the British Army in one day. By the time the Battle of the Somme ended on 18 November 1916, there would be more than 620,000 Allied casualties and 465,000 German: over 310,000 men would be dead.

Sunday 6 August 1916
It was so strange to be really gazing on English hills and English everything. It was rather disappointing to find everything brown instead of the beautiful green we had always been promised, but it was England and safety. Even the birds seem at home here and rested by the waters peacefully. Never saw a bird rest once on voyage.

Colonel Standish told his wife that our trip had been the most dangerous since the beginning of the war: four submarines had been caught in the last few days, one yesterday just on our track. Only 12 miles from us, 40 ships were held up in Plymouth until this morning because it was too risky to let them out. One of the submarines caught was a minelayer.

We left the boat after lunch, had to show our passports and be inspected first. Soon it was goodbye to the *Remuera*, which had given us a very wonderful experience. On reaching the wharf we had to go into a vast shed affair, and wait in queues to get our tickets. Os did that part, and we sat and waited. Then we had some afternoon tea, then waited in queues again to go through Customs. It was very tiring and Roger was like a caged lion. We got through in time and then had to run for train. The English trains are quite different from ours. They are little compartments to hold eight people, after the style of our bird cages.

We got one reserved for ourselves and I had ordered a tea basket for four which cost 12 shillings, and it didn't have a drink in it when we came to investigate. It had chicken and ham with lettuce with salt, pepper and mustard, also bread, plates, knives and forks, even paper serviettes but no drink, and I was almost crazy for one. The heat was awful and after the strain of things we were almost too tired to enjoy the wonderful beauty of Devon as we flashed along, and it is beautiful and such fields, such a cultivated look everywhere. Such a lot of beautiful trees dotted everywhere and well-kept green fences around each small paddock, and some such sweet-looking homes and ducky farmhouses. Two aeroplanes were circling about on one part of the journey.

We went to Bristol and then on to London town, arrived at our lodgings at 12.50 a.m. after a desperate time at Paddington Station trying to collect our luggage. Then when we did, we couldn't get a taxi. One old man on the station ran off somewhere and succeeded in unearthing a bus affair, which took all our luggage and ourselves off. The old scamp driving us couldn't find our place of rest, and drove round and round in the eerie hour darkness of the streets of London, asking first one and then another where Bedford Place was, and we were so tired.

Monday 7 August 1916

Went to Bank of New Zealand and taxi. Mr Mills was very nice, and also found that New Zealand Records [actually Record] Office is just round the corner from where we are staying and that Mr FitzHerbert is in charge.[1] He was awfully decent to us and gave us news of most of our boys. Wid and Dad went across to New Zealand War Association,[2] which is run by New Zealand women, Mrs Empson, Fitzherbert etc., etc. They hoped to find Mr Cecil Wray, but didn't.[3]

Tuesday 8 August 1916

Went to high commissioner's but as he wasn't there the boys had to interview the secretary, who gave them letters to War Office, left our names there. Went shopping in afternoon, round Bourne & Hollingsworth,[4] bought two cheap blouses.

Annie is quick to appreciate the retail possibilities offered by London – 'The shops are a wonderland to us' – and she shops throughout the war, often extravagantly.

---

1 Lieutenant-Colonel Norman FitzHerbert (1858–1943) had fought in the South African War. He was made a CMG in 1919. The New Zealand War Record Office was the information centre for New Zealanders in London wanting to find out about relatives and friends in the forces.

2 This was in fact the New Zealand War Contingent Association, formed in London on 14 August 1914 at a meeting called by New Zealand High Commissioner Sir Thomas Mackenzie. The aim, in the words of L.O.H. Tripp in *War Relief and Patriotic Societies*, was to 'assist New Zealand soldiers by providing them with comforts, visiting them in hospital, securing accommodation for convalescents after they had passed through the hospitals so they might be taken in hand and gradually brought back to health, also by keeping in touch with the soldiers and their relatives'. The association also helped to establish No. 2 New Zealand General Hospital at Walton-on-Thames.

3 Cecil J. Wray (1867–1955) was a Wanganui lawyer and well-known sportsman who had moved to England with his wife in May 1914. He was the chair of the Visiting Sub-Committee of the Hospitality Committee of the New Zealand War Contingent Association, which organised visits to wounded New Zealand soldiers in Britain. He also visited and, with others, gave regular concerts to entertain the men. He later became an eminent New Zealand sports administrator.

Arrival in England

Wednesday 9 August 1916

Mrs Whiteman rang up before breakfast, arranged with Wid to come round and come shopping with us. Boys went to War Office, Dad came with us. Then went shopping to Peter Robinsons,[5] bought two frocks. It's a lovely shop. Os didn't get to his destination but Seton interviewed Whitehall authorities, had to decide by Saturday. Coming back from Peter Robinsons in tube we came across some NZ boys who had just come over from Egypt. Gerry Barton had come with them and we ran into him at the New Zealand Records Office, had him round to dinner.[6] Went in tube to Piccadilly in afternoon then found our way to Buckingham and walked back from there. Dead tired.

Thursday 10 August 1916

Boys asked Mr FitzHerbert's advice about their movements and he was awfully good to them. Seton is going to be a gunner until he is of age for a commission. Os is still unfixed. Went shopping with Mrs Whiteman this morning, also saw St Paul's. It is glorious, saw the pigeons too, and heaps of places with interest. This afternoon went to Walton-on-Thames to see Willie,[7] found him very bright and happy and had a delightful afternoon.

Friday 11 August 1916

Went to Peter Robinsons to be fitted, got back for lunch and rested all afternoon. London is very tiring and the heat is trying. Wid went to Richmond with Gerry and spent an hour rowing on the Thames. Fergie turned up this morning and had lunch with us;[8] he is quite in the inner circle and flourishing. He advises Seton to go into the Artists Corps.[9] New Zealand hospitals won't do [operate on] Os. Colonel FitzHerbert has written to the English RAMC [Royal Army Medical Corps] one. He is a brick to the boys.

Summing up her first week in London, Annie writes, 'It is a wonderful city and the shops and streets are fascinating ... The tubes are eerie and confusing to a new chum, but they get you there.' She deems St Paul's 'beautiful in a solemn fascinating way' and 'just revelled in Windsor's age and charm'. But she refuses to be too impressed and remains loyal to New Zealand.

Windsor Forest didn't raise much admiration – our own bush is a thousand

---

4   Bourne & Hollingsworth, originally a draper's shop, was by this time a large department store on Oxford Street. It remained in business until the 1970s.

5   Founded as a draper's shop in 1833, Peter Robinsons, on Oxford Street, grew into a major emporium that sold women's clothing and accessories. By the 1960s there were branches throughout Britain. The store became Topshop in 1964.

6   Gerald Arthur Arnold Barton, 10/272, originally left New Zealand on 16 October 1914 with the Wellington Infantry Battalion. He was wounded in 1915 and returned to New Zealand but went overseas again in August 1917.

7   No. 2 New Zealand General Hospital at Walton-on-Thames, about 17 miles from London, began on 1 August 1915 as a civilian hospital, funded by the New Zealand War Contingent Association and the New Zealand government. In August 1916 it became an official New Zealand Expeditionary Force medical facility. No. 1 New Zealand General Hospital, opened not long before, was at Brockenhurst, to the south.
    Willie was Archibald William Montgomerie, 7/532, the son of Roger's brother, who had left New Zealand on 16 October 1914 as a member of the Canterbury Mounted Rifles.

8   This is Robert Arthur Fergusson from the *Remuera*. He is the son of Robert and Constance Fergusson of Temple Avenue, London EC4.

times prettier – but everything here is ordered and neat and comfortable. Virginia Water [Lake, in Windsor Great Park] is not so very wonderful either – we have lots of finer sights – but taken on the whole it was an afternoon full to the brim of interest. We all loved it. Going in the train to Windsor we passed Sutton Seeds gardens. They are beautiful masses of bloom, even the little gardens in front or back of houses are bright with flowers. [The rose] Dorothy Perkins is a great favourite. We saw Buckingham Palace one day in our jaunts. It isn't inspiring on the outside anyway. Nothing about London really overawes one, but its vastness, its rush and bustle and heat are very tiring. Haven't seen anything overpowering in the shape of men or women yet, but all the best people are supposed to be out of London in August. I think they must be.

Tuesday 15 August 1916

Went to fur shop in Islington, in East End, Wid chose a coat, £10 10s. I also tried them on but didn't buy one. Mrs Buck bought one too. Afterwards we went in the bus to an East End shop, a big shop and fairly cheap … Such miserable-looking women singing about the streets and calling 'Lavender'. Fairly wet all day, had to buy umbrellas at East End shop. Seton went to see Willie, who was in bed after his operation on Saturday.

Wednesday 16 August 1916

Went out for a short time but too wet to go far. Wid and Os went into NZ War Association and asked Mrs Empson what work was open for her. Mrs E was most affable. There seems to be plenty to do, voluntary work.

Thursday 17 August 1916

Pouring wet day, nothing doing. Roger got a letter from Aunt Bettie [in Ayrshire, Scotland] this morning just as we were going out for morning tea. He stayed behind to digest it but we went on. Wid had a letter from NZ War Ass offering her motor driving, VAD work,[10] or clerical work, so she soon got a choice.

Friday 18 August 1916

Seton, Al and I set off to see Westminster Abbey, got there at noon just as midday service was on so did not get far. We went round to south door to

---

9 The Artists' Rifles was a volunteer regiment of the British Army formed in 1860 and consisting of painters, sculptors, engravers, musicians, architects and actors. The regiment fought in the South African War and in the First World War, during which over 2000 of its men were killed.

10 The Voluntary Aid Detachment was a voluntary organisation providing a variety of nursing and other services such as cooks, clerks, drivers and maids. The great majority were women.

see if we could go round Royal Vaults but found a service going on there too. Standing at door the first thing I noticed was a tablet to one Gideon Mason – can't even keep them out of Westminster. We went to Thames Embankment past Whitehall, then War Office and the Houses of Parliament. Saw the Thames and two of its bridges. Then walked along to St James Park and on to Trafalgar Square, got tube for lodgings. Felt very giddy and blind and was glad to get back. Seton and Roger went to museum this afternoon. Cyril arrived by 8.7 p.m. train.[11] Os, Wid and Set met him at Waterloo Station, went out to get some supper for him. He slept with Os.

Saturday 19 August 1916

Cyril and boys hunted up National Bank this morning and saw St Paul's. Wid, Al and I went shopping, looked at Shaftesbury Avenue and ended in Peter Robinsons. Wid bought a skirt, I bought a pair of gloves. After lunch Cyril, boys and Dad went to see the zoo and the sights of London. All so glad to have Cyril. Dad's parcel arrived from Peter Robinsons while Dad was away and I had to write 'p.p.' cheque. Guy Seton's name is on a list of wounded from Egypt.[12] Boys went to *Ye Gods* this evening.[13]

Sunday 20 August 1916

Cyril arrived from Sling Camp on Friday evening.[14] It has been lovely having him and the boys have been very happy together. He is looking very well, a little older and bigger in every way, quite filled out … We saw him off by the 10.8 p.m. train at Waterloo this evening.

Hampton Court was full of interest but our time was far too short, some day I hope to go back again and see things better. Now it is a jumbled memory of courts and courtyards, fountains, lawns and beautiful trees, rooms with funny old bedsteads and chairs, pictures everywhere, some quite ugly, but some with the most wonderful colouring possible. One could spend days among them. Window seats with glorious outlook on gardens, Al, Cyril and I sat down on one and pretended we were some of the older times ladies and knights.

Tuesday 22 August 1916

Stayed in all morning, Os and Set presented their papers at their separate destinations, Os got orders to go into St Bartholomew's [Hospital] at

11 Cyril Hector Douglas McLeod, 12814, a clerk from Wanganui, left New Zealand with the Field Artillery on 26 May 1916. Os and Seton always called him Mac.

12 Guy Wilmot Seton, 11/498, from Wanganui, left New Zealand on 16 October 1914 with the Wellington Mounted Rifles. He was wounded on 5 August.

13 *Ye Gods* by Erie Hudson and Stephen Roberts was a three-act revue which had begun its season at the Kingsway theatre on 20 May. The musical director was future British composer Arnold Ketèlbey.

14 Sling was a New Zealand wartime training camp on the Salisbury Plain in Wiltshire. A large kiwi is carved into the white chalk hillside above the former site of the camp.

6 o'clock this evening. Seton goes into khaki next Tuesday, and into camp next Wednesday. Boys, Dad, Al and I went in tube to Peter Robinsons then wandered up to Selfridges. Afterwards had afternoon tea at Lyons corner shop in Trafalgar Square.[15] And on home, the rest of us took the tube back.

Os, Set and I went in taxi to hospital, saw the sister and got cards of admission, also saw the ward Os is in. Wid went to Coliseum with Gordon Pettigrew.[16] A letter from Grandma [Roger's mother] this evening, also news that Dick is wounded in Egypt.[17]

Wednesday 23 August 1916

Stayed in all morning, in afternoon Wid and Seton went to see Os. He was feeling pretty lonely, dear old kid. Mr Charles Owen called, found our names at high commissioner's. Mrs Whiteman came while he was here, then she and Wid went to Record Office and Mr (Colonel) FitzHerbert does not think it's true about Dick as they have no record of it. 6 p.m. Seton and Al took me to hospital, and waited for me. Os was in bed. Took him two books from Mudie's and a paper.[18] Sister says his operation will be about 3 p.m. tomorrow, Mrs Whiteman says it's the best hospital in London. It's a wonderful old place and the sisters and nurses look capable and nice.

Thursday 24 August 1916

Stayed in all morning, Mrs Whiteman called to tell us about her interview with Colonel Parkes (Dr).[19] Seton went to Walton-on-Thames in afternoon. Wid and I went round to St Bartholomew's, saw Os for a little while before his operation and waited in sisters' sitting room until they brought him back. He was an hour and a half away. Sister is very cheery and brisk and capable-looking like Aunty Jen [Annie's older sister Janet, also known as Little Tommy]. She gave us afternoon tea, and as soon as possible came to tell us he was all right. We were with him when he was coming out of the chloroform. He was very restless and struggled quite a lot until I stroked his head, then he soothed down quite nicely. He said, 'That you Tiny?' He liked having his head stroked and after a bit Tiny took my place. We stayed at hospital from 3 p.m. to 7.20 p.m., then the nurses said we must go. Poor old son was glad to have us and didn't like us going, the darling old son. Sister gave us afternoon tea while we waited.

---

15 The first Lyons Corner House opened in London in 1909 but soon there were many of them and they were substantial, filling four or five storeys (each with an individual restaurant style and its own orchestra) and each employing some 400 staff. There was usually a big food hall on the ground floor.

16 Gordon Thompson Pettigrew was a lieutenant in the Royal Flying Corps. He died in 1973.

17 Trooper Richard Burnside Mason, 11/1341, from Wanganui, Annie's nephew, son of her oldest brother David, who died in 1911, and his wife Jessie. Dick left New Zealand with the Wellington Mounted Rifles on 14 August 1914.

18 Mudie's was the famous lending library started by Charles Edward Mudie in 1842.

19 Lieutenant-Colonel William Henry Parkes of the New Zealand Medical Corps, who had been head of 2 New Zealand Stationary Hospital in Egypt.

Friday 25 August 1916

Stayed in all morning, darned socks for Seton. Got telephone message from hospital sister to say Os was bright and had good night. Wid and I went to see him at 4 p.m. and found him in great distress with flatulence. Poor kid said he had gallons in his 'tum' for sure, had a good hour and a half go of it. We thought the nurses very callous. After an enema which they gave him about 6 o'clock he got relief. Why they couldn't give it before, goodness only knows. Zepps [Zeppelins] raided outskirts of London in the early hours of the morning, Woolwich and Lewisham etc.

Saturday 26 August 1916

Went out with Seton this morning, had morning tea at Lipton's.[20] Then went to ICS about Customs letter to Os,[21] then to library to change book, after lunch went to hospital calling at dairy shop on way to tube and buying some eggs for Os. Found him much better, stayed three hours. Dad not very well, got some chlorodyne for him.[22] Louie (the maid) says 200 people were killed at Woolwich in the air raid.[23] It's horrible.

Sunday 27 August 1916

Mended and taped Seton's socks,[24] Seton and Allie went to hospital in afternoon, and Wid and I went at 6 o'clock. Os doing well. Saw wounded soldiers returning from motor ride with huge bunches of flowers.

Monday 28 August 1916

Wid, Al and I went to St Leonards-on-Sea, then took motor to St Mary's. It is a dear old school. Both girls loved it and the mistresses. Got back about 7.30 p.m. The hop-pickers in compartment going down were a revelation, quite priceless. St Leonards is very interesting, The school is in the country. Seton went to see Os with my white [admission] tickets, found him doing well. Roger spoke to policeman about windows showing lights into square last night.

Tuesday 29 August 1916

Went out en famille to Lipton's for morning tea, then went with Wid to have her hair shampooed in Oxford Street. They waved and dressed it beautifully. Went out after lunch with Seton and Al and bought Seton's

---

20 Lipton's tearooms were part of the tea empire of magnate Sir Thomas Lipton.

21 ICS was probably the Institute of Chartered Shipbrokers.

22 Originally designed to treat cholera, chlorodyne, which was a mixture of laudanum, cannabis, chloroform and morphine, became one of the most popular patent medicines in Britain, used for a variety of purposes, such as treating diarrhoea, migraines, insomnia and neuralgia. It was very addictive and responsible for a number of deaths caused by overdoses.

23 Louie had her facts wrong: nine were killed and 40 injured.

24 That is, sewed name tapes on.

watch (wristlet luminous dial), changed library book for Os, Seton and I went round to hospital at 6 p.m., found him looking very well.

Wednesday 30 August 1916

Went out blouse hunting with Wid and Al, tried Bourne & Hollingsworth, no luck. Tried Peter Robinsons no luck, waiting for new goods now. Seton came back with his camp outfit this morning, after being sworn in, two khaki suits etc. He went along to Shipping Office and collected his uniform, £8. In afternoon he polished up his buttons etc. Al and I went along to Oswald at 6 p.m. She and Wid had been there from 3 to 4, Os very bright. Set, Wid and I went across to Southampton Row and had supper about 10 o'clock after Seton had finished his packing up.

Thursday 31 August 1916

Seton left for camp just after breakfast. I was very upset after he was gone. He came down to breakfast in his Tommy uniform and looks very nice indeed. The Italian at the table opposite said, 'Another shock for the Kaiser.' Our diminished family went out to Lipton's for morning tea, and Roger and I were changing to go out to lunch with cousin Jack Tilley when in came Seton once more.[25] They had to leave at 1.20 and had been let away for lunch. He got something to eat at Southampton Row and then went off. Jack Tilley is a pet, nicest relation I have met yet. I just hope we didn't stagger him. Lunch at the Criterion is a little bit complicated to plain folks straight off the turnips.[26]

I do miss my boys – my darling old Seton, a Tommy Atkins.[27] Oswald has made wonderful progress. Each day he looks better; he has his appendix in a bottle on shelf beside him. The operation was necessary. The appendix was too long, twice as long as it ought to be, and was twisted towards the liver round the colon, and was adhering to it. Oswald couldn't be in better hands. He likes all his nurses and it is a most interesting old hospital. Founded first in 1100 [actually 1123] by a monk, Rahere (Oswald is in the Rahere ward). Added to by Henry VIII and others and it is a most imposing old place. First time I saw it I thought it was a grim old fortress but I love it now.

---

25 Cousin Jack was distinguished diplomat John Anthony Cecil Tilley (1865–1952), who was British ambassador to Brazil 1921–25 and to Japan 1926–31. He was knighted on 3 June 1919, as Seton notes in his diary.

26 The Criterion in Piccadilly, founded in 1874 and still going strong, is famous for its opulent neo-Byzantine architecture rich in gold, marble, mosaics and mirrors. It has numbered many famous people among its patrons, from Winston Churchill and Sir Arthur Conan Doyle to Russell Crowe.

27 Tommy Atkins was slang for an ordinary British Army soldier.

SETON IN UNIFORM

CHAPTER THREE

The grim and costly fighting on the Western Front continues throughout the rest of 1916 and Zeppelin raids cause great fear in London. Letters from Seton and Annie's diary entries now tell the story.

Letter from Seton, 31 August 1916
Hut 6A, A Company, 2nd Artists' Rifles, OTG [Officer Training Group] Hare Camp, Romford, Essex

The first word that was said to me when I arrived here, was would I like to get into flying. They are forming a new school for flying just out of London. If you sanction it I will get good pay and an officer's kit right off if I go flying. Flying is far easier although there is hard mental work. They are a very decent lot here and I have learned a lot in about three hours. I find that if I spend anything over three months in the ranks here, and another three months in the OTG, that is if I was staying the course, then when I am 18 years six months I cannot get a place in the Artillery School unless there is a vacancy. There are 150 men here who have passed their exams for infantry and cannot get out, and 100 artillery men cannot get in Artillery School.

Friday 1 September 1916
Went in morning to Islington with Mrs Watson. Dad came too and I bought my fur coat. Mrs Watson had a sealskin coat made up into a stole and muff. Roger went to see Mr FitzHerbert to thank him for being so good to the boys. He came back with the dreadful news that our boy Dick had died of wounds on the 10th of August [actually the 9th], four days after we landed here. So the report of his wound was true but even then he was gone. Fate couldn't have struck us a harder blow just now. Had a letter from Seton this morning asking me to let him go into Flying Corps. They asked

him to join as soon as he got to camp, but I can't. He will be in the firing soon enough, God knows. Dick was hit during the day and died that night at Oghratina (Egypt).[1] It seems like fate picks out the very best. I wrote to him when we heard the rumour about him being wounded and have been waiting for his reply, only for this. Dear old Dick … it's a sore, sore blow. 'When to be alive was glorious, and to be young was very Heaven.'[2]

Letter from Seton, 1 September 1916

I have already put my name down on the flying list, to be scratched off if you object. A bit of push might be necessary. I wish now I had stayed out until I was old enough to enter the Artillery OTG or that I tried flying from the beginning. I am convinced that it would be hard to find a better lot of men, or get a more comfortable camp, but strict is no name for it. There is a post office, a book stall and very good afternoon tea can be obtained from the YMCA for 6d. A penny cup is quite delicious. Visitors are allowed between noon and sunset Saturdays and Sundays, so if anyone feels like a trip here take a ticket to Gidea Park, the next station from Romford. When I have been here a fortnight I can get leave from Saturday at four till Sunday night and after three weeks from Friday to Sunday. Romford is about a mile and a half distant. Every night we are free from 4 till 9.45, but dinner is at 6 and meals are very good considering. If I get inoculated I will get two days' leave.

Saturday 2 September 1916

Just after breakfast Allie Tripe came to see us.[3] He is at Codford Camp, Salisbury Plains.[4] Aunt Bettie had told him where we were. He is a nice boy now. We all went out and had morning tea at Lipton's. Then Al and I went to Mudie's to change Oswald's books and Dad and Wid went to high commission to get Dr Innes's address. Al and I went to hospital 6 p.m.; Oswald ready to come out next Wednesday I think. Wrote to Dr Innes tonight, want him to see Al before I arrange definitely about school.

Sunday 3 September 1916

Zeppelin raid at 2 a.m., wakened by gunfire. Roger jumped up saying, 'Those d_____ Zeps are here.' It just sounded as if two or three of them were dropping bombs all around us, but luckily for us they were some distance away. My first thought was for Wid and Al, who are two floors

---

1 Dick Mason, who was serving in the New Zealand Machine Gun Squadron, died of wounds at Oghratina on the Sinai Peninsula, in the Battle of Romani. He is buried in the Kantara War Memorial Cemetery.

2 Annie is slightly misquoting Wordsworth: 'Bliss was it in that dawn to be alive, But to be young was very heaven!'

3 Trooper Alexander Montgomerie Tripe, 7/280, from Marlborough, served with the Canterbury Mounted Rifles. He left New Zealand on 16 October 1914. He was wounded and admitted to a hospital in Cairo on 7 September 1915 and taken to London in October. He would have been convalescing at Codford.

4 Codford, on the Salisbury Plain only a few miles by road from Sling Camp, was a large New Zealand reinforcement and training depot and home to No. 3 New Zealand General Hospital. Although as well equipped as Walton and Brockenhurst, Codford did not generally receive such serious cases because of its distance from the ports and its smaller capacity. Attached to Codford was a Venereal Disease Section, a detention hospital enclosed by barbed wire and constantly under guard.

higher up. I picked up my dressing gown in my arms, also shoes, and rushed for them. They had heard the row too and were soon down, and we watched from our bedroom window. Roger and girls saw one Zep focused in a searchlight and later on all saw it blaze up and fall to earth. And we couldn't feel sorry for them either. To look out of one's window on the sleeping city and see those fiends up there dealing out cruel death to helpless men, women and children dries up one's human feelings. Everybody was a bit 'strung' but there was no panic. God knows what it would be like though if they were above one. It's too awful to think about. We went back to bed at 20 to 4 and as it was getting daylight we slept, but it was a nervy experience.[5] After dinner went out to Gidea Park to see Seton, found him and had afternoon tea with him at YMCA. Then walked to Romford and caught train.

Monday 4 September 1916

Went out to Brompton Road and looked at a couple of flats, went to Harrods first, had quite an enjoyable morning. Roger is getting more used to knocking around. After lunch started off for Bank of New Zealand, met Allie Tripe round corner and took him. At the bank met Miss Clere and all went to corner shop afternoon tea. Walking home, Miss Clere and I got lost. The others walked on ahead and thought we were following. We asked a policeman and got back safely to find Roger had gone back to look for us. Miss Clere had a look at our 'dugout' [lodgings] and then Allie Tripe and I went round to see Os and Dad showed Miss Clere the Holborn underground. Allie came back with me for dinner and stayed all evening, then went to Soldiers' Club.[6] Os was up in chair, tootling round.

Tuesday 5 September 1916

Wid stayed in bed for breakfast, Al and I ... went to Cuffley to see the historic field where fell the Zep ... [7] The Zep field is picked as bare as a bone, just got some wire and aluminum tube, a fragment of glass and a screw.

Letter from Seton, 5 September 1916

There has been an influx of 215 men, Honourable Artillery Co., don't understand why. It is only natural but some of the fellows were struck with the 'Kid'. [Fourteen-year-old Alex had been visiting.]

---

5   Sixteen German airships were involved in the raid. One was shot down by an incendiary bullet – hence the flames – over Cuffley in Hertfordshire, near Waltham Abbey. Pilot Lieutenant William Leefe-Robinson became an instant hero.

6   The New Zealand Soldiers' Club in Russell Square, opened on 1 August 1916, offered accommodation, company and food. As L.O.H. Tripp noted, 'It should have been always a comfort to the mothers, wives, and sisters of the soldiers to know that such an enticing home was provided in the midst of London, with its temptations and its great loneliness. The Soldiers' Club was never empty.'

7   Annie and her daughter were not the only sightseers. In the 48 hours after the airship came down 10,000 people took the train from Kings Cross to visit the scene.

Wednesday 6 September 1916

Roger went to Romford to see sale, Wid, Al and I went up High Holborn looking at the shops and came back in the tube. After lunch got taxi and brought Os back from St Bartholomew's, Mrs Watson called to see him and stayed some time. Dad came back up in great feather from his sale. He saw one pig sold for £10 and sheep for 69/-, cattle £40. Thinks England is the country to do a bit of farming in.

Friday 8 September 1916

Wid, Al, and I went to Gorringe's and ordered Alex's school frock and pinafores.[8] Rested until afternoon tea time. Got message by phone from Seton to say he was coming up for two days off, inoculated for typhoid. Got here before dinner. Lovely to have my flock complete again. Found Dad in Southampton Row and bought some grapefruit and apples (first fruit we have bought in London).

Saturday 9 September 1916

Dad and Wid went to Shipping Company's office and Seton, Al and I changed library book, had morning tea and went to chemist with Al's prescription from Dr Innes. In afternoon Set, Dad, Al and I went to see the Tower of London. Most interesting – need days and days to do it justice. Saw the spot where Lady Jane Grey and Ann Boleyn had their heads chopped off. Poor things. The armoury was very interesting and the Crown Jewels a treat. Pretty rough old diamonds they must have been in those olden days.

Sunday 10 September 1916

Stayed in all morning. This afternoon Set, Al, Dad and I went to see Hyde Park, a great place for sure and we enjoyed our afternoon tea under the trees with the pigeons coming for scraps. The park orators amused us, also the brazen behaviour of the numerous couples. No British reserve there.

Monday 11 September 1916

Went shopping with Wid and Al this morning for matching boots etc. for Wid's brown turn-out. Had a good old poke round. In afternoon set out to look at some flats, but Wid jibbed as we weren't sure of our localities. We

---

8 Gorringe's, a large department store in Buckingham Palace Road, began life as a small drapery in 1858 and closed in 1968.

looked at one deplorable place in Southampton Row, came back and rested. After dinner got letter from bank, one from home. Our section is let for £50 and Clifden [the Mason family property] is in the market. Doesn't seem to matter so much now that Dick is gone.

Tuesday 12 September 1916

Al and I went flatting this morning but reached the wrong place, a dreadful-looking locality. Came back to Lipton's and had morning tea, then poked about Holborn Street, met the Glasgow crowd [Scottish friends]. After lunch Al, Wid and I went to look at some new service flats, new and clean but unfurnished, and not what we want. Went back to afternoon tea and had a talk with lame Frenchman, also with an American woman, who boasts of being connected by marriage with the Duke of Norfolk – ahem! Perhaps she has dollars to recommend her, no visible other qualities.

Letter from Seton, 12 September 1916
No. 8213, Hut 46

I am getting rather sick of filling in forms. I have stated that I wished to go in the RFC [Royal Flying Corps] and to keep out of trouble I stated that I didn't wish to go until I was 18 years six months …[9] The recruit squad that I am in had rifles served out today, and with them came some more work and more new recruit joy. I am the only one in the squad that has done previous arm drill and time moves very slowly in that case.

Letter from Seton, 14 September 1916

I am 'grub' orderly today and seeing that the people in our battle-scarred hut need dinner soon I had better assist in obtaining it from the cookhouse. It is a job that consists of getting the 'grub' and washing the greasy plates and knives generally in cold water, it is not as pleasant as washing up at Taukoro [home]. Then make arrangements for going on leave …

    Second edition – Late war special – bad newspapers. This letter tells of the unforeseen. Being 'grub' orderly I wished to make sure I would have my letter posted by 7.30, so I wrote before dinner. During dinner orders came round for only 10% leave … this order came from Eastern Command so only one from this hut got his leave. It is all to be expected in the army. I am quite happy.

---

[9] The Royal Flying Corps, the air arm of the British Army, would merge with the Royal Naval Air Service on 1 April 1918 to become the Royal Air Force. RFC pilots originally carried out aerial reconnaissance and photography but later became involved in attacking enemy aircraft and bombing German targets such as industrial areas. New Zealand had no air force at this stage so young Kiwis who wanted to be war pilots had to enlist in Britain.

Saturday 16 September 1916

Al and I went to hairdressers. Al was clipped shingled and shampooed, I was shampooed and waved. Roger doesn't like it. We changed library book and then poked round second-hand shops, saw some beautiful cameos. Os went to War Office but couldn't have interview, has to write and make appointment. Captain MacNab called this morning when we were all out but Os. He is off to Scotland. Rested in afternoon and in walked Seton, second inoculation for typhoid. Got leave until Monday night. Went out after dinner to watch crowd going into theatre.

Wednesday 20 September 1916

Al and I went to Gorringe's in morning, when we got back we found Leo Addenbrooke waiting in hall.[10] He is looking fairly well but is much older and thinner. He stayed to lunch and it was very nice seeing him. After lunch Al, Os and I went to Peter Robinsons to get warm 'undies' for Os. It was so cold today that I was glad to give my fur coat an airing. Leo says Dick's death is quite confirmed. Dear old Dick. Wid and Roger went to high commission to get letter for Wid for her War Office venture. Leo says there will be very heavy casualties from France. God help the mothers and wives. Wid went to afternoon tea at Mrs Meldrum's 'dugout'.[11]

Letter from Seton, 20 September 1916

The Eastern Command had its order washed out and old leave is reinstalled and I have again made application for flying. The passport is a certificate of character, also the 'Old Man's' letter [Frank Milner, rector of Waitaki Boys' High School] but how they bear on the subject I don't know. I expect I will have to parade before the officer here and he can see what he likes. I have to find a responsible person who can testify to my character for the last four years.

Sunday 24 September 1916

Miss Clere came to dinner and spent afternoon with us in Hyde Park. Heard Mrs Dacre Fox speak.[12] Seton went back to camp this evening. Saw flash signals in square tonight. Another Zepp raid early this morning. I was sleeping in girls' room as Seton was in mine. We all grabbed our dressing gowns and made for downstairs. Met Roger coming up to call us. Seton

---

10 Lionel Stone Addenbrooke, 11/598, of Mangamahu, left New Zealand on 16 October 1914 and fought at Gallipoli, as did his cousin Hugh. Hugh's brothers, Jack and Sidney, enlisted later.

11 Nora Meldrum was the first wife of Colonel, later Brigadier General, William (Bill) Meldrum (1865–1964) CB, CMG, DSO, who commanded the Wellington Mounted Rifles from 8 August 1914 to 27 April 1917, at Gallipoli and in the Sinai. He then led the New Zealand Mounted Rifles in the Middle East. The Meldrum's son, Alexander (Alick), was serving with the New Zealand Army. Nora Meldrum was the great-aunt of Susanna Norris's husband, Mike.

12 Norah Dacre Fox (1878–1961) was the fiery general secretary, chief organiser and spokeswoman for the Women's Social and Political Union, Britain's foremost militant pro-suffrage organisation. New Zealand women had had the vote since 1893 but British women would have to wait until 1918 for partial suffrage and 1928 for full suffrage. Dacre Fox was also an anti-vivisectionist and later a fascist: she joined Oswald Mosley's inner circle in the 1930s. She was imprisoned in May 1914 as a suffragette and went on three hunger strikes. During the Second World War she was jailed as a fascist.

took quite a bit of waking, also Os. Both boys are very disgusted because there was nothing to see this time, although one girl on top floor saw the burning Zepp come down, just as we did last time. Very few guns were fired, and not close. Hardly a searchlight out and very dim, it was very foggy too. We could hear lots of bombs dropping a long way off and saw the glare of the falling Zepp [hit by incendiaries]. It is wonderful luck getting one twice running. Zepp came down [at Great Burstead] about 1 a.m. and they were selling papers in street by 3 a.m. and calling out the news. Reports says a second one was brought down, which has since been confirmed, came down intact [at Little Wigborough, near Colchester]. The brutes landed off it, 22 of them, and gave themselves up to the first constable. The first 'enemy landing' in Britain for hundreds of years. Just after leaving the Zepp there were two explosions: I suppose they were destroying the Zepp secret as usual. They really did a lot of damage and 28 people were killed and 19 wounded [in Sheffield].[13]

Monday 25 September 1916
I had a letter from Mrs Thomassett asking me to aft tea at the Criterion tomorrow. Roger is invited too but he is wild with me because I am interested in catching German spies who flash signals in our square so I expect he will be a bear. Saw one flash signal tonight, wasn't watching long.

Wednesday 27 September 1916
Got letter from Roy this morning and my one to Dick returned.[14] Dear old Dick was wounded on the 9th of August and died that night; that is all that Roy mentioned. I was glad to hear from him. Guy Seton is better. The big guns have been booming very distinctly today and yesterday, testing guns at Woolwich [Arsenal], they say. Darned stockings nearly all day. After dinner kept watch for spies. Miss Bernacchi caught them signalling on top of Bonnington Hotel. We sent Os out for constable but he couldn't find station. Wrote to Roy and Seton. Dad is recovering again and becoming interested in spy work, came up to Miss Bernacchi's to watch.

Thursday 28 September 1916
Dad, Wid, Al and I went to Lipton's for morning tea, then Dad went to police station about the signals and we others went to Peter Robinsons. After

13 In the 12-Zeppelin raid on the night of 23–24 September eight airships attacked the Midlands and the North-East of England and four bombed the London area, where 15 people were killed and 57 injured. The entire crew of the crashed Zeppelin was killed. The landed airship was set alight by its crew, who then walked south and were arrested at Peldon. The wreckage gave the British valuable information.

14 Sergeant Robert Egrement Mason, known as Roy and Robin, 11/635, 2nd Squadron Wellington Mounted Rifles, left New Zealand in October 1914. He was the son of Annie's oldest brother David and brother of Dick.

lunch Dad and Al went to Hammersmith exploring, Os went to Record Office to get Colonel FitzHerbert to sign Seton's blue paper and Wid and I rested. The policeman is coming at 9 p.m. tonight to watch our signals. Wrote letters to Jen, Roy, Mrs Watson and WSPU [Women's Social and Political Union] … Officer (38) arrived at 9, he watched a few flashes, then went off to investigate. Came back again to say he had been all over the roof of place and could find nothing. Twenty-two flashes in the hour we watched.

Friday 29 September 1916
Great excitement tonight when the two constables arrived to watch flashes, one stayed here and the other went over to the hotel. Later on he came back with the mystery solved: only the 'lift' working. They fixed up the trouble and all's well that ends well.

Saturday 30 September 1916
Went to Records Office with Os and Al, then to Peter Robinsons, Os ordered 12 dozen Cash's names [woven name tags] for himself. Then Al and I did some shopping and Os was to wait outside. When we got out found the streets lined with people and no Os. The excitement was because the French Guard band was coming; we managed to get a glimpse as they passed. A London crowd is a fearful thing.

Monday 2 October 1916
Al went to St Mary's. Another Zepp down. Family party went out to morning tea at Colonial Restaurant, Mrs Stephens came too. Then Al and I went to hairdressers for shampoo for Al. Al also had tooth stopped by Mr Smith at 10 o'clock. There was another Zepp raid in early hours of morning and another Zepp brought down in flames.[15] We all slept through the whole thing; there was very little gunfire. Mostly airplanes work. Os, Al and I went to Victoria in taxi, and Dad and Wid in tube. AL OFF TO SCHOOL. The girls look quite a nice lot. Poor little Al, I am sure she will be homesick. A music mistress went with them. I do hope it will be a decent school.

Tuesday 3 October 1916
Dad, Wid and I went out to Lipton's, called at Records Office on way. A terribly long list of names today. Had a note last night from Mrs Thomassett

15 The Zeppelin crashed near Potters Bar. All 19 crew were killed.

asking me to let her know about Jack Addenbrooke should his name appear … Wrote to Dr Innes and Mrs Thomassett. Os went to high commission for copy of Mr Milner's [reference] and enclosed it in War Office answer.

Letter from Seton, 3 October 1916
The Zepp did pay us a visit on Sunday after all and all I saw of this one was the red glare. Our lights went out half an hour before time. We watched for Zepps, but it was nothing but searchlights so I retired in my clothing. The next thing I knew was a howling mob was loose in the hut and camp. I struggled to the window and caught a sight of it. The buzz of searching planes was heard quite distinctly. Tonight is the last night of the Zepp season, no more special picquets for that purpose.

Wednesday 4 October 1916
Letter from Seton and WSPU, thanking me for donation (5/-). Roger and I went out to Lipton's, then walked round to Lincoln's Inn Fields, quite a peaceful spot right in the heart of bustle and rush. After lunch Dad, Os and I got on bus and went a long long way down through East End, saw nothing tragic but the sordidness of it all. The same rush and bustle there, as in West End, just a different strata of the human English race – the same article evidently, only polished to unpolished.

Thursday 5 October 1916
Letter from Alex, seems happy. Whole family except Os went to morning tea at Lipton's, Mrs Stephens included. Met Mrs Meldrum at RO [Records Office], and asked her also. Roger and I came back to RO and had to wait a long time to look at lists, very long lists, but thank goodness none of our boys. Mrs Meldrum, Wid and Roger went to Walton, Wid to see Les Curtis, Roger to see Jack Harrison … [16]

6 October 1916
After lunch Roger went to WO [War Office] and was refused for motor transport (as he is not an engineer!!). Has offered for horse transport. After afternoon tea Dad and Wid went to RO and Os and I went to Mudie's, then to umbrella shop with Al's umbrella. Walked back to RO. Then Os stayed for Wid and Dad and I came home, getting some mending for Al on

16   Captain Leslie Ralfe Curtis, 26/53, had left New Zealand on 5 February 1916 with the New Zealand Rifle Brigade. He had been wounded in the Battle of the Somme. At Walton-on-Thames he helped to maintain the ambulances. Jack Harrison was probably Wanganui man John Shafto Harrison, 10/3589, the manager of Y.G. Turnbull & Co., who left New Zealand on 8 January 1916 with the Wellington Infantry Battalion. He was wounded in the back.

way. Wire from Cyril: 'can't come'. Heard that Mr Glenn is at St Thomas's [Hospital, Lambeth] suffering from shell shock.[17]

Saturday 7 October 1916

Dad, Os and I went out to Brixton, saw some of the Zepp damage, had morning tea at a queer old show: Davis's is no good. After lunch Mrs Stephens left for Salisbury Plains. Wid went round to Soldiers' Club to help, I fixed up Al's work box and washing for postage. Fergie arrived unexpectedly, looks awfully well in his cadet uniform.[18] Just as we finished afternoon tea Seton arrived; a little later we went out. Dad, Set, Os and I posted Al's parcels then on to Records to look over another big list.

Sunday 8 October 1916

Seton went back to camp just before supper. Wid went to Soldiers' Club at 10 p.m. for all night work, Os took her round.

Monday 9 October 1916

Roger got letter from WO accepting him for horse transport,[19] to be ready on 27th this month. He will have to go to Aldershot to train. Wid got home a little after 7 a.m. this morning and went straight to bed; she enjoyed her work. Os and Roger went to bank and then to view the Zepp remains. After lunch Roger, Os and I went to the zoo, had a very enjoyable afternoon … After dinner Roger went to RO to see Major Watson, who satisfied him about WO letter … Darned stockings all morning. Roger brought me a bunch of violets, just like Taukoro ones.

Tuesday 10 October 1916

Auckland Weeklies [*Auckland Weekly News*] came this morning, but no letters. Os got answer from WO, quite a civil one. He interviewed them this morning and has to go to doctor to be passed. Mrs Stephens came this morning and she, Wid, Dad and I went to morning tea at Lipton's. Called at RO, met Captain MacNab. Roger got Hugh's number.[20] Captain MacNab told us there is little hope for Alick Meldrum.[21] After lunch went back to RO to have a thorough look through those dreadful lists. Hiroti, the Maori,[22] came up and spoke to us, and he and Roger started off together for St Thomas's Hospital to see Mr Glenn. Found him out, however.

---

17 Early in the war William Spiers Glenn, who was farming near Wanganui, and had been a member of the 1905 All Black team that toured England, 'went home to offer his services to the War Office', as the *Wairarapa Daily Times* put it. Aged 37, he got his commission in the Royal Field Artillery in October 1915 and while serving in France in June 1916 was awarded the Military Cross 'for conspicuous gallantry and ability – as observing officer. He was exposed to heavy shellfire for several hours, but with great coolness and judgment corrected the fire of his battery and sent back constant reports on the situation.' But as the *Hawera & Normanby Star* reported on 19 September 1916, 'Word has been received, we regret to hear, that Lieut. W. S. Glenn has: been invalided to England from the front owing to an attack of fever.' This was, perhaps, a euphemism for the shell shock that Annie mentions. Glenn was promoted to lieutenant in December 1916 and by January 1917, when he visited Cecil Wray, he was convalescent.
  Shell shock was a loosely defined term in the First World War but generally was what would now be described as post-traumatic stress disorder: a severe reaction to the noise and terror of warfare that could take the form of panic, sleeplessness, dizziness, an inability to speak etc.
  St Thomas's was designated 5th London General Hospital during the war.

18 Fergie was in No. 12 Officers Cadet Battalion, Newmarket, training to be an officer.

Letter from Seton, 10 October 1916

Just a bit more frightfulness. The whole battalion was vaccinated yesterday, very few exemptions, the physical 'narks' [bad-tempered people, spoilsports] and other degrees of 'narker' all taking their dose. You should have seen the fainting that commenced as soon as it was known what was contemplated. One man started then and others fell out at various stages from when they had their arms washed, disinfected sounds better, till after the operation was over. It was purely a case of stomach and does them no credit. If you hear of my funeral in the next fortnight … U-boats [German submarines] arrived just in time is all I have to say, although it would have added interest to our eventful journey if we could have 'bagged' a sub before entering the danger zone. The *Remuera* made her return home none too soon; it shows she has got luck.

Wednesday 11 October 1916

Got NZ mail, also one from Mrs Watson and one from Mrs Thomassett with the sad news for Hubert Addenbrooke's death yesterday.[23] Jen's letters too were all tinged with the dreadful sadness of Dick's death … Oswald passed his military doctor and sent in his papers …

Friday 13 October 1916

Oswald's birthday, 20 years old today. Got letter from school telling me that Al was bright and happy. Also one from Leo, which was very sad. Os and I went to Colonel FitzHerbert after breakfast and asked him to get leave for Leo. He is always splendidly helpful and kind and he sent off at once about it. Then I wired Mrs Thomassett about it and I hope it will be all right. The family went to Lipton's, then Os, Wid and I went to buy a Treasury note case for Os, and Roger gave him the first £1 note to put in it. Os and Wid went to Brooklands [aerodrome] after lunch; G. Pettigrew sent card of admission. They quite enjoyed it.

On Saturday 14 October Annie and Roger visit Al at school, catching the Hastings train at Charing Cross. 'Allie was looking very bright and well and Roger has quite fallen in love with the school too.' They take their younger daughter to St Leonards for afternoon tea and buy her a pencil box. Annie, ever alert, spots 'several bargains in shops today, solid silver spoons especially'. The shopping, and the taking of tea,

---

19 This was the transport section of the Army Service Corps. On 5 December the *Wanganui Chronicle* reported that 'Mr Montgomerie has received a commission in the Motor Transport Service and is now in training'.

20 Hugh Alexander Anderson, 12543, who left New Zealand with the Wellington Infantry Battalion on 6 May 1916, was Roger Montgomerie's nephew.

21 Captain MacNab was too pessimistic. Former law student Alexander Francis Meldrum, 22740, the son of William and Nora Meldrum, left New Zealand on 27 May 1916. He received a gunshot wound to his right hand on 1 October and after being taken to Etaples, then Birmingham, was transferred to Walton-on-Thames on 11 October, then sent to Hornchurch in November. He went on to serve in the Middle East and returned to New Zealand on the *Willochra* at the end of 1918.

22 Perhaps Lieutenant Turu Hiroti, 16/392, a civil servant from Wanganui, who was wounded in 1916, or his brother, Jack, 16/532, who was a chemist in Wanganui before the war and had a distinguished military career in the Second World War. A third brother, *cont. over...*

cont./... Rangi-hiwinui, died of disease in France in June 1916. All three left New Zealand with the 1st Maori Contingent on 14 February 1914.

23 Hubert Addenbrooke was a Wanganui friend and Leo's father. He died on 10 October.

24 Fuller's, in Regent Street, was one of a chain of tea shops: there were 24 branches by 1909.

continue when she is back in London: 'Wid bought two frocks, one blue crepe de chine and one black velvet. Went to Fullers to morning tea,[24] then went to Italian restaurant in Dean Street … After lunch Os, Wid and I went blouse hunting, Wid got pink one at Bourne & Hollingsworth. Looked at fitted dressing cases at shop in Oxford Street.'

Letter from Seton, 17 October 1916

I went on the Mountnessing [village to north-east of Brentwood, south Essex] stunt [attack] again. The aeroplane landed at Brentwood and this time it was not an aeroplane I got, but about half a Zepp. Two aviation men brought some Zepp for us and it is just as well some of us filled our pockets because one of our thoughtful sergeants at the end of the journey commandeered the remainder for himself. There were two large pieces, one of ordinary girder trestle and the other a very substantial junction of some description. I should have secured the junction for NZ. It was worth some money for novelty alone, as it was more than the ordinary Zepp, the Billericay [another nearby town] Zepp, the second to come down. I have a dozen pieces of both large and small.

25 Flag days, instituted by Agnes Morrison in Britain on 5 September 1914, raised large amounts of money for the war. Prisoners of war and the wounded were among those who benefited.

Thursday 19 October 1916 Flag Day[25]

Os, Wid and I went to Lipton's. A flag seller came in and we all bought a NZ flag. Then we went to Peter Robinsons to get frock fitted (Wid's). Looked at dressing cases at J. Pounds … Received invitation to Mr Massey's reception on Tuesday at Hotel Cecil.[26]

Sunday 22 October 1916

The whole family set out for Hyde Park, walking round, picked up Miss Clere. Watched riders in Rotten Row and didn't think much of their riding … After dinner family and Miss Clere went to hear Mrs Pankhurst speak,[27] enjoyed it.

Tuesday 24 October 1916

Dad was measured for uniform this morning then went to high commissioner's to get a ticket for reception at Hotel Cecil for Mrs Innes. Wid, Mrs Innes and I went shopping at Madame Louise, P. Robertson and Bourne & Hollingsworth. After lunch got ready for reception, went in taxi. Shook hands with all the notables, met Miss Calder, Mrs Whiteman, Mrs Palmer (Mrs J.B. McLean's sister), Sister [Elizabeth] Nixon (matron of Codford), Colonel FitzHerbert, Mr Glenn and Mrs Glenn, Mr Mills (our banker). Watched the flashlight photograph being taken, taxied home, taxied to Kings Cross with Mrs Innes. Os came with us. Taxied back home to dinner.

Letter from Seton, 24 October 1916
[Cousin] Allie Tripe is out of blue now and on the Military Police here.[28] In that capacity he has some dirty work and far-reaching work. They can go anywhere in the British Isles after men that don't like particularly any locality [those absent without leave or deserters]. Or they can be in charge of batches going to Sling etc. and the usual work of rounding up those that take a fancy to Romford at 12 p.m. Flu? I woke up about three feeling restless and when I got up at six thought it best to take a little quinine. When breakfast came the taste of food gave me the feeling of a bad sailor so the army lost nothing in that meal. At nine we went for a 4-mile march and when I had finished it and another hour's drill I had overcome the distaste for nourishment. I must say I have not enjoyed today at all, but now I feel quite all right.

Wednesday 25 October 1916
Os, Wid and I went to Hyde Park this morning and saw 40 Inverness Terrace, very pleased. Had morning tea at Maison Lyons then went to Lexington Gardens but did not like it; anyhow it was full. Mrs Stephens came to lunch, very upset because her brother has gone to France. After lunch Wid and Ina went to Chelsea and Os and I went shopping for Al. Back for afternoon tea, then went to Inverness Terrace and arranged to go next Wednesday. Dad told Miss Abbot [their landlady in Bedford Place] tonight. Dad was fitted for his uniform today. Heard that submarines are shockingly busy again, 16 boats yesterday and 26 previous day. Nothing in papers.

Letter from Seton, 26 October 1916
I have not been killed with the Zepps yet but I had as good a chance as anyone in England tonight. It is only six and the warning has been received already and it seems they are determined to make life happy here, and the whole camp saw the performance. The fellows in my hut watched her [the

26 Prime Minister William Ferguson Massey (1856–1925) had sailed from New Zealand on 24 August 1916, with Joseph Ward, his co-leader in New Zealand's wartime coalition government. He would remain in Britain until 25 June 1917. This trip was the first of five lengthy overseas trips that Massey made in the next five years to attend meetings of the Imperial War Cabinet and to visit New Zealand troops in France.

27 Emmeline Pankhurst (1858–1928), leader of the British suffragist movement and founder of the WSPU. She would have been speaking in support of war effort as militant suffragism was suspended during the conflict.

28 Seton is referring to the blue uniform, with red tie, worn by wounded and convalescent soldiers, who were sometimes known as 'blue boys'.

airship] in the rays of the searchlight as she sailed past on one side of the hut, and there were many curses from their lips and running to the other side saw three red lights around her and the gunfire crossed, then she lit up and settled down, finally taking the usual nose dive. The gunfire here was heavy as she passed and when she dropped some of her bombs the concussion was fairly strong. This one is fairly well guarded, it seems. There must be some secret that was not in the Cuffley one for them to take such precautions. We don't hear anything of the intact one that fell. I have taken the job of batman to Captain Peach. It means getting up before six, but it means no guard, no fatigues,[29] no hut orderly and leave every fortnight for sure. He is an 'old sport' or I would not take it on …

[29] Work such as cleaning or cooking, often for punishment.

Friday 27 October 1916
Waited in all morning for Roger's parcel [containing his uniform]. Os went round after breakfast and was told it would be sent immediately. Then he rang up and was told it couldn't come before 11.30 (and Roger was due to report at 11 a.m.) then they promised to send it in half an hour so we all went to Lipton's for morning tea. It was raining fairly hard and coming back we got a drenching shower. At 12.30 we knew it was useless waiting for uniform and Roger went off to explain. He was told he must report at Aldershot, so rushed back for his warm coat and started for 3 p.m. train. When he got there he could hardly get back again. A sergeant major fixed it up for him or else he would have been stranded there just as he stood. Found his way in dark to station and got back at 10.30. We both went to Southampton Row for cup of tea, still raining. Parcel arrived after 3 p.m. Found Aldershot a very rough show.

Saturday 28 October 1916
Dad, Os, Wid and I went to Angel [Islington] this morning to look at fur sets. Have to go back again with costumes on … Wid went to Records Office and brought back the sad news of David Stewart's death in action.[30] Dear good old David. It's terrible to hear of our boys dying while these thundering idiots here are still left to make fresh blunders. Wid went to club in afternoon. Roger tried on his uniform tonight, looks A1. Raids on Channel last Thursday night and the Germans got the best of things. Someone is blundering all the time. Funny where our navy is at these times.

[30] David Reid Stewart, 8/2482, left New Zealand on 13 June 1915 with the Otago Infantry Battalion. He was killed in action on the Somme on 21 September 1916 and is buried in the Caterpillar Valley Cemetery, Longueval. He was 22 years old.

Sunday 29 October 1916

Roger, Os, Wid and I went out about 1 p.m. to Colonial Restaurant so that Roger could have snax before he left. We got taxi in Russell Square and came here for suitcase, Os went to Waterloo with Roger. After dinner went to see Seton. Al's 14th birthday and Roger gone to Aldershot by 2 p.m. train. Wid at club tonight.

Monday 30 October 1916

Os and I went to Records and asked them to look up Hugh's whereabouts. They said he was all right, thank goodness, but that's all we can know. Morning tea at Lipton's, then to Peter Robinsons to order pillow slips for putting away dress suits …

Tuesday 31 October 1916

Had letter from Roger this morning, doesn't sound bubbling with happiness poor old dear.

CHAPTER FOUR

THE MOVE TO '40'

Wednesday 1 November 1916
40 Inverness Terrace
    Busy packing then went out to morning tea at Colonial with Miss Bernacchi. Then out to Angel and bought set of furs (musquash). After lunch took parcels to post office to send to Auntie Jen. Over weight so had to open them there and take out one skirt and waistcoat which I posted separately. Valued each box at £1 and small parcel at 4/- … Arrived 40 Inverness about 5 p.m., pouring rain, shining wet street with every light from cars reflecting, red one side of street, clear the other. First hot water in London: had piping hot bath going to bed. Os has room on top floor for ten days. Enjoyed our dinner and didn't go in [to the lounge] for coffee. Too tired to be bothered, so went to bed early.

Letter from Seton, 1 November 1916
I cease to marvel at anything from this time forward. The net result of today's move has been to put as many men as possible in new huts, in new companies. We have all changed beds and friends, much to our sorrow. They have at last woken up to the fact some men in this camp are more advanced than others and this has caused all this upheaval. I changed my lodgings to B Company but what I object to is that I had got nicely settled down.

Annie declares their new accommodation a 'great improvement' on 7 Bedford Place and is out shopping again the next day – nightdress, stockings, bedsocks, spencers and a costume (suit) plus a dressing case. For the latter she writes 'cheque for £18 18/- to be sent next Wednesday after initials and cover are done'. On Friday 'poor old Os' is very disappointed to get 'napoo' (no) from the War Office and clearly decides a night on the town is in order: 'Os didn't turn up for dinner, no sign of him all evening.' Seton arrives that night but has to stay at a hotel along the street as Miss Ibbotson, the landlady at 40 Inverness Terrace, cannot get him a room next door. Os, 'the villain', reappears on Saturday morning: he and a friend had had dinner together and gone to the Hippodrome.[1]

Sunday 5 November 1916
After breakfast Dad and Seton came along, my three men sat in smoking room and Wid and I sat in lounge reading newspapers until lunchtime – pouring day. In afternoon we all went to Maison Lyons and had afternoon tea. Roger went off to Aldershot before dinner and Seton to Gidea just after. Wid goes to club for her all night work.

Monday 6 November 1916
Wid got home from club just before breakfast. Had breakfast and went to bed feeling very miserable with a horrid cold, which seems to have settled on her chest last night. Os is also wretched with a cold. Ordered wine this afternoon but the wretches haven't sent it. Os and I went to Peter Robinsons this morning and got air pillow, balaclava, socks and bedsocks for Roger. In afternoon went to St Paul's and got a hussif (6/6d) for him.[2] Letter from Al this morning, Wid had one from Aunt Bettie. Rubbed Wid's chest with St Jacob's oil and then put on castor oil on brown paper.[3] Wrote to Miss Burnett, repacked Jen's parcel.

Tuesday 7 November 1916
Wid stayed in bed all day but is getting better. Os didn't turn up for breakfast so went next door to look him up. Found him having breakfast in bed, after a miserable night. He just got up to lunch. After lunch we took parcels to post office but they wouldn't take postman's authority for our not having to pay again, so have to go to central office to fix it up – heigh ho!!! Ordered bottle of 12-year-old whisky. Went to Whiteley's with Os, did some shopping and had afternoon tea there.[4]

Letter from Seton, 7 November 1916
There is a rumour Major Blundell is going to interview RFC men on Friday. The new hut improves the outlook considerably. Our new captain is a very good and considerate soldier, but seems rather too fussy – only natural when he is over 60. We could have some good laughs if only laughing was allowed when he is giving the orders, but in spite of this he would take a lot

---

[1] The Hippodrome, built in 1900 on the corner of Charing Cross Road and Leicester Square, was then a music hall and variety theatre.

[2] A hussif or housewife was a pocket sewing kit.

[3] St Jacob's oil was a turpentine–ether–alcohol tincture used as an 'anti-neuralgic'. Vinegar, or in this case castor oil, and brown paper was an ancient remedy. Jack in the nursery rhyme has his injured head wrapped in vinegar and brown paper.

[4] Whiteley's, founded in 1863, was London's first department store. The building Annie shopped in was finished in 1911 after a huge fire in 1887 destroyed the original premises. It was *the* retail destination in the city in these years.

of beating. The colonel announced last night that he was giving a lecture on the Artists' Rifles Regimental Association. He called us gentlemen several times and talked promisingly of our commissions amongst other things. He thanked us for attending, rather a stiff one as it was in our own time.

Wednesday 8 November 1916

Have been a week at 40 Inverness Terrace. Like the place extremely but the people are a queer collection of unattached females of, to me, a general English type. Plain, unattractive women without any more signs of leisure and intellect than any ordinary crowd of hard-worked New Zealand women. In fact less of the latter. Their complexion, ye Gods, I have looked in vain for the 'English Rose'; parchment skin and powder predominate. Their hands, which I did expect to show signs of ease, are quite ordinary both in shape and colour. My own after all the years of toil are better than lots – and feet! One can hardly realise what a lot of ugly-footed women and men one sees. It's appalling. Little NZ doesn't need to stand aside for anything. I overheard two women talking at breakfast today about the American presidential election. One remarked that Mr Hughes seemed to have a chance of winning,[5] and she supposed from the good opinion of the people when he was here, and general impression that his speeches were very straightforward and sensible, that he really was a very good man. The other one chipped in saying that that was the Australian Mr Hughes, not the American one. Oh, they are a brainy crowd. One woman asked Ina Stephens about her trip through Panama: 'And did she see the Suez Canal too?'

English people are just soddenly complacent. London is one rush and bustle of shopping, eating and pleasure seeking. The shops are filled, the restaurants are overflowing, the crowds are idle and well dressed, and looking on, one wonders if they know we are at war, or do they still think that after the last two years of horror that war is only flag waving and drum beating with the spruce, lithe, khaki officers interspersed to take the girls to afternoon tea and dinners at the restaurant? They won't wake up, they won't realise that while they are fooling, fooling their time away, the Germans are organising every man and woman.

The exemptions are hideously unfair. Compulsion from the start was the only just thing;[6] still these sodden imbeciles play with it, and they haven't the pluck to enforce it in Ireland. And they take it for granted that

---

5   Charles Evans Hughes, 1862–1948, the Republican candidate who lost narrowly to Woodrow Wilson.

6   Annie seems to be talking about conscription. Under the British Military Service Act, passed in January 1916, all men between the ages of 18 and 41 could be called up unless they were married (or widowed with children) or in reserved professions (which included the clergy). Legislation of the same name passed in New Zealand later that year also introduced conscription but exemption was limited to those members of religious bodies who had declared, before the war, that military service was 'contrary to divine revelation'. New Zealand was very tough on conscientious objectors: 14 were shipped to the front.

our boys should come over and die for a country that holds such crowds of people that won't fight for it themselves. It is comforting! to the boys who are fighting to know that these slackers will be the ones left to carry on the race. Nothing matters to them. They go on with the same smug satisfaction in everything English, while the Germans are practically doing what they like on land, sea and air.

Thursday 9 November 1916

After lunch we took tube to Trafalgar Square to go see the Lord Mayor's show but we had not a hope of getting into line; the place was packed and packed. However from where we stood we saw a bit and anyhow we did see the Cinderella coach with its gold and red, with its absurd little umbrellas over each horse's ears and its red reins.

Friday 10 November 1916

Had afternoon tea here then went to Hotel Cecil to call on the Masseys, found them out so left cards. A soldier grabbed me by the arm and said something I didn't catch in a very thick voice as we worried our way through the throng in the darkness of 5 p.m. Didn't wait to investigate! Rushed for Wid and got along as quickly as possible. Wid was tickled to death over it, but I wasn't. Wid's chest was feeling tender all day so called at chemist and got thermogene wool, cologne and quinine.[7] She went to bed immediately after dinner. Seton rang up to say he has been accepted for RFC, dear old son I hope it will be all right …

The next two days introduce the Montgomeries to a London fog of record thickness: 'one queer old party cannoned into me, she was meandering about with a tiny electric torch in her hand. The fog even came into our bedroom.' Wid and Annie are alarmed by nocturnal fog signals, mistaking them for Zeppelins.

Letter from Seton, 15 November 1916

I was interviewed today together with about the whole camp, by a lieutenant colonel for the RFC. My interview consisted of sitting down like a hare in a dog trial, while the three present discussed the climate and general conditions of NZ. He was a very decent old sport, and when they had settled matters he told me it was 'All right', or orders to quit. So you see, I am no wiser, but I

[7] Thermogene wool was an Italian-made medicated dressing containing capsicum. It was applied for muscle or joint pain. Quinine was widely used as a tonic, often in port wine, and to 'cure' colds.

hope to be at roll call tonight. The most important rumour is that an orderly room nark says that only two of B were washed out. Again it is said only 50 were wanted. One needs some push in this world, no doubt about it.

[Later] I am washed out of the RFC, but whether permanent or not I have yet to find out. I am going to see the company commander tomorrow. It seems that the RFC men were prejudiced against NZ as facts turned out, or I should have asked more questions … I have not given up by any means.

Annie, Os and Wid socialise in a cold, wet London, visiting, writing letters, having afternoon tea (one day at Lyons a ragtime band is performing) and shopping. Seton and Roger appear on 17 and 18 November, respectively, and return on the 19th.

Monday 20 November 1916

First War Office money. Went to post office nearest the bank to fix up my separation allowance paper.[8] One of the girls there signed it and I drew £4 13/-.

Letter from Seton, 21 November 1916

We were in the trenches or rather tried to get in them today. The rain thoroughly wet the ground and as fast as we dig we run into water and the result of our labours looks somewhat like our first line after being attended to by German artillery on a wet day. If Ernest Barron [the Taukoro manager] could see me in full equipment, pick, shovel and rifle with me, he wouldn't give me any peace to the end of my days. You would say 'How cruel' but we have to be soldiers and it won't be such a job to go to the front and develop trench feet and fever.[9] Anyone who can keep out of the trenches should keep out, that's that. There is panic among the accepted flying men as they have to go the War Office in threes and be examined as regards nerves. There might be some 'washouts'. They must be going to do things thoroughly to only take three daily and they must have chanced upon some nervous wrecks in their past schools.

Wednesday 22 November 1916

Had letter from High Commissioners this morning inviting us to presentation by Queen Alexandra of Colours to Indian troops!!! After breakfast posted papers, had morning tea at Whiteley's and went to Eastman's to pay

---

8 Separation Allowance for Dependants of Soldiers.

9 Trench foot, caused by constant exposure to damp and cold, was widespread in the First World War trenches. The men's feet would develop a dreadful infection which, left untreated, could result in gangrene (and possible amputation).

for my frock being cleaned 6/9d … Afterwards went to Strands to ask if an answer was required for letter [the invitation]. It was so came back, had afternoon tea, then answered, and got Os to post it. Seton's letter came at dinner time, had fire in bedroom, wrote to Seton.

Thursday 23 November 1916
After lunch sat about in room expecting HC [high commissioner] tickets, which never came, so we were disappointed after all. Don't know what happened. Paper tonight mentions the ceremony. That blankety, blankety man said he would send tickets this morning …

Friday 24 November 1916
Wid got home before breakfast and went to bed. After breakfast I wrote letters … Didn't go out all morning. Wid had lunch in bed. Her night work is not proving too good for her and has not improved her cold … After dinner Os got a letter from HC asking if he had fulfilled his declaration of joining Officers Corp and I got one from Mrs Glenn …

Monday 27 November 1916
Wid got up a little before lunch and we went down to lounge. After lunch she was wretched again so we lit bedroom fire and sat there until afternoon tea. Os and I went to bank and PO. In morning Os went to HC and asked for interview in answer to his letter but he couldn't see Sir Thomas [Mackenzie, New Zealand's High Commissioner in London] as he was too busy and has to write an answer. He is asking for an interview …

Tuesday 28 November 1916
Zepp raid on northern counties last night, two Zepps brought down in flames.[10] Wid had breakfast in bed, after breakfast I sat in room and wrote letters … Just after we began dinner waiter told me a gentleman wanted to see me. It turned out to be Willie Montgomerie, to our great surprise and joy. He had dinner with us but couldn't get a room for the night. Had to go out with Os and hunt, got one at Seton's 'No. 2' [Inverness Terrace]. He has a fortnight's furlough. Wid was still miserable and went to bed after dinner. A German aeroplane dropped bombs on London at midday and got away, nine [in fact six] people injured.[11]

10 This seven-Zeppelin raid on the north-east coast and the north Midlands dropped more than 200 bombs, killing four people and injuring 37. Two airships were shot down.

11 Six small bombs were dropped between the Brompton Road and Victoria Station. This was the first raid on London by a fixed-wing aircraft.

Seton, too, has experience of enemy aircraft. 'The Zepps are busy again and so are we,' he writes on 28 November. 'We got orders to cover our lights at 6.30 tonight, these nights are too cold for Zepp seeing so I hope they don't come. I like to hear that the devils are getting their own back with interest, compound interest too. It must be no little job working a land plane at sea at night, I expect a few airmen were drowned, but that news is not for us.' A couple of days later he is under orders to go to the Officers' Training Corps at Cambridge, from where he reports, 'We have arrived here safely. We were kindly told by Major Blundell that the reason for sending us here was that they wanted a few more officers to kill in the spring offensive, which they hope will be the last effort.'

Friday 1 December 1916

Willie was here to lunch. After lunch he and Os went to Ponting's Pictures of Captain Scott.[12] I wrote letter to Roger, Al, and GPO. Went down to aft tea with Wid, then came up to bedroom and lit fire, Wid rested, I wrote to Jen. Seton arrived just before dinner, after dinner all the boys came up and sat in bedroom until bed time. Seton slept with Willie at 22. By late post in evening got letter from WO asking to go before a JP and make a declaration as I can't produce marriage certificate.

Sunday 3 December 1916

Os and I went to Aldershot by the 11.15 train, got there sooner than expected so went and had cup of tea and came back to station where we found Dad. Wandered all about, saw Roger's hut and stables training ground etc … The town itself is not very exciting and the crowds of 'English' soldiers were very poor specimens of manly physique, splay-footed, spindly, dwarfy, round-shouldered specimens – heaps of them – and Aldershot is a cold bleak place. Them's my sentiments.[13]

Coming back in the train some 'English' passengers were discussing their affairs. One of their relations was evidently under orders for China and they were discussing its geographical place on the globe. One asked if it was much further than Salonika; none of them had the haziest notion where it was or how far. Then the paper boys began crying out 'Lloyd George resigns',[14] which drew from them the brainy comment, 'Let him.' One asked sarcastically 'which job' he had resigned. These working people are crassly ignorant in comparison to ours; even their better classes are often stupidly ignorant.

---

12 Herbert G. Ponting was Captain Robert Falcon Scott's 'camera artist' on the fateful 1910–13 British Antarctic Expedition. His travelogue *With Captain Scott in the Antarctic*, with a lecture and cine film alternating with lantern slides, at London's Philharmonic Hall, had been a huge hit when it was first presented in 1914. Willie and Os would have seen the exhibition of Ponting's photos, *Photographic Pictures of the Scott Expedition*, at the Fine Art Society in Bond Street.

13 Annie's less than complimentary opinion of Tommies was not without factual foundation: as many others had observed, small, undernourished men from poor urban areas of Britain could not be expected to compete with much taller, fitter and well-fed New Zealand and Australian soldiers.

14 David Lloyd George (1863–1945), then Secretary of State for War, resigned because, as the *Wanganui Chronicle* back home reported, he had 'arrived at a definite conclusion that the methods, dilatoriness, indecision and delay characterising the action of the present [War] Council endanger the prospects of winning the war. He demanded a smaller council empowered to make prompt and binding decisions.' Prime Minister Herbert Asquith 'declined to accept that view' so Lloyd George resigned on 5 December. Asquith followed suit the same day and Lloyd George became Prime Minister on 7 December.

The Move to '40'

Monday 4 December 1916

Wid had breakfast in bed, after breakfast Os and Willie went to the high commissioner, Os interviewed his secretary. I finished writing Jen's letter and got some papers ready for post. After lunch Os, Willie and I went to PO and then to bank, where I interviewed accountant about the JP business. He fixed up the passport for post, and told me to try it first. He thinks it will fill requirements, came back and wrote note to enclose.

Tuesday 5 December 1916

Everyone is in a fearful state of depression today, Cabinet affairs and Romanian peril has set our nerves on edge.[15] We are wondering now if invasion of England will be next.

Wednesday 6 December 1916

Hurrah! [Prime Minister Herbert] Asquith has resigned, thank God. Went out to morning tea with Willie and Os, to Whiteley's. Then rested, feeling seedy. After lunch sat in lounge all afternoon. After dinner Willie and Os came up with NZ mail which upset me very much as it told us about Dick's death. Dear brave old Dick.

Friday 8 December 1916

Lloyd George is forming a cabinet all right, and Mr Balfour will be in it – thank goodness.[16]

Letter from Seton, 9 December 1916

We are stationed in the students' rooms [at Queens' College], six of us being in our sitting room. The usual is to have single rooms and the others all sleep in the larger room. We have our meals in the dining hall; they are some meals too. Breakfast is at 7.40, dinner at 12.40 and tea at 5. It is rather peculiar to have dinner at noon. There is no jam for breakfast, but marmalade can be bought for 1d a pot from the buttery, which is a sort of pantry. All those from 'M' down are in this 'New Court'. This place was, I believe, erected about the time of Henry VIII so it is a little ancient. It is compulsory studying from 9 till 10 at nights and lights out 10.15. We in this sitting room have supper every night, each subscribing to its fund. I am against a rock now as the captain told us it was not likely RFC men would

---

15 The Romanians had entered the war on the Allied side in August but were now being routed by the Germans.

16 Conservative politician Arthur Balfour (1848–1930), who had been Prime Minister from 1902 to 1905, was foreign secretary from 1916 to 1919. He is perhaps best remembered for the 1917 Balfour Declaration, which supported the establishment of a Jewish homeland in Palestine.

be called for a long time, if at all. He requires humouring, and I shall wait till he knows me a little and then see what can be done in my case. He is a Scotsman and always wears a sneer, and if you don't behave yourself the sneer can turn out very nasty ... I am glad to hear Father passed his exams; he ought to be commissioned soon. If you do come and see me please bring my raincoat and stick. I have not seen a newspaper since I came here – we don't follow the fall of H. Asquith!

Sunday 10 December 1916

Wid got up for breakfast! And Roger had his in bed. He and Os are both pretty miserable. Sat in lounge after breakfast and read papers to let Roger have a sleep. Shined Roger's buttons with patent cloth and nearly spoiled his coat, got it right again. Malcolm Stewart came to lunch and afterwards all went for walk in park.[17] Then the young people went to Mrs Hutton's club and Roger and I went to Maison Lyons. I got on tube train without Roger, waited at next station and got him again. Roger got sandwiches to take to camp, went off about 5.30. Os and Wid got back at dinner time, a little late.

Monday 11 December 1916

Bought Christmas cards for boys at front and ordered 'Great Push' to be sent, 5/-.[18] After lunch took velour hat to Anna's, Wid bought blouse and camisole 15/6d. Went to Colonial for afternoon tea, called at Records Office. Posted Christmas cards. Os had letter from Willie from Newfield. Ordered two bottles of wine and one of whisky 10/-. Willie got here tonight from Scotland, he and Os went out to try and get some supper, enjoyed his trip, he wired for extension of leave as soon as he got here. Got the blues today.

Tuesday 12 December 1916

Os stayed in bed until lunchtime. His cold is worse and he has earache badly. I sat in lounge most of morning. Wid and Willie went to RO to see Colonel FitzHerbert about Willie's extension ... His Codford wire came tonight refusing his leave, so it's a blessing the colonel fixed it for him. Os stayed in all day. I went out this evening and bought him some cigarettes and evening paper. Wrote to Roger, Set and Al. Very dumpy all day.

---

17 Malcolm Reid Stewart, 12/2568, a law clerk from Aramoho, Wanganui, had been in the advance party that seized German Samoa early in the war, then served with the Auckland Infantry Battalion.

18 The public was greedy for accounts of the war. *The Great Push: An episode of the Great War* by Patrick MacGill was published in 1916. As he said in the introduction, 'I have tried in this book to give, as far as I am allowed, an account of an attack in which I took part. Practically the whole book was written in the scene of action, and the chapter dealing with our night at Les Brebis, prior to the Big Push, was written in the trench between midnight and dawn of September 25th; the concluding chapter in the hospital at Versailles two days after I had been wounded at Loos [in September 1915].'

Wednesday 13 December 1916

Put peroxide in Oswald's ears this afternoon and this evening syringed them and rubbed outside with St Jacob's oil. After dinner the dear old thing got his call from War Office to go to Denham on the 28th.[19] He has gone to bed with his ears and throat tied up with thermogene wool, but much happier, poor old kid. Had postcard to say Al may be home on 16th.

Letter from Seton, 14 December 1916

I have to consider the 'glad rags' for Christmas. This old tunic is getting to be like what it would be after a month in the trenches and not very presentable. I think I should bribe the tailor 10/- to do it before I go on leave. You had better send me along £1 or I shall be broke soon. I have bought some football boots and trousers and I only have 10/- to run on now. Games are compulsory here so it was a case of buy something. I am bucking up as I want to get in the company team: it all helps to get a 'star' [rank] and the RFC. This is not an impossible place to reach. You can travel at 50 miles in 1½ hours on the Great Eastern, London and North Eastern and the great Northern [railways]. The GE ought to be the most convenient from Liverpool Street; the fare would be 8/4d. I came in contact with a student who patented the Zepp 'strafing' projectile and the authorities would not acknowledge his letters now. The usual official sympathy and encouragement.

Saturday 16 December 1916

Wid and I went to the city today to interview a notary and for me to sign a declaration as to my maiden name and date and place of marriage. A liveried factotum from the bank piloted us to the notary's den, a dark grubby hole. Our NZ notaries' dens are luxurious in comparison. Imagine me, after being a highly respectable married woman for 23 years, having to attest before a notary to satisfy the muddling imbeciles in the War Office here. Anyhow signed the declaration and sent it. It's a great pity they wouldn't exercise their officiousness towards the enemy aliens that they let flourish within their gates instead of worrying loyal British subjects who have done more for Empire than they ever dreamed of. I wish the Montgomeries could suddenly become as powerful as they were 800 years ago, and I would see that the lot of them were taught manners.

19 Denham in South Buckinghamshire was a training and transit camp.

Letter from Roger, 16 December 1916, Aldershot

Have arrived safely but have not met of my school yet though it's eight o' clock. Much love to all, Your Roger.

This is a rotten pen in the post office.

Sunday 17 December 1916

Os had breakfast in bed. Wid and I had early breakfast and caught 10 a.m. train to Liverpool Station for Cambridge. It is a great station with its huge glass roof all dirty and black. The many platforms and the many engines puffing up clouds of smoke into the foggy murky air. Then as the train puffs out of station the first thing that strikes one is the multitude of chimneys, such rows and rows of them and endless vista of chimneys popping out in the mist. Later we saw snow, real picture postcard views. The land is very like our Waikato as one journeys along. At Cambridge Station we managed to get a taxi and soon reached Queens College, where Set was standing at the doorway to meet us. He took us up to see his room, also sitting room and dining hall, which is intensely interesting. We walked through the stone corridor where the flagstones are quite worn in the centre and out over the bridge across the Cam. The wonder of it all to be gazing at Cambridge on the Cam, the famous seat of learning that I have learnt about in the old days at school. I ought to feel my increased knowledge oozing from every pore. There is certainly an atmosphere of repose and peace and stability and solidness about it all. Set is looking so well. He took us to The Bull, a nice old place where we had lunch, not Seton: he had to go back to college and do some drill and then he came back again. We sat in lounge by a comfy fire and had a good chat. Then we peeped at museum, which had plenty to see but a very bad light to see with. So then we went into shop and had afternoon tea and then to station for London again. Wid wrote a note to Al on The Bull notepaper and posted it in Seton's mailbox to commemorate the occasion.

Monday 18 December 1916

Os had breakfast in bed, then he went to the recruiting office with registration paper as requested and found it was only a form he had to go through. Then Wid and I sat in lounge all morning. After lunch Os and I went to bank and PO, then to Peter Robinsons to get Os a warm Jaeger coat 37/6.[20] Ordered wine 5/2d and back for afternoon tea. Os and Willie went out after

---

20 Jaeger was an upmarket clothing chain founded in 1884 by Lewis Tomalin and named after German zoologist and physiologist, Gustav Jäger, who believed in the health-giving properties of woollen clothing. There were six Jaeger 'depots' in London when the Montgomeries were there and Jaeger clothes were stocked in other stores.

tea and I went round to chemist to get something for Wid's sore throat …
Painted Wid's throat three times [with glycerine], tied on wet compress and
gave her some whisky.

Wednesday 20 December 1916

Got NZ mail this morning, wrote to Roger. Os went to Whitehall and
attested. Wid and I went to Petit Palais and had morning tea there, then on
to Victoria Station to meet Al. Os met us there and acted as porter. Such
a rush at station: mothers, aunts, uncles and brothers all wheeling trolley
affairs. We caught a taxi and got back a little late for lunch. After lunch
went shopping and had afternoon tea at Peter Robinsons, bought ribbons,
hairpins, gloves and khaki handkerchiefs. Had coffee in smoking room after
dinner. Al has an excellent report and is looking well and bright. She has
No. 14 for her room, quite close to Os and us.

Thursday 21 December 1916

Wid, Al and I went to Whiteley's and had a good poke around. When we
got home we found Dad and Seton had arrived and there was great joy.
After lunch Dad, Seton and Os went to see Colonel FitzHerbert and then
round to see Mr Bernacchi. Wid, Al and I went to Gorringe's and bought Al
a raincoat and crepe de chine blouse. Had a bother to convince them we are
the 7 Bedford Place Montgomeries. Had afternoon tea there, then home,
then the boys and Dad came and we sat round fire in bedroom until dinner
time. Had coffee in smoking room after dinner, Seton has his glad rags and
looks awfully nice.

Friday 22 December 1916

After breakfast Roger and Al went to Bank, and Os, Set, Wid and I went
to Peter Robinsons, bought shirt, collars, braces and cholera belt.[21] Had
morning tea at Fullers … After lunch Roger, Set and Wid went to Victoria
Street and had photos taken …

Took Al round to 65 Onslow Gardens [to visit the Tilleys]; Os came
in tube with us so that we would not get lost … Mrs Tilley and I had
afternoon tea together. She said she had two brothers in the 'strategic' retreat
from Mons and they told her it consisted in running back as fast as their
legs could carry them.[22] … A man from Romania lunching with them lately

21 Cholera belts were originally worn as a preventative measure by British soldiers serving in India, where cholera was endemic. Basically a waistband or cummerbund made of flannel or silk, the belt was supposed to keep away the cold and damp, the theory being that a 'chilled abdomen' would lead to cholera, dysentery, diarrhoea and other gastrointestinal ailments.

22 The Battle of Mons, which began on 23 August 1914, was the first clash between British and German forces on the Western Front. The British, heavily outnumbered, fought bravely and were responsible for many German casualties, but were finally forced to retreat in the face of the greater enemy numbers and because the supporting French Fifth Army had suddenly retreated. Although it was a properly planned withdrawal, the British retreat ended up taking two weeks.

was telling her about the wonderful Romanian retreat and compared it with the English retreat from Mons. She laughed and said she knew all about the retreat from Mons: they had simply run as hard as they could and he said 'Exactly', that is just what the Romanians did.

Saturday 23 December 1916

After breakfast Roger, Os, Set, Al and I went to Peter Robinsons. Wid stayed at home. Dad bought a raincoat and Jaeger vest, Seton got some socks. Then boys and Roger went to Thresher & Glenny to get a particular kind of coat Seton wanted.[23] Al and I stayed behind and tried to get some suitable Christmas cards. Then we walked to Bond Street and took tube home. After lunch Wid rested and Al, Roger and I went to Whiteley's and had a poke around. Bought a 'Tommy's' cake and some sweets on the way back.[24] Boys met Irene Thomas in Piccadilly. Lex Butler for dinner and took Wid to *Chu Chin Chow*.[25]

Monday 25 December 1916

Seton and I went out to purchase some chocolates to take to the little Tilleys, it was the very first time I have ever seen empty London streets. We have been a complete family since the 21st and it has been a great joy to me, especially after all the panics about leaves being washed out. Miss Ibbotson has managed to fit us all in, which is a great comfort. Al has a touch of influenza and is pretty miserable. She didn't want to go to the Tilleys but finally decided to make the effort so off we started. We sat in the library for a while and talked then we went to the dining room for a sit-down afternoon tea with Christmas cake and crackers, which latter caused lots of fun for the kiddies. The lights were turned off to see the little fireworks, snakes etc. that came out of them. Then we all trooped upstairs to the drawing room in which there was a very pretty Christmas tree and Father Christmas arrived on the scene. He had presents for everybody, even the 'Taukoros' [i.e. the Montgomeries]. Then he disappeared, to the amazement of all the little kiddies, who searched everywhere for him, behind curtains, up the chimney etc etc. Miss Forbes was the Santa. The big children played battledore and shuttlecock etc.,[26] and the little ones danced round the Christmas tree and played musical chairs. It was all very homey and Christmassy and nice and Mrs Tilley was a most thoughtful hostess and

---

23 Still going strong, Thresher & Glenny, established in 1683, is one of the world's oldest tailors, shirtmakers and men's outfitters.

24 A Tommy's cake was a chocolate buttermilk cake. The name had no connection to soldiers.

25 *Chu Chin Chow*, a musical comedy written, produced and directed by Oscar Asche, and with music by Frederic Norton, was hugely popular after it premiered on 3 August 1916 at His Majesty's Theatre in London: there were 2238 performances over the next five years. There was also a successful season overseas and later a film.
   Lex Butler was Alexander Edward Butler, 3/388, from Ohakune, who left New Zealand on 14 December 1914, as a member of 1 Field Ambulance, New Zealand Medical Corps. Twice turned down because of his eyesight, he became a stretcher bearer.

26 Shuttlecock and battledore is an earlier version of badminton.

a real sport. We asked for the children to come to a pantomime with Al and Mrs Tilley was quite agreeable.

We just had time to get home and dress and then start off for the Savoy where Seton had engaged a table for 8 p.m. We had fish, turkey with cranberry sauce, leeks (no potatoes), Christmas pudding (alight) and rolls and cheese (Gorgonzola). Roger had whisky and soda water and the rest of us a bottle of claret and it cost us £2 10/-, which sounds like thieving to me, but that was soldier's price too. The crowd was very disappointing, the women, either painted or ugly, and the men most ordinary. All of them fairly good at dining and wining. Nothing there to command one's respect or admiration. It was a beautifully cooked meal and the waiting was excellent but that was all. But the 'Taukoros' dined en famille at the Savoy and that was all they wanted.

Tuesday 26 December 1916
Al had breakfast in bed, but is quite bright again. After breakfast settled up a big washing and hunted up soldier's belongings. Had tin box brought up from boxroom, then all but Os went out for morning tea to Petit Palais. After lunch all went to Round Pond [in Hyde Park] to feed the birds. Then Roger and Wid went home and Set, Al, Os and I went to Ponting's pictures and enjoyed them immensely.

Thursday 28 December 1916
Os had an early breakfast and reported at Horse Guards to get his railway pass. He came back about 10.30 to collect his luggage to go off to Denham. The Bernacchis came just after he returned and waited until he left. Dear old son, I do hope he will be comfy and not feel it too much at first. God alone knows how hard it is to see them going off. Mr Bernacchi is very keen to have the boys to manage his angora goat farm island after the war. Wid, Roger, Al and I went out to Fullers, Queens Road for morning tea. After lunch rested for a little and then went to Maison Lyons for afternoon tea to let Al hear the ragtime band, and afterwards went to Grafton Galleries to see the Canadian war photos.[27] They are very wonderful photos but very sad. Felt very sick and wretched this morning and throat is still sore.

Friday 29 December 1916
After breakfast Roger packed up his kit. Then he went to Pope & Bradley

27 The Canadian Official War Photographs Exhibition for the Benefit of the Canadian War Memorials Fund, December 1916. One hundred and fifty-eight works were shown.

to get his Star up.[28] He didn't get word from the War Office, but he has to have it up to report at Aldershot tomorrow morning at 9 a.m. … He started off in taxi about 3.30 to catch his train for Aldershot. He will stay some place tonight and be ready to report tomorrow. Poor old dear. How I do hate this hateful war, and all the muddling imbeciles whose hateful smug complacency has jeopardised everything we hold dear. If every woman feels like I do, they have a day of reckoning ahead. Had two letters from Os today, he sounds cheerful. Wrote to Os and Set.

Saturday 30 December 1916
After lunch was lying down when Roger walked in. More WO muddling: they ought to have had a wire telling them not to go until sent for. Anyhow it's a muddle that can be appreciated this time … WO graciously pleased to return Al's certificate and acknowledge me.

Sunday 31 December 1916
Last day of 1916. Most wonderful year for the 'Taukoros'. God grant that the end of 1917 may find us all happy the same.

Letter from Seton, 31 December 1916
I arrived here 12.30 and was lucky to get here as soon as that. We spent about two hours at Liverpool Street Station and when we made the stampede for the train, about 2000 of us, I lost Fergie without saying 'Goodbye'. The train crawled as far as Bishop Stortford when the fog cleared and we paced it out. On Friday evening we had that exam and it was not as hard as I expected it to be by any means. This is a land of rumours … It is about 500 cadets are to be taken for a 10 days tour of France, to give them practical experience. I believe that some of the Inns of Courts cadets did that some time ago, and personally I like the idea immensely. In church today I found myself next to an NZer. During our hushed conversation I found he was a Wellington man … He asked me if I knew the Hawke's Bay Williams, as one lived at Trumpington Street and she was always pleased to see NZers! No further comment is necessary … You say Father put his stars on, but you don't say he was in the Gazette.[29] I understand that unless he received word he would return as a cadet … We played a match of rugby yesterday and beat F Company 21 to nil … A Company can be pleased with its opening matches.

---

28 Pope & Bradley were civil, military and naval tailors in Bond Street. This addition to his uniform marked Roger's commissioning as a second lieutenant: on 13 January the *Evening Post* stated that he was 'now in the O.T.C. [Officer Training Corps] for the A.S.C. at Aldershot'.

29 Rank had to be officially gazetted, i.e. appear in the *London Gazette*, which listed appointments, commissions and promotions, and medals awarded.

ANOTHER YEAR OF WAR

CHAPTER FIVE

Three major events stand out in 1917, the fourth year of the war. The first is the Russian Revolution – Tsar Nicholas II abdicates in March and the Bolsheviks take power in October – which leads to Russia leaving the war on 3 March 1918. The second is the United States' declaration of war on Germany on 6 April. The third is an indictment on the British high command: its horribly misconceived and costly Passchendaele offensive in Belgium. On 12 October alone there will be more than 2700 New Zealand casualties.

Monday 1 January 1917
Went to Bond Street, gazed in such windows as the crowd would give us the chance to. It was the first day of the winter sales and the crowd was 'some' size.

Wednesday 3 January 1917
Roger got word from the War Office saying they would not give a commission, but in consideration of his age and circumstances they will not enforce the usual military custom of 'placing you wherever they like to put you', but will give him his discharge on Saturday. It was a bit of a bomb for Roger, especially as he had put up his Star and got several military requirements, however I am sure it is for the best. I have never liked the business. Roger and I went to the bank to clear up the £100 mystery [they had been told they were £100 better off than they were]. My calculations were right. So it will mean we have to 'go steady' [save money], especially as Roger is 'washed out'. Roger wrote a cheque for £10; credit at present is only £140. There is a visitor here: she lost her only son in the war and her husband is a colonel at the front. She has the most glorious head of white hair, and is very distinguished looking. Her hands are the only disappointment. A really good-looking woman is such a rare thing that I had to mention her.

Thursday 4 January 1917

At breakfast I opened a communication for Oswald from that Officers' Recruiting Office at Paddington. Dear old son has had no end of annoyance since he registered there on the advice of that man at the high commission. I want to keep the paper as a sample of English muddling impudence, and the thundering cheek of these English, insulting loyal Britishers and letting Huns and Aliens crawl about all over the country.

Friday 6 January 1917

Went to the new Princes theatre to see *Bluebell in Fairyland*.[1] Met the Tilley children. The nurse brought them and little Edith hadn't come because they didn't think she was included. However the nurse hurried back for her and she only missed a little. We had a box; the place was packed from floor to ceiling.

Letter from Seton, 6 January 1917

I am glad I was not accepted for Gidea. While waiting for the train at Liverpool Street I met one of the 'Accepted' and he was still in the same place and likely to remain there for some time ... I did well in that first exam, I got 63 out of 67, but in the one last night there were 50% washouts. This place is getting stricter every day and it takes one working full pressure to keep out of the 'crime sheet' and 'black mark' list. This war, from Captain Vick, is likely to peter out in another six months. This seems to be the general opinion and we hope so.

Saturday 6 January 1917

Roger got up early and went off to Aldershot to get his discharge. He came back in the afternoon and changed into civilian clothes again. His colonel was very nice to him and said he was a sport to have tried it. Letter from Ruth Mason [Dick's sister] was very sad and contained two Christmas cards found in Dick's kit bag, one from Al and one from me. Ruth says Dick's grave is in shifting sand and may be lost, which seems too hard. Surely we can keep his resting place. All the letters are full of hard work and tiredness. NZ was always a cruel place for work, but it must be far crueller now.

Sunday 7 January 1917

Went to afternoon tea with Captain and the Hon. Mrs Parr. The captain

---

[1] First produced in 1901, this Christmas season children's entertainment was written by Seymour Hicks, Aubrey Hopwood, Charles H. Taylor and Walter Slaughter.

talked away about New Zealand but he knew it in the very early days, the days of stage coaches and no railways. Before we left he took us down the dining room and showed us two pictures of the Pink and White Terraces by Blomfield.² He was interested to know we had one of our homestead by the same artist.

Monday 8 January 1917

Roger got a letter from his Colonel expressing his regret at his 'washout' and admiring the spirit which inspired his trying. Called at War Records Office and Roger saw Colonel FitzHerbert, who also was sorry … and suggested he return to NZ, but thank goodness Roger isn't keen on that. Wid went in to see Mrs Empson at the 'dugout' [War Contingent Association] about doing clerical work in the mornings and is to go on Wednesday to do records. Coming back on the tube we lost Roger. He was in the smoking carriage and busy talking to a soldier boy and didn't notice in time to get out at our station. He had our tickets so we had to pay over again, but the lift man gave him back our sixpence when he came along shortly after us. After lunch we went to St Thomas's Hospital: we got out at Westminster and crossed old Father Thames on the Westminster bridge. We found James Howie without much trouble,³ out on a balcony overlooking the Thames and bridge. Oh, it was cold sitting there talking – such a wet, cold day with sleet falling. He chatted away. We took him some cigarettes, and a good thing too, as they only issue Woodbines to the patients.⁴

Tuesday 9 January 1917

Roger posted back his uniform this morning. After lunch we went to Southampton Row, to Pope & Bradley, and chose material for a new suit for Roger. Roger met one of his old Aldershot school mates; he was very disgusted with Roger's 'washout'. Got Calox, quinine and cinnamon to send to Os also, shaving stick and boric ointment from chemist [5/-] …⁵

Wednesday 10 January 1917

Wid [most unusually] first to breakfast, which was due to the fact that she was going to the 'Dugout' in Southampton Row to start some clerical work there.

2 Charles Blomfield (1848–1926) was an English artist who settled in New Zealand and is best known for his paintings of the Pink and White Terraces, which were destroyed in the Tarawera eruption of 1886.

3 This was in fact Harold George Howie, 12/2622, who had been working on his father's farm in Morrinsville before he left New Zealand with the Auckland Infantry Battalion on 14 August 1914. He had received a severe gunshot wound to the abdomen on 28 September and been hospitalised in France before being sent to St Thomas's (5th London General Hospital) in November. In February 1917 he would be sent to Walton-on-Thames where he was listed as 'seriously ill' both because of his wound and because he was suffering from emphysema. Judged 'no longer physically fit for war service on account of wounds received in action', he was sent back to New Zealand on the hospital ship *Maheno* in March 1917.

4 Strong unfiltered cigarettes made by W.D. & H.O. Wills between 1888 and 1988, Woodbines were popular with soldiers in both world wars.

5 Calox was Indian tragacanth, used as a bulking laxative or even a denture fixative; quinine and cinnamon capsules were used for cramp and malaria (the cinnamon disguised the bitter taste of the quinine); boric ointment was a topical antiseptic. Mild in its effect, it was easily made as boracic acid was readily available.

Thursday 11 January 1917

Wid was not so energetic this morning, got down last. London is white with snow this morning but it was very soon slush. Seemed quite funny to see Wid trotting off after breakfast. She likes the work.

Letter from Seton, 11 January 1917

Don't encourage Father to go back to NZ. There is something to do here and it keeps the family together. Besides, this war is not going to last much longer … I made another record shoot yesterday. The practice was firing 10 shots and leading in 45 seconds, the target was 200 yards off and I fired all 10 and put them all on the target. Most of them did not even get eight. This is when the old 'air rifle' tells at Taukoro.

Friday 12 January 1917

Got a letter from Os this morning to say he was in Southall [Auxiliary Military] Hospital with influenza. His letter is very cheerful and I am glad he is in hospital being taken care of. The Bernacchis came to lunch. Mrs Bernacchi is very keen for Oswald to have one of the islands near Tasmania, Clarke or Schouten or part of Maria, to try angora goat farming there. He is very enthusiastic about it all.

Saturday 13 January 1917

Met Mr Chapman in the tube. He thinks the war will be over in a month – if it only could. Al gave two little girls a penny each this morning. Their mouths opened and their eyes bulged. They looked at each other and then at the penny. It was worth a good many twopences to see their amazement.

On Sunday 14th Annie and her daughters travel to Cambridge to visit Seton. After lunch at the Blue Boar – 'Lounge was full of young officers enjoying coffee and sundry other refreshments' – Seton arrives, 'looking so well', and the afternoon is spent sightseeing. The following Tuesday it is Os's turn for a visit. 'We went to Shepherds Bush, got out there and took the train to Southall, a most slow tiring journey of about an hour. All the way along the line was snow, snow, snow. A lot of Australian boys were snowballing themselves and their friends. We found Os in a hospital which was formerly a margarine factory.[6] Saw an English airship sailing about as we journeyed along. It was quite close enough to see the men in her.'

6 Southall was one of the biggest and best equipped auxiliary military hospitals in Britain. It was established not in the margarine factory owned by Otto Monsted & Co. (a Danish firm), but in the Maypole Institute built in 1910 as a recreation centre for the staff. In 1915 the workers willingly helped to turn their institute into a hospital and the company paid for heating, lighting and X-ray machines. It was staffed by VADs and local trained nurses.

Letter from Seton, 18 January 1916

I expect you will have noticed in the papers that the Queen's [College] chef hung himself by his braces last Sunday night. Nobody seems to know what was at the bottom of it. I did all right in the last exam, 89 out of 104. We are all 'windy' or panicky tonight, as the Duke of Connaught is having an inspection tomorrow. All the companies have different roles: ours is to charge 50 yards over trenches and wire entanglements killing sundry Huns on the way, with gas masks on. The helmets are worse than a dose of gas, but makes no odds.[7] Ask Father what he thinks of them … We are kept quite busy with this inspection, the exams, football, cross-country runs, boxing and generally trying to keep out of the orderly room. I shall be exceedingly glad when this lot is over.

Saturday 20 January 1917

The windows rattling last night was caused by an explosion, a huge one at munition works, causing a heavy loss of life. It's very terrible.[8]

Sunday 21 January 1917

After dinner sat in the smoking room, Mr Jardine annoyed me by saying Mahomet was a wonderful man and had knocked to pieces the belief in the Trinity and the Athanasian Creed [which emphasises Trinitarian doctrine]. I said Buddha and Confucius were far ahead of Mahomet and he got quite wild. Wish I had some books to read it all up. Al packing to go to school tomorrow.

Letter from Annie to Seton, 22 January 1917

It was the most terrible explosion on Friday, wasn't it? It has quite put me off munitions work for Dad. I am enclosing you some luck, which I meant to give you at Christmas. I hope it will bring everything you wish for, dear son. Goodnight and tons of love, dear boy. Very loving Mother.

Wednesday 24 January 1917

Got a letter from St Mary's from Sister Dora saying Al has influenza. They put her to bed after midday yesterday with a temperature of 102, which is very worrying when one is so far away.

---

7   Chlorine gas was first used by the Germans in 1915; then came the deadlier phosgene gas in 1916 and, in 1917, mustard gas.

8   The massive TNT explosion, at a munitions factory in Silvertown, East London, killed 73 people and injured 400, 94 of them seriously. Nine hundred homes were destroyed or damaged. The inquiry found that the heavily populated urban site was completely unsuitable for a munitions factory – TNT is extremely unstable – and that Brunner Mond & Co., whose chemical works had been turned over to the government, had failed to look after its staff. The findings were not released until the 1950s.

Thursday 25 January 1917

Went to Whiteley's to order fruit for Al. Got one bunch of grapes, six oranges and one pineapple, which with postage was 5/9. Cheapest fruit I have seen in London. [The doctor would not allow an indignant Al to eat her pineapple, claiming it was indigestible.]

This is a week of freezing temperatures and family sickness: Roger is 'very ill' with a stomach complaint. The Round Pond is 'thick with skaters, crowds of children sliding and everyone enjoying themselves to the utmost'.

Letter from Seton, 27 January 1917

Did seven miles in one hour 35 minutes, 10 minutes being used up in a rest. The majority have exceedingly sore muscles in their legs and of course our old friends the blisters must have their day.

Thursday 1 February 1917

A letter to Roger from his mother: she thinks we ought to go back to NZ … but I am not going to ask anyone's advice about going or staying. 'No funds' would be the only power that would move me on. After lunch Roger and I went to the Strand to see about getting a window or some place where we could see the Opening of Parliament function, but 'napoo'. Got to trust our own 'push and shove' qualities. Germany begins her 'sink everything campaign' at 6.30 tonight.[9] America has another chance now, her last one, to take her stand as a decent nation.

Friday 2 February 1917

Big guns were booming this afternoon, Roger says the sound came from Woolwich [Arsenal], which means gun testing. I hate the boom of guns and bombs.

Letter from Seton, 2 February 1917

The last exam was not as bad as I expected. I managed 79% and was sixth, but about 30 found it extremely hard and failed. I don't know how the ones who have failed all four exams are going to get on, they are going before the colonel sometime soon. The first of the 'washout' started last Tuesday when two left our ranks and returned to Gidea Park for 'not having attained

---

9 On 31 January Germany announced a campaign of unrestricted submarine warfare. The aim was to cut off Britain's imports and starve the British into submission.

a sufficient standard' … I don't think there will be any argument about my desire for the RFC until near the end of the course, so I don't think help will be needed until then, but there is always a possibility the captain will be busying himself about the matter any old time.

Sunday 4 February 1917

The papers contain the best of news: America has severed relations with Germany. The ambassadors of each country are recalled; hope she doesn't waver now. I would like to be able to do without her but coming in will end the war quicker and that counts more than anything. Ever so many cracks showing up today on the Round Pond but everyone said they were a sign of safety. Can't say I felt like that.

Tuesday 6 February 1917

Got a reply to my letter to the high commissioner saying that no provision had been made for overseas ladies to see the Royal Procession. So Wid rang a friend who is trying to get us a ticket for some balcony from her cousin Lord Somebody or other. After lunch got ready to see *The Tanks in Action* at Scala theatre.[10] The pictures were very good but sad and depressing to me anyhow. I hate war with all its cruelties and injustices.

Wednesday 7 February 1917

A friend rang to say it wasn't possible to get tickets and that the Duke of York steps near Whitehall would be a good place to see the procession from. We went by tube then walked through St James Park, all white and beautiful under the snow through the Mall. A dear thing of a policeman gave us the edge of the pavement (gave him 1/- tip) and we had a splendid view of everything, Queen Mary's smile and all. After lunch we went to Westminster Abbey, saw the Chapter House where Lord Wolsey held a great meeting. Came by Whitehall, saw Number 10 [Downing Street], a most shabby-looking front entrance. From there we went to the 'The Old Curiosity Shop', such a dark tiny place. Only a genius like Dickens could have found inspiration there. Near by found a second-hand shop and I noticed a sweet cameo brooch in the window and went in and bought it [£2 2/-]. I felt extravagant but I knew I would never see it again.

---

10 *The Battle of the Ancre and the Advance of the Tanks* was a follow-on to *The Battle of the Somme*, a documentary and propaganda film released the previous year. Tanks had been used on the Somme in 1916, with only partial success; their first successful deployment would come in the Battle of Cambrai in November–December 1917.

Letter from Seton, 7 February 1917

The weather has been really cold the last three days, only 18 to 21 degrees of frost, but being the army we carry on as usual, which means cleaning ice-cold rifles and equipment, and firing on the range when the only warmth is from the explosion of the cartridges.

Friday 9 February 1917

Fergie came to visit. He had seen the Times and found himself gazetted as second lieutenant. Roger and I congratulated him and he kissed me for his mother. Later Mrs Whiteman and I set off from Waterloo to go to Walton to see Harold Howie. In train going down a NZ boy told us we should get out at Weybridge to get to Oatlands.[11] Saw Sister Woodward.[12] It is a fine roomy place with a nice drive. The sun was shining like a huge scarlet tail through the leafless trees and the ground was white with snow. We walked back to Walton and got a taxi there with three NZ boys to take us to the station. A nurse says that 250 of our boys are isolated behind barbed wire at Codford diseased,[13] confirmed by another nurse.

Saturday 10 February 1917

Went in to Trafalgar Square and listened to suffragettes speaking, but as they were almost inaudible we moved on. Went past Cleopatra's Needle, on to Blackfriars. Roger made me furious by passing on family affairs to Mrs Whiteman; she is such a news send-on. Men are donkeys. Wid is thinking of taking work at War Records Office, 35/- a week. Just the same work as she is doing now.

Letter from Seton, 10 February 1917

Don't worry about me. The cold, I don't feel it as much as the people who have lived here all their lives, thanks to Waitaki. The only places I feel it are on the face, hands and ears, but not as much as I did with a good old NZ frost.

Sunday 11 February 1917

After breakfast sat in lounge, read paper and talked. Mr Jardine came in and he and I had an argument about the qualities of men and women. He says they are emotional and imaginative with no practicalness. I say that they are far more practical and far-seeing than men and the world would have never

---

11 Oatlands Park was an historic hotel not far from Walton-on-Thames recently taken over by the New Zealand authorities and converted into a hospital for medical, limbless ('limbies') and tuberculosis cases.

12 Sister Katherine Adelaide Woodward of the New Zealand Army Nursing Service, from Invercargill, sailed on the first voyage of the New Zealand hospital ship *Marama*, which left Wellington on 4 December 1915.

13 They had venereal disease.

been in such a muddle as it's in just now if they had had a 'say' in matters. After lunch set off for Gerard's Cross to see Oswald. It was a real Weary Willie train and we had to change twice. At first he was looking flushed and well. He is finding the training a bit strenuous, but he is as keen as ever, dear old thing. We walked to a sleepy little village and found a place to have tea [2/9] and a talk, got some lozenges [9d] for Os as he still has a cough. Sat by the fire at the station waiting room until the train came along. The country was very uninteresting, cold and wet.

Monday 12 February 1917

Wid and I went to Southampton Row to interview Colonel FitzHerbert and she has arranged to go to work at the War Records Office on Thursday morning. Then went to NZWCA [New Zealand War Contingent Association] to tell them about Wid's new arrangement. They say they will be pleased to have my help when I feel ready. Mrs Simpson and Mrs Wilson said they were sorry to lose Wid. Mrs Wilson is the wife of Dr Wilson of Captain Scott South Pole fame.[14]

Tuesday 13 February 1917

… Came home and found Fergie had been here since 3 p.m. However he stayed for dinner and kissed me 'for his mother'. When he was going away I gave him a little monkey charm and he hung it on his whistle. Having guests to dinner is rather a tricky problem just now, to see them helped to about two square inches of meat, and a scarcity of vegetables.

Thursday 15 February 1917

Wid went off to her new job at the War Records Office. Mrs Whiteman called as she wanted us to go to War Loan demonstration in Trafalgar Square. We managed to get fairly close to front line, had a weary wait and after all the speeches were fairly feeble. Our Mr Massey spoke a few words, or rather roared them, but he isn't an inspired orator. Mr William Thorne, MP Labour member,[15] was the liveliest one of the lot in his own way. The Coldstream Guards played a selection, would like them to play something decent. The Lord Mayor and other mayors, the sheriffs, the choir boys of Westminster and other churches and the Boy Scouts were the chief features of the scene. Wid liked her work today.

14 Dr Edward Wilson (1872–1912), explorer, physician, naturalist, ornithologist and artist, perished with Scott and four others in the Antarctic.

15 Will Thorne (1857–1943) was a unionist, activist and one of Britain's first Labour MPs.

Letter from Seton, 15 February 1917

I am picked for the march-shoot, second man on the list, only eight in the team. It is a terrible fag. We have to march from 5 to 7 miles every other day and practise shooting and it means running 100 yards with loaded rifle, flinging oneself on the nearest ground, usually a puddle or snow, and repeating this three times, doing our best to hit sundry targets and plates that are stuck upon sticks. We feel like mutiny at times but we have stick it out. I sometimes wonder what you would have thought of me at Taukoro if I was to clean up my rifle, boots and everything else, and after a shower of rain charge out and fling myself in puddles that were precisely 100 yards apart, and on the next day repeat the performance. It is from little things that one sees what discipline means in the army …

I said I was in for some boxing. It started on Tuesday and I found my weight was 11 stone 3 pounds, just about a stone heavier than I expected. I fixed up my two opponents and am living for the semi-final, which is tomorrow. In the first contest I boxed a man of my height and build, evidently interesting to the spectators because it was the only contest in which the applause was drawn out at the end. The third and last drew the same applause. About an hour later I had a contest with a man a little taller than myself. He had learned my fault of not guarding my face, and was all out for a win, but at the start of the first round I nearly outed him and gave him a similar one in the third round. Captain Vick mentioned to the major I was from NZ. That was Major Rose, the NZer in charge of C Company; he remembered Uncle Jack Montgomerie. I have made a bit of a hit at boxing. I have the name of taking all the blows on the face and not feeling them. But against all this I failed the exam by one mark. The time was too short and I panicked, but what a jar to come down by one mark only.

Saturday 17 February 1917

Roger and I went to Edgware Rd to see the Employment Department, but 'napoo'. It was a very common show.

Letter from Seton, 18 February 1917

You had better busy yourself and see what regiment you would like me to go in case I have to go in one before the RFC.

Letter from Seton, 22 February 1917

It is now two months since the Christmas leave and through layers of work I see four days leave next Friday. We had the march and shoot today, thank the Lord, but we don't know how we got on yet. We were by far the smartest 'turnout' and we marched the distance faster than any other team but I bet I am pounds lighter. We carried 45 pounds without counting our clothing.

Later

Sorry to say but it's bad news of the march and shoot. After all our days' toil at marching and cleaning up it was only shooting counted.

Friday 23 February 1917

Letter from Al: she is not feeling too good and her heart a bit shaky. Roger and I found our way to the Agricultural College to see the horse fair. It wasn't my line, and there very few women there, but Roger found it interesting. After lunch went out and bought some Widow Welch's pills and posted them to Sister Dora,[16] and also a bottle of Dr Paget's stuff for palpitation and asked her to look after Al. Then went out and posted them. Mrs Stevens [Wid's office mate] came for dinner then they went to a dance in Elysée Rooms, Queens Road given by the NZ Soldiers' Club.

Saturday 24 February 1917

Got tickets for *Peg of my Heart*.[17] It was Wid's half-day so went to the Globe Theatre. I did enjoy it, even though there is nothing really clever or uplifting in the play. However it is quite wholesome and clean and acting is good. In Piccadilly I saw some of those wretched outcast creatures [prostitutes], even saw one speak to a man, but he passed on without the slightest notice. It's a great nation that allows such hideousness in its open streets. My blood just boils over at its manmade laws.

Sunday 25 February 1917

There is no fresh news from New Zealand, every one is waiting patiently for mails now. This U-boat war is bound to make a difference to our getting the mails regularly.

---

16 Widow Welch's Female Pills had been used since at least the 1850s 'for all female complaints, nervous disorders, weakness of the solids, loss of appetite, sick head ache, lowness of spirits, and particularly for irregularities in the female system', as an 1874 advertisement in the *Otago Daily Witness* claimed.

17 *Peg o' My Heart* was a popular comedy written by J. Hartley Manners in 1912.

Letter from Seton, 25 February 1917

Regarding the choice of regiment, you can turn on as much 'influence' as you like in this place, so carry on with all vigour.

Monday 26 February 1917

Letter from Seton. He is amongst a room full of 'flu' so sent him some quinine and cinnamon capsules to ward it from him. Wid saw George Lethbridge [a cousin] at the Records office and he was meant to call here so after dinner Roger and I went to Waterloo Station as we knew he was returning to camp by the 9.30 train and we found him![18] As soon as the gates on the platform were opened George and a large number of decent boys went and then for the next half-hour we saw the sickening sight of boozed boys trailing, some with 'hussies' and some without. It was not a pleasant sight. One cheap-faced 'hussy' in particular enraged me, the boy was giving her such long lingering kisses. Why can't the grubby little brute be locked up? It's shameful.

Tuesday 27 February 1917

NZ mails this morning. Fergie wrote to Wid and said he was under orders for France and Os says their two-monthly course at Oxford is to be reduced to three weeks and he expects to have his commission in five weeks now. It's just a shame that these dear boys, almost babies, are rushed through to fill up numbers that ought to have been there without them if really we had decent men in power, but our boys have to be sacrificed for their mistakes. I hope history will drag them in the mud. After lunch Mrs Whiteman and I went to St Dunstan Hospital for the Blind in Regents Park.[19] It was very sad to see all those blind men, but it was wonderful to see them all, so bright and busy, learning Braille or typewriting or making string bags or cane baskets, even mending boots and shoes. The sister said they always ask how many visitors have been, if they bought anything, so I purchased two string bags [6/6] and a cane basket.

Money affairs have been featuring in Annie's diaries for some time and on 2 March she and Roger go to the bank and then to New Zealand Loan and Mercantile 'to arrange about transferring money to BNZ, fixed it up, having £250 put in now and later the rest. I have the power to call it in.' And this on the very day she is

---

18 Lance Corporal George Montgomerie Lethbridge, 31865, from Wellington left New Zealand on 15 November 1916 as part of the New Zealand Rifle Brigade.

19 Now Blind Veterans UK, St Dunstan's Hostel for Blinded Soldiers and Sailors was founded in 1915 by Arthur Pearson to rehabilitate and train blinded servicemen.

pricing silver hairbrushes in Queens Road. Annie spends up large in London, always noting the price of her purchases. The money probably comes from the estate of her father, who died in 1910.

Saturday 3 March 1917
Roger went to St Irwin's Hotel to try to interview the National Service creatures but couldn't get an interview, has to write again. Seton, Wid and I went to the Savoy theatre to see *The Professor's Love Story*;[20] it was charming. Henry Irving and his wife Fay Compton were the leading actors,[21] but I liked the woman who was acting Agnes Goodwillie the best.

Sunday 4 March 1917
After breakfast set off for Paddington to go to Oxford to see Os, who is now at Jesus College. Seton had to get his ticket: they wouldn't give him any reduction, 15/10½d like ours, gave him £1. Saw the silvery Thames threading his way amongst fields with banks about two inches high, saw some hills!! Saw Taplow and Newbury, then the spires of Oxford and old Os at the station. Saw some impressive old buildings and the Martyrs' monument to Cranmer, Latimer and Ridley. It stands by the spot where they were burned for their faith. After lunch set off to see Jesus College, also Trinity and Keble colleges, but can't get the same beautiful glimpses of courtyards as at Cambridge. Lovely to have the two boys together, they both looked bonny.

Monday 5 March 1917
After breakfast went out and ordered seats for Gaiety Theatre [10/6d] for Seton and Wid, ordered Madeira cake and dates for Al [4/2], also had café au lait and cocoa and milk for Seton [2/1d],[22] coathanger for Wid [6d], then had morning tea [1/5d], poked around for a while. After lunch Seton and I went to look at apartments in Museum Street, napoo. Went to Kingsley Hotel to ask tariff, 6/6d a day for bed and breakfast. Went to Selfridges to get naso-pharyngeal for Os. Financed Roger and Seton 10/- each. Found Fergie here this afternoon, financed him 30/- but got his cheque for amount. He went to the theatre with Wid and Seton. They had to get a taxi as they were so late getting away [5/3d].

20 By J.M. Barrie of *Peter Pan* fame.

21 British stage actor and manager Henry Brodribb Irving (1870–1919), the eldest son of the great Sir Henry Irving. Fay Compton was not his wife. He was married to actress Dorothea Baird.

22 Made by Nestlé, café au lait was a tinned ready-mixed coffee and milk powder to which boiling water was added to make a hot drink. It was a staple both for men at the front and for civilians.

Tuesday 6 March 1917

Letter from Sister Dora to say Al has influenza on top of her measles: poor wee kid is having a run of bad luck. After lunch went to *Maskelyne's Mysteries* [9/9d].[23] Dad came too and we enjoyed them very much. Soon after we got back Fergie came. He wouldn't stay for dinner as he had to pack up, but he came back at 8.30 and took Wid to the Palladium. He goes to France tomorrow. The tragedy of it all, it just makes me blue all over. He is a very loveable boy. We are all very fond of him and I hope and pray he will come through. It was lovely having him a few days, but it makes it harder going back, though he looked so much better for his little holiday. I am very tired tonight and depressed. I just hate my boys going back to camp and I hate Fergie going away. I've seen too many go away now. It's all a tragedy and I just hate all the bungling muddlers. Roger wrote to his Forest Department [Timber Supplies Department of the War Office] for fuller details.

Friday 9 March 1917

The daily papers are full of Gallipoli Commission report.[24] So went into smoking room after breakfast to digest them. The report only confirms what I have said from the very beginning about it; I am thankful those muddling blunderers are uncovered at last. They can't be hung but they should certainly be prevented from ever holding a position of responsibility again, in justice to those poor boys who had to bear the brunt of their ghastly ignorance and ineptitude … After tea had a great argument in the lounge about the Gallipoli business and its muddling instigators. These English people will hold Kitchener up as a little tin god.[25] They won't look at his feet of clay at all. They won't look anything in the face, that is an unpleasant fact, and they will never learn. Narrow-minded, stiff-necked, smugly self-satisfied crowd of blind idiots.

Tuesday 13 March 1917

Nine o'clock Roger's taxi came and off he went to his forestry venture. Oh, I do hope it will turn out well. Later went to chemist and ordered salicylic and collodion …[26] Wid has had pain and collywobbles all day at office, gave her a dose of chlorodyne tonight.

---

23 Founded in 1873 by John Nevil Maskelyne and George Cooke, this was a show of conjuring and entertainment, including a levitating lady. When Cooke died in 1904, the show was run by Maskelyne and his son and staged at St George's Hall in Langham Place.

24 This was the very critical report of a parliamentary commission into the Dardanelles campaign of 1915, which concluded that the extreme difficulties of attacking the peninsula were greatly underestimated, there was a lack of resources and both the April and August landings were flawed.

25 This admiration of Lord Kitchener, Secretary of State for War and the face on the First World War's most famous recruiting poster, was perhaps enhanced after his death in June 1916, when the warship on which he was travelling to Russia was sunk by a German mine.

26 Salicylic acid has long been used to relieve aches and pains and mitigate fever. Better known for its use in photography, collodion was also used as a surgical dressing.

Annie photographed in March 1917. She turned 50 the following May.

Right: Winifred, also known as Wid or Tiny, in London.

Far right: Alex, usually Al in the diaries, who attended boarding school during her stay in England.

Right: Os, probably in his Royal Flying Corps cadet uniform.

Far right: Seton, aged 18, while studying to be an officer at Queens' College, Cambridge, from December 1916 to April 1917.

Roger and Seton. Roger was briefly in uniform early in 1917 before beginning forestry work.

Above: Guy Seton, who served with the Wellington Mounted Rifles. He was wounded in August 1916.

Right: Seton and Os, standing, with Cyril McLeod, known as Mac. The three boys were all at school together in Wanganui.

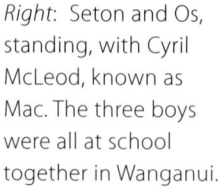

Far left: Fergie, Robert Arthur Fergusson, of 6 Battalion, Royal Fusiliers, was killed in the Battle of Arras in April 1917.

Left: Hugh Anderson, who was a nephew of both Roger and Annie, as Roger's nephew married Annie's niece. He served in the Wellington Infantry Battalion on the Western Front and is frequently mentioned in the diaries.

Left: Annie and Winifred with Os, centre, and an unknown friend in Hyde Park, where the family often walked.

Edited by the New Zealand Press Association's London correspondent G.H. Scholefield, the *New Zealander: Home News for New Zealanders on Active Service* was published fortnightly in London from December 1916 to August 1919. It provided a summary of New Zealand news for those serving overseas and listed those killed and wounded.

Left: Diplomat John Tilley was a close relation through his Montgomerie connections. In 1916 he was working in the Foreign Office and was later British ambassador to Brazil and then to Japan.

Below left: Alan Payling's lunch invitation to Winifred, written shortly before he was killed in Belgium in October 1917. Annie described him as a 'bright, jolly boy'.

Below: Winifred's Lloyd's insurance policy, taken out in case of injury or death by bombing.

> Will you come to lunch with me to-day. Will wait at the corner at one o'clock.
> Alan Payling

Right: Annie's letter, from Devon, asking the Record Office for information on New Zealand soldiers Leslie Potts (a relative) and Charles Morgan, and (*far right, below and below far right*) the reply from Norman FitzHerbert. Potts was a Cambridge farmhand before he left New Zealand in June 1916. Morgan was a farmer in the same area.

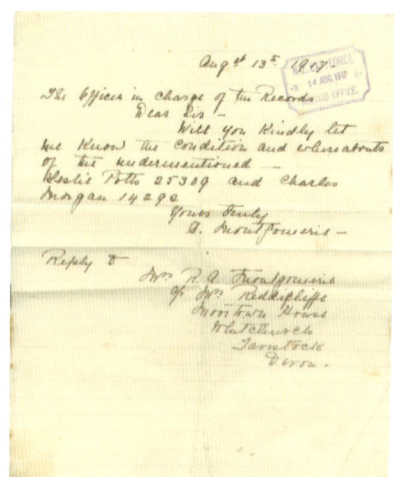

Flying Outfit
Tunics 2
Flying & Infantry
Trousers 1 pair
Breeches 1 pair
Boots tan 2 pairs
Puttees 2 pairs
British Warm 1
Ties silk 4
Collars 4
Shirts Khaki 4
Flying Cap 1

Binoculars 1
Revolver 1
Valise Containing Blankets Folding Bed Wash stand etc etc } 1
Suit Case

The 'shopping list' for the clothing Os needed for the Middle East. The 'British Warm' refers to a knee-length great coat.

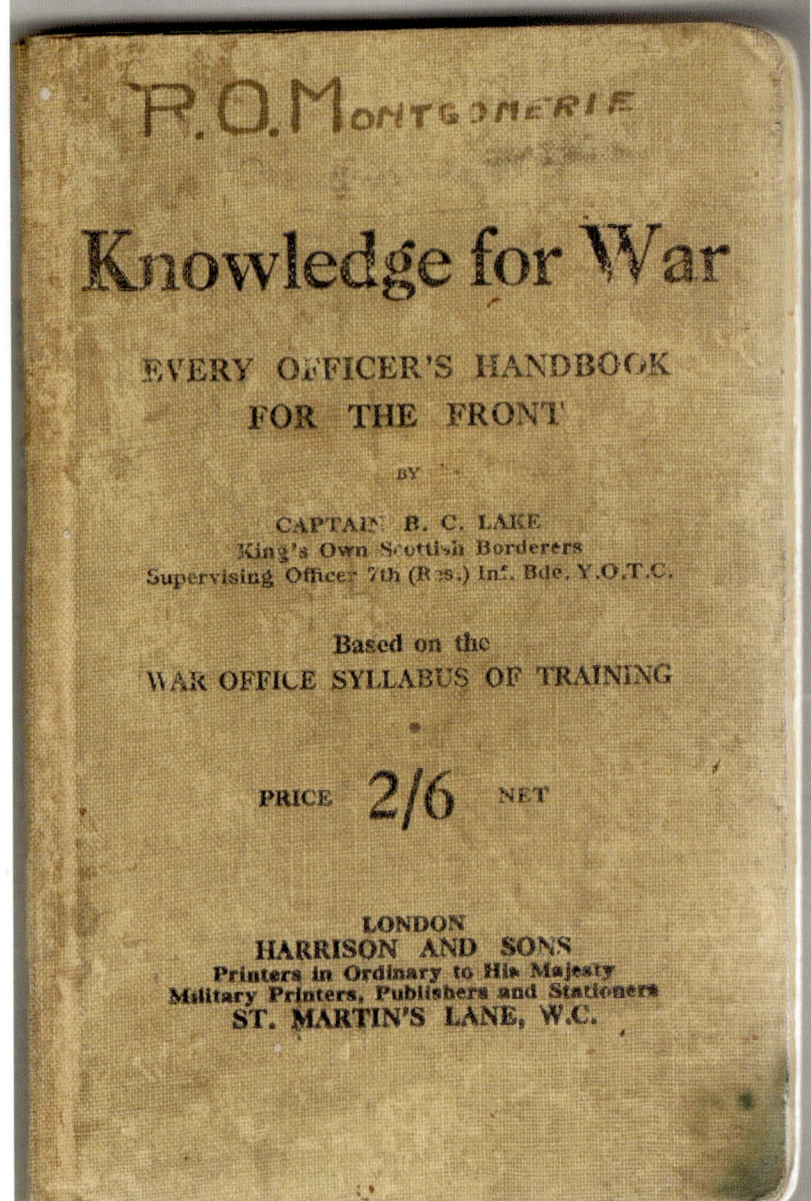

Os's copy of *Knowledge for War: Every officer's handbook for the Front* by Captain B.C. Lake, which, among other things, listed the kit required at the front.

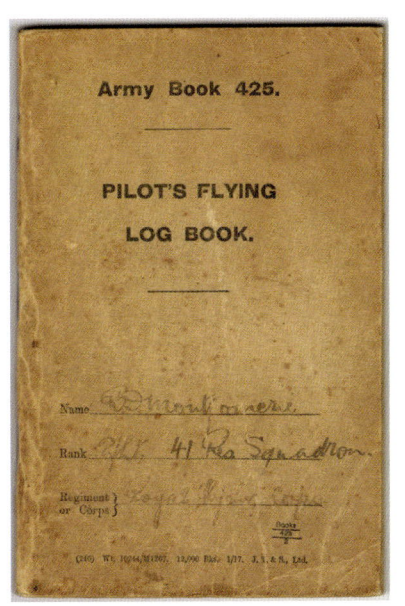

Above and left: The cover and first page of Os's *Pilot's Flying Log Book*, when he was a second lieutenant in 41 Reserve Squadron, showing circuits and landings made. Entries start on 14 April 1917.

Above: Os's wristwatch, worn throughout the war. Until the end of the nineteenth century wristwatches were mainly a female accessory but this changed as men on horseback, and then on bicycles, began to wear their timepieces on their arm rather than in their pocket. Wristwatches were also obviously much more practical on the battlefield. Omega made a luminous watch that was popular with officers.

Above: Os's identification bracelet, showing his religious affiliation as Church of England. This would have been privately made or purchased. Although each soldier, or in this case, pilot, was issued with an identity disc, the official requirement to remove it from a body meant that the dead could remain unidentified, so such bracelets were widespread. The inclusion of 'C of E' meant that, should the need have arisen, Os would, if possible, have been buried by an Anglican padre.

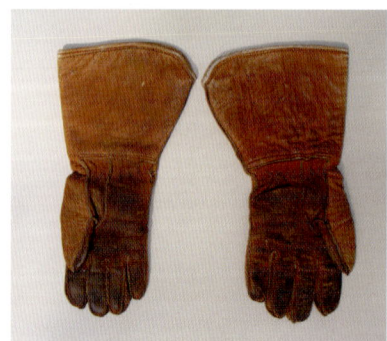 

Above: Os's well-used flying gloves, made of sheepskin with the wool on the inside.

Above: The jacket pocket and RAF wings from a jacket issued to Os near the end of the war. The Royal Air Force was formed on 1 April 1918.

Left: Os's war medals with the original envelope and sealing wax in which they were posted by registered mail after the war. The large ones on the left are the Victory Medal – the wording on the back reads 'THE GREAT WAR FOR CIVILISATION 1914–1919' – and the British War Medal 1914–1918. Both were campaign medals for war service. On the right are the miniatures and Os's tunic colours.

Left: The New Zealand government telegram sent to the troops at Christmas, 1917.

Far left: Os and Seton.

Roger worked for the Timber Supplies Department of the War Office at Heckwood, by Horrabridge, near Tavistock in South Devon. The pit props were sent to France for use in the trenches.

Right and far right: Annie was a great admirer of actor H.B. Irving. The family often went to the theatre.

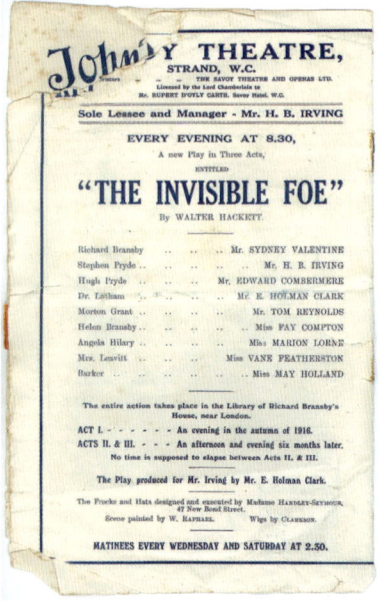

NEW GALLERY TEA ROOM Open to the Public.

NEW GALLERY KINEMA
SOCIETY'S PICTURE PLAYHOUSE.
PATRONIZED BY ROYALTY
REGENT STREET QUADRANT, W

SLIDING ROOF.   PERFECT VENTILATION.

OPEN DAILY from 2.0 till 11 p.m.   SUNDAYS 6 till 11 p.m.

Monday, Tuesday, and Wednesday, August 27th, 28th, and 29th.

Programme

THE PRINCIPAL ITEMS OF OUR PROGRAMME ARE ADVERTISED IN ALL THE LEADING DAILY, EVENING AND SUNDAY PAPERS.

THIS PROGRAMME IS SUBJECT TO ALTERATION AT THE DISCRETION OF THE MANAGEMENT

1 **PATHE FRERES TOPICAL BUDGET**
   Including all the latest WAR PICTURES.

2 **CHARLIE CHAPLIN**
   In his Latest Farcical Absurdity, in Two Acts, "THE IMMIGRANT."

3 **The Romance of President Wilson**
   Highly Interesting Cartoon.

4 **The Winning of Sally Temple**
   In Four Acts, featuring
   FANNY WARD
   SALLY TEMPLE. an Actress at Drury Lane Theatre, is the benefactress of the people of Pump Lane.

SPECIAL NOTICE —For the convenience of the Medical and Professional gentlemen attending the Theatre

The House of Thrills, Smiles and Tears

Teas can be served to Patrons in their Seats or in the New Gallery Tea Rooms.

Above: Captain Bruce Bairnsfather (1887–1959) was the best-known British humorist and cartoonist of the First World War. In 1917 his most famous creation, the elderly Tommy, Old Bill, became the subject of a successful musical called *The Better 'Ole*, which had more than 800 performances in London.

Above: As this programme for the New Gallery Kinema shows, films were an important source of both entertainment and information in wartime London.

Above: *Chu Chin Chow: A Musical Tale of the East* was the *Cats* of its day, a long-running theatrical success seen by many soldiers on leave in London.

Right: The 'Britannic Tablet' Winifred used as her address book in 1916 when all the young soldiers she wrote to, including her brothers, were cadets. Note the inclusion of the poignant little poem: 'If a body write a body/Getting no reply/May a body ask a body/Who the____? What the, Why?'

Wednesday 14 March 1917

Wid got up feeling very sick and came into my room on her way down to breakfast. I gave her a dose of chlorodyne and she was very sick after it. Had a cup of tea, then she had some port and whisky to steady her and she went off to work. Later went to Southampton Row to see how Wid was getting on, found her quite ready to come home again. She got leave from one of the authority, got a taxi [2/3]. Went to the chemist, he says she has gastric influenza, also bought some grapes [6/10] and bottle of Bovril [1/1-]. Roger came back this afternoon, couldn't get forestry work. When one sees for oneself how they muddle the simplest matters, is it any wonder that one loses heart about the war they are muddling through. Roger had a very cold uncomfortable night and looks flushed tonight and eyes bloodshot. He had to tramp about looking for accommodation and had a palpitation after it. The man told him he didn't think he could do the work.

Letter from Seton, 15 March 1917

We had quite an experience today: we went in the gas chamber for the first time. Don't get alarmed, it is no worse than wandering round in the fresh air but our buttons thought differently.[27] When in the gas helmets one feels as safe as a bank, though when one first tries it on it seems as if the helmet is sufficient without any gas. It certainly does give one confidence and the German gas has not the terror it used to have. The battalion had a lecture last night from a Dr Ross of the university, on Germany's and Austria and Hungary's eastern ambitions. It only becomes increasingly evident that 'statesmen' must have known of the proximity of trouble. He was a splendid speaker and very clever.

Friday 16 March 1917

Read the paper, every one got a shock this morning to find there has been a Russian Revolution and the Czar had abdicated. I wish we could strike our Unseen Hand traitors as they have done theirs.[28] Roger went to the War Office this morning and reported the man at Harlestone. The War Office man who saw him was very annoyed about things and said that it was no way to treat a colonial. He took some notes.

27 The chlorine gas they had to walk through would have discoloured the metal buttons.

28 The Unseen Hand, made much of in the media, was said to be a 'mysterious organisation … considerate to German interests' as the *Hawera & Normanby Star* put it on 27 December 1916. Under the headline 'Hun Businesses in London' the paper wrote of 'the privilege extended to comfortably-housed and well-fed Germans in British internment camps to go out from time to time, unattended, to look after their businesses in the City'.

Letter from Seton, 17 March 1917

You will be surprised to hear I am quarantined. One of the fellows in our room has developed German measles and the five of us are semi quarantined … he had a rash last night and being in the army means sick parade is only in the morning … five of us were separated for the exam … we have our meals in our 'sitting room' and parade separately at the end of the company.

Monday 19 March 1917

After breakfast helped new maid make our beds. She is Swiss and she thinks we ought to have made 'peace' when Germany offered it. She can't see why we go on with such a hopeless war. She says the Swiss would have been ashamed to let Germany get through as easily as the Belgians did. She hasn't much respect for the power of the Allies and it was quite funny to hear her point of view.

Friday 23 March 1917

Wid brought home word that the *Rotorua* was sunk off the mouth at the Thames, her passengers and mail were put off at Plymouth, also the *Otaki* was sunk in the Atlantic, both NZ boats.[29] Thank goodness some Americans were drowned in the last American boat sank, surely old 'Won't Fight Wilson' will have to play the man now.[30] Mrs Watts is very worried about her boy in France. It's pitiful to see the anxiety these poor mothers go through.

Saturday 24 March 1917

At Maison Lyons I overheard an American wounded boy. He said one of his mates had a shell explode in front of him and he was picked up and taken to the dressing station. The doctor said, 'Well, Yank, I'm sorry for you. I'm afraid you will never see again.' 'That's pretty hard times,' said the boy and the doctor said. 'Yes, it's pretty rough on you.' Then he sent him to wait outside for an ambulance to take him to hospital. The boy sat down, unswung his gun, loaded it, put it to his neck and pulled the trigger with his feet, and was gone, poor, poor boy. Another mate had both legs and arms off and asked the doctor constantly to put him out of things. Poor maimed wreckage of life. It stuns me to hear these things. Another of his tales was about a lady visiting his hospital. She came to his bed and said, 'You are an American, aren't you?' He said, 'Yes.' 'When is your country

---

29 The New Zealand Shipping Co.'s steamer *Rotorua* was sunk in the English Channel on 22 March after being torpedoed by a German U-boat. One man, a steward named Williams, was killed. The New Zealand Shipping Co.'s *Otaki* was sunk off the Azores on 10 March in a battle with a German raider. Six men died, including the master, Archibald Bissett-Smith. The rest of the 71 crew were taken prisoner and not released until after the war. Bissett-Smith was awarded a posthumous VC in 1919.

30 Annie is referring to US President Woodrow Wilson (1856–1924) who had been re-elected in 1916 on the policy of American neutrality. The 'American boat' was the merchant vessel *Vigilancia*, which was torpedoed on 18 March 1917: 15 Americans were killed. Two other American vessels were sunk by U-boats that same day.

coming into the war?' she next asked. 'Never. Why should it? Weren't there enough countries spoiled without it?' Then the lady said, 'You don't show very much spirit.' 'Don't I?' said the boy. 'I have just put in fourteen months in the trenches anyhow.' The visitor moved off and the matron, who had been scowling at him, came and said, 'Why did you speak like that? Don't you know who it is?' He said, 'I don't care either if King George came here, I would say the same.' It was Lady Haig.[31]

Sunday 25 March 1917

Went with Wid to Berner's Hotel to see Moira McNab [who had been at school with Winifred]. She came to Plymouth last Thursday from the *Rotorua* at 2 p.m. By 6 p.m. the ship was sunk in the mouth of the Thames by a torpedo with all its valuable cargo on board, not a destroyer within 9 miles. It's always the same hopeless muddling. If they couldn't protect it after it left Plymouth, why in the name of common sense didn't they land the cargo there. How I wish Lord Fisher was in power.[32]

Letter from Seton, 25 March 1917

It seems the Huns are contemplating an Easter surprise on the east coast. Don't be surprised if this son of yours has some rather perculiar [*sic*] experiences in the near future.

Tuesday 27 March 1917

Went to lounge and had little 'jarring' note with Mrs Fairfield about the colonials, which was a sudden surprise to me; she is such a nice old thing. The England she worships does not exist today. We who have to suffer for her faults have the right to criticise her. They are so hide bound, insular, smugly self-complacent muddling fools, and even now they do not realise this war, as little NZ does. They have never made any real sacrifices here in England apart from this awful one of blood, but they still have endless comfort and extravagances. Spent afternoon at Whiteley's, saw their live model display, which I thought was a bit lavish. One costume we saw was only £29 10s – no sign of war there today. Sodden, stupid, selfish extravagance.

Thursday 29 March 1917

Small argument started again about colonials. The English think we have no

---

31 Lady Haig was the wife of Sir Douglas Haig (1861–1928), the controversial British general whose command of major battles on the Western Front won him opprobrium for the high number of casualties.

32 John Arbuthnot 'Jacky' Fisher, 1st Baron Fisher of Kilverstone (1841–1920), admiral and promoter of naval reform, was recalled as First Sea lord in November 1914 but resigned only a few months later over Churchill's Gallipoli campaign.

right to blame England for her 'street traffic' [prostitutes] and think we are very one-sided in our patriotism etc., etc. I guess I know who is one-sided. They think we should come as 'daughters to Mother's house'. Just so, and if we do and find that Mother's house keeps open leprosy we have the right to say so, also to object for her blunders and mistakes. When we are not consulted in the policy which brings about such blunders, also we have no right to be treated the same as aliens and super-taxed here.

Friday 30 March 1917

Al arrived for the holidays. Roger took her for a row on the Serpentine and I rested as I am feeling sick and aching all over. Roger got a letter from the War Office offering him work as foreman of timber work in Exeter.[33] Heard that some are rather scared of employing colonials as they are scared that colonial methods may upset their ways.

Saturday 31 March 1917

Woke up with German measles all out on face and chest. Great consternation, Miss Woolley, assistant housekeeper, very upset. The doctor came about midday and there is every likelihood of my being sent to London Fever Hospital, which is a fearful hurdle for me, much worse than the disease. Wid was sent home from the office and they say no one can go out to work from this place if I stay. A case of quarantine – don't know the exact truth yet. Finished two letters for NZ, told them to 'cook' [sterilise] their letters even though the doctor says letters don't carry infection. When he wrote my name he asked if we were Ayrshire Montgomeries: he had been at Oxford with Hastings Montgomerie. Al has been in quarantine with me all day, which has been horribly dull for her, poor kid. I expect it would be better all round if I do go to hospital. Miss Woolley was furious because she thought Wid had mentioned 'measles' downstairs, but she hadn't.

Sunday 1 April 1917

My eyes were too sore to even read my usual Sunday papers today. The doctor came at lunchtime and said I was splendid and went off again. He said if I used the carbolised vaseline jelly I would not be the slightest bit infectious. I simply smeared myself with it: nice, oily-looking object. The lounge-ites are rather embarrassing in their kind inquiries and Wid had to

---

33 The timber was used to make trenches, roads, railways and military camps on the Western Front. There was a desperate shortage of wood, partly because Germany had declared all timber contraband at the beginning of the war, blocking Britain's access to timber and wood pulp from the Baltic. A Directorate of Forestry was established in France in 1915 and in 1917 forestry was made a reserved occupation in Britain. A Director of Timber Supplies was appointed to report to the War Office. The Forestry Commission was founded in 1919 to replant and restore British forests decimated for the war effort.

fence like a diplomatist. One kind creature wanted to come and see me but Wid had to say the doctor said no visitors. Page [at the lodgings] was quite nice the way he asked if I were better. I asked if he was frightened of me and he said, 'Oh no, Madam' and then added in a whisper, 'I have had measles.' Roger is suspicious of Mr Thompston, who had a temperature last night and too sore a throat to smoke his pipe tonight. Al is being quite a good little nurse but it's hard for her to be locked up.

Tuesday 3 April 1917

Two letters from dear Little Thomas [Annie's sister Jen], with some four-leafed clovers enclosed. Expect they brought me luck because I have not been 'sent out' to hospital. I am getting on wonderfully well, apart from some nasty flatulence round my heart last night …[34]

Wednesday 4 April 1917

Hurrah! America is going to play the game at last. Seton was out until 11 p.m. last night on the Gogog Hill doing wire entanglement and trench work under star shells etc, freezing and snow lying all over the ground. They make things pretty strenuous for our baby boys.

Tuesday 10 April 1917

Got up this morning and sat by fire in bedroom all day. Roger came up and said 'Goodbye' before I got up, and then went off to Exeter to his forestry work. I do hope he will like it. Seton arrived from visiting Os at Oxford about 12.30. We entertained him in our measles room yesterday and today. Miss Ibbotson suggested Al have her dinner downstairs, which she did. Seton took her to see *Maid of the Mountains* this afternoon.[35]

Wednesday 11 April 1917

Letter from Roger: his address for the next few days is City Hotel Exeter. He will be away at Okehampton for several days, railing timber in company with his boss. Al had a disinfecting bath after lunch and had her room disinfected with a formalin candle. Miss Woolley is a victim; she went to hospital today. Went through a lot of old newspapers today, ready for our fumigation next Monday. It was snowing this morning and this evening it has been hailing – great summertime.

---

34 Annie's 'heart flatulence' may have been palpitations or arrhythmia; symptoms of heart problems often mimic indigestion. Her health must have been reasonably good, however, as she lived until the age of 91.

35 This famous operetta, produced by Oscar Asche of *Chu Chin Chow* fame, opened at Daly's Theatre in London on 10 February 1917 and ran for 1352 performances.

Thursday 12 April 1917

Doctor called before Wid was [had made herself] beautiful. He wanted to see that no complications of any sort had seized us, however we completely satisfactory. After dinner read paper and was just lying down when in came Oswald. Dear old kid had his 'pip' up and his Sam Browne on as a full-blown second lieutenant.[36] He looks A1. We managed to get a room here for him; it was 9 p.m. when he arrived. We celebrated his 'pip' in port [Gilbey's Invalid] and soda water with some petit beurre biscuits, and sat talking till 12 p.m. He is very keen and happy with his work but says he is rather disappointed with the stamp of boys going through with him. He says he owes the government here a debt for all the useful knowledge he has garnered these past few months: with what he knows now he could make the old 'Krit' [the family car] go if he handled it again.[37] We received him in the measles room. We just had to see him. We have come to the conclusion that if he doesn't get them any worse than what we did, it would only be of benefit by keeping him a few weeks longer from the front.

Letter from Seton, 12 April 1917

Today we had a mock battle against the Fifth Battalion and it was quite exciting. There was one bad casualty of a seriously sprained ankle, one of our boys … it is a wonder someone was not blown up with all the bombs used by the Fifth. The Gogs [Cambridgeshire hills named Gog and Magog] did not look like themselves at all, with a tank, aeroplanes, a sprinkling of brigadier generals and civilian onlookers and the 'movie' men strove to do justice to our efforts. You will see it advertised at the Scala or elsewhere soon: the cadet battalions at battle, striking war film. He has me fighting with a coil of barbed wire, doing my best to help the company win the entanglement competition, which we lost. They attacked us and we attacked them and the judges and the brigadier said we won; they did not have it all their own way. Smoke bombs are great ideas. Green manuka [being burned off on farmland] is nothing to them and we all got a good idea of what a battle is like, those that have not already been in one. The aeroplanes swooped down to within 6 feet of the ground and dropped bombs on us. The 'tank' was a Ford converted and was not effective.

---

36 The pip is on his epaulette, to show his rank. A Sam Browne is a wide leather belt with a strap that goes over the right shoulder.

37 K-R-I-T or Krit was a small and short-lived (1909–16) car manufacturing company based in Detroit, Michigan. Seton seems to have discovered the car while at Waitaki Boys'. He sent letters home about it, and an advertisement from the 10 May 1913 edition of *The Autocar*. The family bought one, presumably for the not inconsiderable sum of 200 guineas quoted in the ad. As the slogan said, 'It isn't so much the Price as the Car'. The company's emblem was a swastika or fylfot, commonly and uncontroversially used in the early twentieth century as a symbol of good luck.

Friday 13 April 1917

Woke Os early so he could have a bath and shave before early breakfast. He came to show us his vaccination marks: he was vaccinated and inoculated before he left Oxford. The porter got a taxi and he was away. However he will be back very soon again: kit leave. He gets his chequebook today and begins his bank account at Cox's [Cox & King's bank]. I think he gets 14/- or 15/- a day, 6/- to 8/- goes in mess allowance. After dinner Al brought a letter from Aunt Jessie in NZ with a photo of dear old Dick's grave. It also included two £2 postal notes for Seton because he was the first in khaki!

Saturday 14 April 1917

Card from Roger. He sounds very happy in his new work. Al had afternoon tea with Miss Ibbotson and she came up to ask if I would mind if her guest, a South African boy, sat at our table with Al. I said I didn't mind at all. Then another request came by Bessie the maid to ask if I would allow Al to go to the theatre with him and Miss Ibbotson. I again acquiesced. So after dinner our flapper set off to see *Vanity Fair*.[38] She was just bubbling with importance and joy. Miss Ibbotson has been very kind to her while I have been sick. She is a real Christian.

38   *Vanity Fair* was a revue written by Arthur Wimperis, with music by Herman Finck, Max Darewski, Shelton Brooks and Jerome Kern. It opened at London's Palace Theatre on 6 November 1916 and ran for 265 performances. One of its songs was called 'The Anzacs'.

Sunday 15 April 1917

Woke at 1.30 am and remembered about Al, so crept upstairs to see if she was in bed. Of course she was and I gave her a great fright too. When she came in the morning I impressed upon her the necessity of coming in to see me before she goes to bed when she has been out like that. It was her first dash, so she couldn't be expected to know. Wid always pops in then I go off to sleep quite satisfied.

Monday 16 April

Had breakfast in bed and then got up and had my disinfectant bath and spent the day in Wid's room while ours was being fumigated. Our room was ready for us soon after afternoon tea but it smelt strongly of formalin so we didn't go down till about dinner time.

Wednesday 18 April 1917

Shopped for silver pendants to hold four-leafed clovers for boys' mascots.

Got satisfaction at Silversmiths' Co. shop. Arranged to have them made to order, monogrammed and crested for £4, two of them. Absolutely tired and aching arms and feet tonight.

Friday 20 April 1917

After breakfast went to Wid's room and just looking down the 'Killed in Action' column of the *Times* I saw our dear old Fergie's name killed on the 14th.[39] It was a stunning blow – just six weeks and three days since he went away. We have been dazed and miserable all day. Winifred has felt it very much, but we all loved him. I'm sure the boys and Roger will be terribly shocked. This sacrifice of young lives is too hideous. It makes me hate with bitter hatred all these muddling idiots at the head of affairs. Why can't they be to made to pay for their blundering, not our precious boys? While in town watched crowds of 'Tommy Atkins' coming from Victoria Station – just made me bitter. They all or nearly all, looked rough uncouth creatures, yet they were back safely and that splendid young life was stilled for ever. And these commonplace, middle class-looking English crowds get on my nerves. They don't look worth dying for, indeed they don't, smug, ordinary-looking lot. To be truly British you don't want to see too much of England and the English. They won't face close inspection.

Oswald had written to report that he had been up flying on the 18th on 'dual' – with an instructor – and flew most of the time himself: he was up 40 minutes and made 10 landings. 'It seems very quick work,' writes Annie, 'and I don't want him to be quick.' On the night the family hears about Fergie, she writes to Seton to give him the 'sad news': 'God only knows what it will do for his poor mother.'

Saturday 22 April 1917

Read the papers just as we went out, but at last our patrols have caught some cursed Hun destroyers that came raiding our coast. Walked in Rotten Row, but I sat down most of the time – am feeling used up. Spoke to Colonel Whiteman. He seemed to think our NZ forces will be taken out of France before very long and sent to Judea. He says the NZ people won't stand much more of the 'wiping' [rejection?] business and the authorities know it. I just hope they do, it's high time. If many mothers felt as I do they would certainly be called to account, and punished too. Went to the Criterion for

---

39 Second Lieutenant Fergusson, 6 Battalion, Royal Fusiliers, was actually killed on the 15th, in the Battle of Arras, which began on 9 April and officially ended on 16 May. By then the British had suffered more than 150,000 casualties. He was 19 years old. Fergie is buried in Bois-Carre British Cemetery, Thelus.

afternoon; it was very restricted tea for that place. I just love to see these greedy people curtailed. It would do them a world of good. Perhaps it will dawn on them that we are at war and that our precious boys have been sacrificed to keep their flag flying.

Letter from Seton, 22 April 1917

Had a 'heart attack' on account of the bad news in your letter … It is very sad about Fergie but he said on board ship [*Remuera*] he was going to be killed and sure enough he was right. I didn't like the way he said it at the time and said he had 'Rats' [no chance], but they say the Gaelic have a premonition of trouble. It is a shame because you could not find a better officer.

Tuesday 24 April 1917

Went to Kew gardens with Wid and Al. It was just a little too early, but the daffodils in one place were beautiful, and blue flowers [bluebells] were worth seeing. We went in bus and trams and weren't impressed with the majesty of the British race as seen from the top of our bus – pretty sordid, a lot of it. English people are in three strata: lowest, sordid, then middle class smug, and third and highest swollen headed and charmingly inefficient.

Sunday 29 April 1917

Went to Piccadilly Circus, had a very wartime tea, very black-looking bread [one small piece buttered and two small sandwiches] with a saucer of cake, one each and about one inch, fruity looking too. In the smoking room heard that the *Ballarat*, an Australian ship with 10,000 tons of food, was sunk an hour after leaving Plymouth, just the same as the *Rotorua*.[40] Aren't they fools?

Monday 30 April 1917

Wid went back to work today. Got tickets for *Hamlet* at the Savoy. Saw H.B. Irving acting. It was very good, great improvement on most of the shows running here [15/9] Something brainier and more lasting, we all enjoyed it. Heard today that the *Medina*,[41] another P & O ship, went down the same way as the *Ballarat* and *Rotorua*. Some people think the 'neutrals' are laying mines. It's very serious anyhow.

---

40 Annie's source had it wrong. The *Ballarat* was an Australian troopship with 1367 soldiers from Victoria on board. On 25 April, as she was sailing up the English Channel, she was hit near the stern by a German torpedo. Although the vessel sank, no one died.

41 SS *Medina* was sunk by a German U-boat on 28 April.

Wednesday 2 May 1917

Al packed her bag in the morning. Seton has heard from headquarters Cambridge, not from the War Office. He passed out 8th of 400, which is wonderfully good … Seton on leave for a few days.

Thursday 3 May 1917

Seton wrote to Jack Tilley this morning. After lunch we set off for Drury Lane to see the picture film *Intolerance*, a most wonderful picture which took two and a half years to produce and cost £390,000.[42]

Friday 4 May 1917 Half a century for me

Letter from Os, the dear old kid, wishing me many happy returns. Went to the Tower of London, got some of the Beefeaters to explain different things. Al and I 3/6, Seton went free in khaki.

Saturday 5 May 1917

Got letter from Roger wishing me birthday wishes. Al back to school today. Seton went off to the post office with a parcel to post. A telegram arrived from Os asking Seton 'to come up as fast as possibly can', which put me in a panic. Hurried off to Whiteley's and changed Seton's ticket to Doncaster, which cost 24/- extra. When they saw the telegram they all declared wire just a usual one, so he set off with Al and I for St Leonards boarding school near Bexhill. Sent Os a wire to reply to Bexhill to the hotel. Had a very uncomfortable journey by train, hot and comfortless, took taxi to hotel. Bexhill is a bright clean interesting place; along the promenade are beds of tulip, all colours massed separately. Saw the Lizard lighthouse blinking away as I sat at my window. Os's wire came so we knew he was all right, but the fear of it upset me.

Sunday 6 May 1917

Got up and pulled blind and drew short curtain across and lay in bed watching the sea rolling in, then we watched two ships on the horizon: Al counted nine in sight at one time. Got a taxi and went to see Battle Abbey [built at the site of the Battle of Hastings]. We had to stand in a beautiful old gateway and ring an ancient old bell. Seton did the deed and then we stood aghast at the jingling noise it made. A woman answered and said we would

---

42 Advertised as 'D.W. Griffiths' Colossal Spectacle', *Intolerance* was three and a half hours long, had four parallel stories covering a period of 2500 years and was then the most expensive movie ever made. It was not a commercial success but is now regarded as a silent film masterpiece.

find her husband at the abbey. We had a good old poke round before we saw him and then he told us we couldn't see the Abbey Battle roll [supposedly listing those who came over with William the Conqueror], 'because it isn't there'. A man named Sir Augustus Webster owns the abbey and has removed the roll to his own house. He lets the abbey – an American millionaire had it last – but at present it is unoccupied. Such a beautiful place and garden. Besides the thrill of standing on the very actual battlefield of Hastings, old 'Cousin William' has left some beautiful old buildings behind him,[43] the crypts, cloisters and old towers and all that remain of the great public hall …

43 A reference to William the Conqueror, who, it is said, was cousin to Roger de Montgomery, who came over in 1066.

Tuesday 8 May 1917

Seton returned from Doncaster at 9 p.m. He found Os very well and happy; he has been flying solo for some days now. The other boys say Os is a very steady flier and has never made a 'dud' landing. I am thankful. I don't want him to be brilliant, it's too dangerous. They had a fatal accident last week: one boy who was very good asked permission to take a friend up and in turning he didn't 'bank'. His machine started to turn and then went turning and twisting and nose dived to earth. Both boys were killed; it's too sad. Seton didn't have a flip as it was too windy, but Os was up before Seton was awake in morning.

Friday 11 May 1917

Went with Seton to Royal Academy picture [2/-], saw some great daubs, loved one called 'The Hills of Lorne'. Heard report from Leo Addenbrooke, who says the newspaper reports about a victory at Gaza were lies, and the general would have to face a searching inquiry.[44] He said if it was a victory, he doesn't know what a defeat is like.

44 The Second Battle of Gaza fought in southern Palestine between the Allies and the Turks from 17 to 19 April 1917. The Allies were defeated and lost almost 6000 men. The commander, General Archibald Murray, was sacked and replaced.

Sunday 13 May 1917

Set off for Rotten Row after breakfast, no bus available: turns out there is a bus strike on. Sat for a while on Monkey Parade and watched the passing show. To me it was a fearful irritation to see the mincing and overdressed, underdressed display of vulgarity. Had no taste at all. Talk about Nero fiddling when Rome burned. These people go on with their empty buffoonery while the Empire staggers. Went to Kew in the afternoon, it was a pure delight. The spring green, the fruit blossom, the tulips, the bluebells.

The water-lily lake and the glimpses of old Father Thames with boats and river boats like Hatrick and Co.[45] Mrs Watts told us that their doctor warned them against primula and cowslips, supposed to bring on cancer and eczema. English beauty is all cultivated, ordered and stately, our NZ beauty is pure nature and stands on its own.

Monday 21 May 1917

Seton's commission papers arrived ... They have put him into the Notts and Derby Regiment [Sherwood Foresters] and ordered him to report to his unit on the 29th, right up in the north of England at Sunderland. Dear old baby son, I do feel sore. Os turned up unexpectedly and a party of us went to see *Bubbly*.[46] Os has ten days' sick leave: his head has been troubling him, he gets giddy.

Tuesday 22 May 1917

Three of us went to Cox's bank to see about Seton's bank account. It was a great sensation to be walking about London with my two officer sons ...

Wednesday 23 May 1917

Os sent an urgent reply-paid wire to adjutant about his leave. Later went to the Tower of London as Seton wanted to get some things from ordnance – policemen, Beefeaters and soldiers all stood to attention and saluted the boys. One old Beefeater called a piquet, at first old guardhouse, and sent him to show us the way. I tipped him to Seton's horror as he was Honourable Artillery Company and might have been Lord Montgomerie or some other swank for all we knew. Ah well, I did it, so it's to be hoped he wasn't. No result at ordnance. Os spent time at Piccadilly boot shop, decided to have pair made to order – £7 3/-. I lent him £9. Os went to post office to ring his adjutant and had to wait one and a half hours for his answer but thank goodness it was all right, and he can stay on. After dinner hurried off to see Gladys Cooper in *Wanted a Husband*.[47] She is exceedingly pretty and acts most naturally. All very tired, night cap and bed.

Thursday 24 May 1917 Wid's 23rd birthday

Os went to West's to be fitted for breeches and Seton and I went on to New's, where he bought most of his kit. Afterwards walked up Regent Street

---

45 Hatrick & Co., founded in the late 1880s, ran the river boats that plied the Wanganui River.

46 Produced by André Charlot, *Bubbly* was a popular revue that opened at the Comedy Theatre in May 1917 and featured a mixture of songs and light-hearted sketches or 'bubbles'.

47 Dame Gladys Constance Cooper (1888–1971) had a 70-year career on stage, film and television. She was only a teenager when her career began, in pantomime and musical theatre.

and Os bought Wid an RFC brooch £3 7/6; Seton went shares.[48] Found Wid at home with a Mr Payling – a NZ boy from France.[49] Stayed to dinner and then took her out to the theatre. Our boys went to *High Jinks*.[50] Heard that Notts and Derby are a good regiment.

Friday 25 May 1917

Letter from Mrs Tilley asking me to go to Ciro's YMCA to have tea with her tomorrow afternoon; she is the hostess for the day.[51] After breakfast Os went to dentist and on to New's the tailor – Seton and I followed on. Then we went to Lincoln Bennett and Os bought a cap there but we like his flying one best.[52] Dressed for NZ dance, Mr Payling came. He danced nearly every dance with Wid, Os was feeling giddy, Seton had a fairly good time. Two policemen came in about half-time: it was about our lights. There were rumours of a Zepp raid, it was a very hot night but they kept it going merrily. Home about 12 p.m.

Saturday 26 May 1917

Letter from Roger and a pot of Devonshire cream. Went to Ciro's; they haven't got into the swing of it yet. Shown the games and writing gallery. Everything was so comfy. Mr Payling came to dinner and then we all went to *London Pride*. Gerald du Maurier was the star, we all enjoyed it.[53] Os headachy, later took a couple of aspirins and some wine to put him to sleep. Mr Payling is a bright jolly boy. Gave Os £5 to pay doctor and dentist. There had been an air raid over east coast early yesterday evening with heavy casualties so no wonder policemen were alert about lights last night.[54]

Sunday 27 May 1917

The doctor is anxious to treat Os himself and forbids him going up solo as he is now. Now we must wait to see what the Medical Board will say about him. He went back to Lincoln from Kings Cross. Seton and I went for a walk by the Serpentine, glorious pink hawthorn, pink and white chestnuts, yellow laburnum and gorgeous green of foliage and grass. It has been a stifling hot day.

Monday 28 May 1917

Seton busied himself with packing. A letter from Roger: he wants me to go

---

[48] Known as sweetheart brooches, these were often worn by wives, girlfriends and sisters of soldiers.

[49] Gunner Alan Eldred Payling, 2/2234, from Christchurch, left New Zealand with the Field Artillery on 9 October 1915.

[50] An operetta written by well-known composer and pianist Rudolf Friml in 1913. Friml's most famous works were *Rose-Marie* and *The Vagabond King*.

[51] Ciro's had been opened in Orange Street, behind the National Gallery, in 1915 as a luxurious private dance club; there were already branches in Monte Carlo and Paris. Strong opposition to such costly entertainment in wartime led to the club being closed in 1917 and used as a YMCA.

[52] Lincoln, Bennett & Co. was a well-known London hat manufacturer.

[53] Written by Gladys Unger and A. Neil Lyons, *London Pride* was a comedy running at Wyndham's Theatre. It was made into a film in 1920. Gerald Du Maurier (1873–1934) was a popular English stage and film actor and manager, and father of novelist Daphne du Maurier.

[54] Ninety-five people died and 192 were injured.

down for a week or two and enjoy the spring beauties of Devon. It would be lovely to be together again, but just now I am too anxious about the boys to be away from London … Seton goes to Sunderland tonight: how he hated going away from London. Oh, how I hate this war. Seton earlier left luggage at luggage office, gave him 20/- for taxi expenses. The dear baby son has went away to face a lot of new faces and new conditions. It's very hard – I can ask God to keep my precious boys.

Tuesday 29 May 1917

Breakfast on my own, missed my boys very much – miss Seton's squeaky boots on the stairs too. Thunderstorm, heavy rain on way to tube. Got letter from Roger. He is happy in his new surroundings, has sent a long list of things he want me to bring him. Was talking to an elderly woman at headquarters this afternoon when waiting for the storm to pass. She asked me if I knew some people in Hobart when I told her I was an NZer. So I told her Hobart was a week's journey away, which was information for her. These English are ridiculously ignorant. Too easy-going and lazy to have got themselves out of this war without help.

Wednesday 30 May 1917

Letter from Os: he is to have a Medical Board, but he doesn't know when. After breakfast found Seton's name in the *Gazette*. Wid had lunch with Alan Payling at Holborn Restaurant. He sent her some beautiful roses today.

Letter from Seton, 30 May 1917

Battn Notts and Derby, Clendon, Sunderland

Clendon is many miles from nowhere. We are quartered in huts with less comfort than Cambridge. There are three companies here and over 30 'subs' [subalterns or junior officers], who have been here a short time and don't know what to do with themselves. As far as I can see they hang on here for three to four weeks and then go over to France. Final leave comes any time: it is four days. This plentiful supply of officers may assist my transfer to the RFC. The colonel is … a very decent old gentleman. The major, the officer commanding this detachment, seems to have a 'good' temper and is not loved. We arrived at Newcastle at 5.30 this morning and waited till 6.18 to catch the train to Sunderland. We then went to the Grand Hotel and went to bed about 8 o'clock. After two hours' sleep we arose and after a clean-up we had some breakfast at twelve. It was very cold in the train last night and in spite of being tired I couldn't sleep.

Second letter from Seton, 30 May 1917
I met the OC detachment … under rather nasty circumstances. This morning I was just going off on a stunt with another fellow when 'a man' in shirtsleeves passed us. As he said 'Good morning' I took it he knew my friend, but 'Come here when I speak to you' cut me short. I reversed and stood to attention and got this: 'When you meet your CO in the morning you salute him and say, "Good morning" and don't you forget it.' We saluted and departed and now we know who Major Phelan is, and I can honestly say I never set eyes on him in my life before and I did not like my introduction. I honestly thought he was the sergeant cook or some such person but I know better now. This afternoon this same man gave his 'subs' a test in map reading, and I created a favourable impression by pouring forth my knowledge in a long stream and he cut me short and told me it was very good … Tell me if I am gazetted as I don't see any papers with the Gazette here. [Later he finds a copy of the *Times* with his name in but cannot keep it as it is the mess copy.] … We have to walk about a mile to the railway station and if we don't want to walk back have to return by the 9 o'clock train. Taxis number about two and horse vehicles are as plentiful.

Thursday 31 May 1917
Went down to afternoon tea and Miss Gaines irritated me by blowing off about England's justice – justice? Conscientious objectors can be considered – Exemption Board can sit and listen to piffle from shirkers. Irish traitors and Sinn Feiners can roam at large and escape any responsibility – of honour or country – but a baby boy with loyal Imperial instincts who gets tangled up in their cursed red tape conventions has to have the screws turned on him and forced into a groove that is absolutely distasteful and can't get any consideration of any kind justice!! They don't know the rudiments. It seems to me that all the decent people, the ones that did the things to make the nation, must have colonised and left the riff-raff of the country behind. These muddling, lazy, swollen-headed smug things never made England what she was. And they would have certainly lost all she was if the grit and loyalty of

the colonists hadn't held it for her. I don't mean men like Mr Balfour – he is a white star among a pall of blackness. But his kind is very rare.

Friday 1 June 1917

Wrote letter to Roger for use in writing to Jack Tilley [to influence a transfer for Seton to the RFC]. Just feel worked up. After lunch had a note from Seton in which he said he they are only kept a few weeks and then drafted to France, and it would take a year to get anything done for him. Went to see Wid about my letter to Dad, but she wouldn't read it. Came home and couldn't settle to any thing. When Wid came home she gave me a letter from Cyril to read in which he said, 'Don't let Seton come over here in the infantry', so that settled me and I went off and posted my firework letter to Dad. Letter came for Roger from Jim Watt [the family lawyer] containing a regular bump: we have to pay severely for war tax etc.

Letter from Seton, 1 June 1917

Tomorrow I will be on range duty … hope I can get the afternoon and evening clear … We have lectures the first four nights of the week and Friday is guest night. On Tuesdays and Thursdays we have night operations so you see we don't get time to go into Sunderland in the evening very often. We are now called cadet officers here; we are rising slowly.

Saturday 2 June 1917

Letter from Os, his friend Collier has been sent to France[55] – so Os would have been sent too if he hadn't had this check of illness. Ah me, I try so hard to trust them to God's care and keeping, but even then I shrink fearfully – but I know I must trust them to Him who has the power to guard and keep them. Seven aeroplanes were circling over London on guard this afternoon.

Letter from Seton, 3 June 1917

Yesterday afternoon I ventured into Sunderland and found some very good shops there, a very nice place for afternoon teas and a dinner at a hotel that only cost 4/6d without full course … There is a river running through the town through a narrow deep valley which allows coasting merchant ships to berth. It is a dirty, smoky, misty view and the locality would compare favourably with the East End. There are one or two possible theatres in the

---

55 Arthur Reginald Collier, 12747, from Wanganui, who left New Zealand with the New Zealand Field Artillery on 27 May 1916. He would be wounded on the left hand later in June 'in the field while cutting grass for sick horses. He was in no way to blame.' After a severe fracture of his tibia and fibula in February 1918 he was hospitalised for some time in Britain and sent home on the *Maheno* in August. Arthur Collier was a brother of the well-known New Zealand artist, Edith Collier.

place but you have to consider your home journey. There are half a dozen taxis but petrol for only one.

Monday 4 June 1917
Letter from Seton: he says he will have embarkation leave in about a fortnight, so just feel crazy to know if Roger has written my blast to Jack Tilley. After dinner Wid got a note from Alan Payling – written at Folkestone on his way to France. He couldn't get hospital treatment for his ears and had to go off. We are both sorry not to have seen him before he went; he is a nice boy. Wid had a sweet letter from Al. School is developing her latent principles and character; she is going to be very fine.

Tuesday 5 June 1917
Forgot to put Jack Tilley's address in my blast to Roger and got a funny little note this morning, very pithy and to the point. Os arrived just before dinner. He is looking very bonny, but is pretty deaf. He hasn't stopped smoking yet, the naughty boy. He is here for the Medical Board.

Wednesday 6 June 1917
Os went off for his Medical Board. There was another air raid on the coast last night; it's too dreadful. Two enemy planes were brought down on the English coast, and six or eight were downed when they got to the other side again, so I hope that will daunt them a bit.[56] When Wid and I were out Os came for his luggage and gone off to Prince of Wales Hospital.[57] I was so disappointed to miss him like that. After dinner had note from Roger to suggest that Jack Tilley may be out of town.

Thursday 7 June 1917
Seton says he may be 'down' this weekend. Wrote a note again telling him to 'push' well his end. Os came round after lunch. He went before five doctors yesterday and he has to go to a specialist on Saturday. They all seem more doubtful about his heart than his ears … Os and I went to Regent Street and he ordered slacks. The tailor promised to hurry Seton's things up but he is an artful dodger. Wid and I went to Rosina, a little hat shop in Queens Rd, I bought a liberty green toque, 23/- got a veil too 3/11. Wid found she left her RFC brooch behind at the dressmakers and she was too tired to go back.

56 It was actually a daylight raid on the Thames estuary and Medway in which 13 were killed, and 34 injured; at least six enemy aircraft were destroyed.

57 The Prince of Wales Hospital for Officers, in Staines, Middlesex, was established in Jamnagar House, the country property of the Maharaja Jam Sahib of Nawanagar, who offered it for the war effort. It opened in June 1915.

Saturday 9 June 1917

Letter from Seton to say his transfer papers have been returned to him with the message that all transfer papers had been suspended at the present. His Cambridge CO had sent word that he was one of the best cadets in his company and would make a reliable good officer etc., which only makes me want them to hold onto him all the more. I didn't need them to tell me that he would make a good officer – anyone with half an eye could see that. After breakfast I hunted up Seton's old letters to find out exactly when he applied for flying and then I got ready to go and see Colonel FitzHerbert. He says he can't do anything to alter War Office but Seton should at once apply for attachment to RFC and we should use all the influence we can bring to bear at once. Personally he thinks Seton is safer on infantry than flying, but I said it was a matter of personal justice. Seton is being moved into a groove he dislikes. Evening mail brought a cheering letter from Cousin Jack for Seton. Wrote to Seton and enclosed Jack Tilley's letter. He is trumps after all.

Letter from Seton, 10 June 1917

Startling news about the RFC, I should have liked to go to the RFC. I have not a clear head as I should have – I don't know what makes my head rather heavy, nothing to worry about but I expect it is my old goitre. On the other hand I might not like it in the air … and don't think I detest the infantry as I am quite reconciled to this life, but you understand there are better places. I expect to get four days' embarkation leave about Tuesday or Wednesday … It would be an advantage to let the army know who I am but if we close down the RFC idea, it would require diplomacy to do so.

Letter from Seton, 11 June 1917

This is the land of adverse news and I am afraid that I go and make things worse for myself … The future unfolds itself in a very nasty way where I am concerned. I wrote to you yesterday and said 'washout' and now on top of it I tell you I will carry on again. Only this afternoon I got another surprise. My OC Company said a cross-country race was coming off in about two weeks and said I should go in for it. I mentioned I would be in France by then, and he told me I was under age.

Monday 11 June 1917

Les Hill took Winifred out.[58] Got a letter from Roger tonight, quite a masterpiece. He thinks we are calling on his mental powers too frequently. I thought my request for him to write to his blue-blooded relations could raise some opposition. It isn't his brains I want to use, it's his cousinship – but thank goodness there is no need for his effort now.

Tuesday 12 June 1917

Sent a telegram to Seton to say I had sent on the letter from Jack Tilley. Mrs Whiteman called to say there was overseas officers' entertainment this afternoon. Went off to Pall Mall, got there early and sat in cool lounge talking. Later went into tea room, got a table quite near one the Princess Beatrice of Battenberg and her party sat at, and we had a good view of them all the time. We all stood when they entered and left. She is no looker but a lot of her party were worse. The concert was very good. The Duke of Somerset was present and a countess one of the hostesses.

Wednesday 13 June 1917

Just before lunch after I had come home from the bank I heard bombs dropping and guessed those German devils were at work. Soon after it was over Wid rang to say they had been fairly close – they had set fire to a place near Gorringe's. I never guessed they were near her. They really are the most alarming things, these raids. I could hear the loathsome thud of the bombs and went and sat in the lounge until it stopped. We were meant to go to a matinee at the Gaiety with our overseas officers' tickets but went to look up Wid instead. We could see the smoke from burning places from headquarters top storey. The whole city is burning with wrath over this raid. It has done a lot of damage and only one enemy plane was brought down. Women and children blown to bits on the streets. It was just a ghastly tragedy – and not one word of warning.[59]

Letter from Seton, 13 June 1917

My letter from Jack Tilley I consider a diplomatic triumph. I saw one of England's airships yesterday and it was a peculiar-looking bus. It looked like three sausages tied side by side together. It looked quite serviceable but was in the fog.

---

58 Possibly former law clerk Second Lieutenant Leslie Gerald Hill, 12/441, from Auckland.

59 This daylight attack by 20 Gotha aircraft (long-range German bombers) killed 62 civilians and injured 432. It was the highest death toll from a single air raid on Britain during the war.

Thursday 14 June 1917

Wid came home to lunch because they were warned of another raid approaching, however it didn't reach London, thank goodness. Yesterday's raid shook poor old Wid up a bit. It's just awful to think of sudden death being dealt from the skies in such a savage way. If they can't protect London a bit better I shall feel justified in taking Wid away. I can't see any reason why I should risk sacrificing her to their inefficiency. Goodness knows they've had enough warnings that this would happen but still the Germans have the best aeroplanes and we are crawling around trying to catch them up. I know Wid is doing good work and I should hate her to be a cold footer [piker], but there is a limit to one's endurance of these endless muddlers and unnecessary sacrifices. Wid has been looking very fagged today.

Friday 15 June 1917

Went to lunch at Holborn restaurant, it was very nice but so unwarlike. The glitter of glass and mirrors, the music and the crowded room with waiters in attendance and food and drink galore. These English really do love their meals.

Letter from Seton, 15 June 1917

You seem horribly panicked about me, and I am sure you are not doing yourself any good. I think you can be peaceful until you find out how this luck runs out.

Saturday 16 June 1917

Letter from Seton to say he was coming from Clendon but he arrived first. Got here a little after 6 a.m. and sat in the smoking room until about 7. He got word at the range that he was on draft for France and had to hurry and pack and depart by the 10.45 train that night. It is not right either as he is still under age until the 25th. We got his things brought up to our room as Miss Ibbotson can't take him and he has to search for quarters for tonight. He had a bath and changed and had breakfast with me. Went to the War Office to interview Colonel More, poor old Seton came back without seeing him so we concocted a telegram to his CO at Clendon asking permission for Seton to have this interview and in the meantime Seton went back at 3 p.m. to try his luck again. Seton came back with a happy face: Colonel

More was awfully nice and has given him a letter for Adastral House [the War Office headquarters]. And at dinner time his answer arrived from Colonel Wise at Clendon saying 'Yes'. So all's well so far.

Monday 18 June 1917
Seton set off for Hotel Cecil to interview RFC authorities. I hoped this awful heat wouldn't make them all too cross to be interested. I threw some shoes after him. Seton had to go back to Hotel Cecil as he didn't get an interview this morning. At first they told him they couldn't see him but when he explained he had a letter from the AMS [Assistant Military Secretary, responsible for junior officer postings] the man stuttered and way was open. Influence is a very wonderful thing so he is to appear before their board tomorrow morning …

Tuesday 19 June 1917
Letter from Dad to Seton. The poor old dear has found out how far away he is when it comes to the pinch. I will be so glad to get down to Devon but I don't want to leave Wid here by herself now that these German brutes are having aeroplane raids. It seems I must be always torn two ways. Seton back to Hotel Cecil: I threw more shoes after him. Seton was back for lunch and had to be back for a medical test at two. Then we went to the War Office and they took him off the French draft as he had passed the board tests. Oh, the joy of it. Went to the bank and found that another credit arrived, £650. Spoke about getting insured against aircraft and he sent a clerk along with us to insurance office in Cornhill. Filled in papers, cost £2: Wid and I insured for £1000.

Wednesday 20 June 1917
A letter from Roger, seems quite unsettled and has refused a promotion. He jibs at any extra responsibility.

Friday 22 June 1917
Ordered two bottles of wine from Whiteley's to be sent and took one back myself [7/6d]. Wid could have plenty while I am away. Called in to see Wid. The general was in her room, also Colonel FitzHerbert inquiring if any of them would volunteer for record work in France. Mrs Prescott did, but I

don't quite fancy it for Wid. Went to the cupboard to get something for Roger and found the moths were having a great time with his dressing gown and everything available. Wid and I both panicked – we looked at our fur coats but thank goodness they are all right.

Saturday 23 June 1917 Devon

Got up at 7 a.m., darned Seton's socks and fixed up his parcel. I got Roger's box brought up and got his telescope. Tickets £2 13/-, had very uninteresting people in my carriage so didn't talk to any of them until just at the end of the journey when most of them had thinned out. Saw oat fields scarlet with poppies, red soil from ploughed fields. Arrived at Tavistock, met by car and came away before sending a wire to Wid. Didn't realise I was coming away from civilisation. Tavistock seems quaint and old-fashioned, then away to wilderness of Dartmoor, which is very rugged and stony with bracken growing from everywhere and some rough-looking ponies feeding. Roger came to meet me, and got in car. He is looking awfully well. We had some tea and hot cake and delicious butter – real and sweet – and then we went for a walk to see logs he has to move about. One could see it is a fairly difficult piece of work and I laughed to see some of Roger's triangle sledges on the spot made by himself – and doing successful work too … Staying with Mr and Mrs Bailey.

Sunday 24 June 1917

A wet morning so we didn't get up till 9 o'clock … Roger is fearfully disappointed about the weather, he wants Dartmoor to 'show off' for my benefit. But it rained all morning, had dinner about 2 p.m.: roast beef, onions and rice with nice brown gravy and then stewed gooseberries and Devonshire cream. No Devonport rations here.[60] Later we braved the weather … Heard a skylark singing as we sheltered under Vixen Tor.

Monday 25 June 1917 Seton's 19th birthday

Got up at 7 a.m. Roger's horses came tramping along then, which is the signal for him to get up. Breakfast 7.30, Roger goes off at 10 to 8. Heard my first English cuckoo; it is a perfectly beautiful day. The postman arrived, sent telegram to Wid and Seton, postman refused a tip. Mrs Bailey said he will never take one from anyone. After Roger came home for lunch the first

60 Hudson Ewbanke Kearley, 1st Viscount Devonport (1856–1934), was the British Minister of Food Control during the First World War.

tractor engine load of logs went past, it came back for a second load too … After tea Roger and I set off for Pew Tor to watch the sun set. I wore Roger's trench coat but even then I was cold and I had his cardigan jacket too … We lay down behind Tor boulders and watched. There was a wonderful panorama stretched out in front of us: Plymouth and its observation balloons floating over a camp and sometimes an airship sailing round Saltash bridge over the Tamar River, villages, towns and farms dotted around. Everywhere the eye could reach the fields of England all fenced in squares like a draught board, some newly ploughed squares a pinky, bricky red, the others varying shades of green, trains rushing round the hillsides leaving a trail of white smoke. The Dartmoor ponies grazing below us and black-faced Scottish sheep feeding peacefully just beside the Tor. A farmer a little way off on horseback driving some cattle, a couple of women picking heather on the slopes and away in the west the sun sinking behind great black banks of clouds, through which the crimson trickled like blood through the black pall of war. Coming back we could see the flickering flash of Eddystone lighthouse and even here amid all this wild remoteness the war grips me and I am worrying about Al being so close to those German daylight raids and Wid too.

Tuesday 26 June 1917
The postman brought me a letter from each of my chicks, also an invitation card from Mrs Tilley for the opening of Ciro's YMCA by Princess Helene Victoria … After tea at night Roger and I went for a walk down among his logs and on to the stream at the bottom … Going and coming we saw 'hackers' at work. They are poor people who come out in the evenings and hack away at refuse branches lying about to get bundles of firewood. One nearly toothless old woman and a very old man and their daughter were very busy when we passed. Roger chopped a very small bundle and carried it home with him. It was nearly 10 p.m. when we got back and quite light. As we went to bed children were playing outside and women and girls walking past. England is a land of extremes: life like it is here and then London with its luxury. Overdressed women and their lap dogs, dogs with bejewelled collars and sometimes even with jewelled rings in their ears. One can only wonder how long these conditions will last. This simple patient endurance of hard colourless lives would be nothing short of heroism if they understood it, but they don't and there lies the tragedy of it all.

Wednesday 27 June 1917

Roger wrote a letter to Jack Tilley. It wasn't worded just as I would have liked it about Seton and I was ruffled, but after all I don't suppose it will matter all that much. Roger's strong point is certainly not his pen. The niceties of a point which means right or wrong to me, mean nothing to him, and he worries over a knot, or a stump of a branch being left on a log as if it was something that really mattered. I expect we are both too fussy over our particular points … After tea changed into a costume and went with Roger to see two timber wagons load up. Mr Beauchamp was there and he promised to bring a railway timetable from Plymouth tomorrow. He is going for the Medical Board. He is quite a nice young man; he has a year's leave for neurasthenia and from his symptoms I feel Oswald's is something similar.[61] He suffers with his head at the back just the same. The doctors told him it was starved nerves.

Letter from Seton, 28 June 1917

I am getting a bank of 'red tape', a real meal of it through putting in those applications of mine. The transfer has gone for good, I hope, but the refund returns regularly every other day for some amendment and particulars. The latter has collected quite a volume.

Friday 29 June 1917

Mrs Bailey got a pamphlet asking her to see her household used less bread, signed Devonport. It has been another miserable day, after tea just stayed inside. Roger has been very tired each night and this change in the weather has been very trying for him. When he came home for lunch his clothes were all damp and that is not good for him at his age.

Saturday 30 June 1917

Up at 7 a.m. Roger is feeling a little off colour this morning. Had a touch of diarrhoea last night. Oswald's letter: has seen the board and given four months' home service. Also will be sent away to Eastbourne or the Isle of Wight and I am more than ever distressed I have been away from him this last week … Got a wire from Os which upsets me very much: he has been sent to Eastbourne. I was more sorry than ever that I had come here until his movements were definite. Roger doesn't understand how I feel.

---

61 Neurasthenia, meaning nerve weakness, was a term used to describe a generalised state of lassitude and extreme tiredness often caused by stress – what is now referred to as chronic fatigue syndrome. It was used in the war as a synonym for shellshock.

Letter from Seton, 30 June 1917

We cadet officers are getting a little work now and our 'guardian angel' calls rolls and keeps a fatherly eye on us through out the day. He is 'loved' and I would not like to be in his boots. The colonel was here last night. He asked me when I was going in the RFC … Well, I am in command of the east coast tonight and I hope England trusts me.

Sunday 1 July 1917

Poor old Roger was very sick and miserable through the night and I was glad I was here after all. It's a dreadful business being dragged two ways. Roger just had a glass of milk and whisky for breakfast. He got up for dinner. We had potatoes I bought yesterday with rice and gravy and he seemed to enjoy them.

Monday 2 July 1917 Back to London

Up at 7 a.m., Roger feeling better but not feeling up to work, I'm sure. He is doing his bit, the poor old dear, and I just hated coming away today …

CHAPTER SIX | DEATH FROM THE SKY

Back in London the air raids continue, destroying lives and fraying nerves. After the big raid of 7 July public pressure forces the government to improve the capital's anti-aircraft defences. In the words of the Times *editorial on 9 July, '[The raid] has produced much anger in the public mind, and the Government must be prepared to face widespread indignation.' Once the RFC starts to use Sopwith Camels against the German Gothas, daylight raids end. On the Western Front the Third Battle of Ypres, and the bloodbath of Passchendaele, begins at the end of July. Seton finally takes to the air.*

Wednesday 4 July 1917
Oswald's letter was very alarming as he suggests going into a machine gun corps as he doesn't think his health will be good enough for flying. So I wrote and told him it wouldn't be any better for machine guns. I think wireless or signalling would suit him better. Went out to post Os's letter; the news boys were calling about a raid early this morning at Harwich on the east coast.[1]

Thursday 5 July 1917
Letter to say we have £1,000 credit, quite satisfactory. Went out to get things together for NZ Christmas parcels. Gave a poor woman 6d. Ordered a set of silver brushes for Jen's silver wedding present [£6].

Friday 6 July 1917
Letter from Al. She was so excited about Os taking her out on Saturday she began 'Dear Os'. Roger wrote to say he is all right again. Did more shopping: two little plates 1/-, two pin cushions 1/9d, handkerchief and glove sachet 7/-, box of pencils 2/-, a work bag and two powder boxes 3/11, two shawls for Gran [Annie's mother] 1/9 each, two sponge ducks and some boxes of soldiers 4/6d.

---

1   Seventeen people were killed and 30 injured.

Saturday 7 July 1917

Helped Alice [the maid] make the beds when bang, bang, bang went the bombardment of an air raid. Went downstairs and soon the whole household was assembled in the hall, then as awful sounds drew closer we decided to go the basement. Several didn't like it down there and came back up again but I stayed down there with Mrs Matthews and Bobbie [her young son]. The maids stood out on the bridge and watched the brutes flying straight at us with three of our planes climbing up to meet them. They flew over without dropping any bombs. I tried to ring Wid's office and couldn't, then she rang me and told me go and look at the fires they had caused. The chemical laboratory of St Bart's [hospital] and the corner of the GPO suffered but most lives were lost in the Whitechapel tenement.[2] And the devils got away without punishment; it's a disgrace. Wid's nerves got shaken up again. It's such devilry, no one can help feeling shaken. One of the staff boys across the road collapsed, he has suffered from shell shock. Later went by bus to Piccadilly to see where bomb had dropped on Swan & Edgars [the famous department store in Piccadilly Circus]. It just grazed the front of the building and didn't explode, which was a mercy. I just feel sick to think the English boast the 'command' of the air and they can't protect the women and children in their capital.

Sunday 8 July 1917

Mrs Jardine is still very upset: the air raid shook her nerves up very much. The general opinion is that our defences are absolutely inadequate. The papers today have two good photos of the brutes flying over us. After dinner we had coffee in the lounge for the first time for months; everyone is nervy and unsettled.

Letter from Seton, 8 July 1917

I forgot to say in my last letter that we had an officers' bombing competition and I was fourth out of 14 and a dozen of them had had months of experience in France … Let me know a little about the raid [on London] and I hope it has not got on your nerves and Tiny's also. They want Os and me up aloft to look after London, don't they?

---

2 In this major raid on Margate and London, the last daylight attack on the city, 57 died and 193 were injured; 11 enemy aircraft were shot down.

Monday 9 July 1917

Went to the bank as it was a wet morning and I thought the German devils wouldn't come. Saw hole in the street of Mansion House where one of their dud shells hit, not many yards from the door of our bank. Did more Christmas shopping. The colonel brought a major from France into Wid's office today and said her room was noted for the best set of cards, which was great praise. Heard rumours of a threatened air raid tonight. They did try to get back today, rain and all, but were stopped at East Ham. Rumour says two squadrons from France have been sent over to protect us. It's a crying shame our defences are so inadequate. Went to bed wondering how much sleep we would be allowed to have. It's a fearful strain.

Tuesday 10 July 1917

After breakfast fixed my Red Cross things in case of need in a raid. About 12 Wid came home unexpectedly. Her nerves had crumpled and she asked permission to come home; she rested until lunchtime. Later we went to the office together and asked sergeant major for leave. He has given her till the weekend and then we will see if she has pulled up again. Wid went to Paddington to send a wire to Eastbourne to try for rooms at a place Mrs Watts told us about. She is in a real need of a holiday – a few days won't do any good. The Huns got as far as Croydon today but evidently got turned back. Was asked to help at Dugout on Thursday morning, which I promised to do but this is going to stop it all right.

Annie, letter to Seton, 10 July 1917

Yes, those German devils did get near us ... Dud shells were dropping all over London. Three came close to Wid, one at the very corner of Mansion House, on the pavement and one at Swan & Edgars, Piccadilly. It now turns out they are our own shells, fired by our own guns, and points to treachery in our munition factories. It also turns out we only had 12 planes to defend London and six of them couldn't go up as some of their parts were missing. We usually have two squadrons but the previous Wednesday one of them was sent to France and on Thursday the second one was sent – and the question is who gave the necessary information to the Huns.[3] The East Enders got a little out of hand and wrecked some of the German shops and threatened to lynch any Germans they found and I don't blame them.[4]

---

3   Annie is repeating a popular rumour about intelligence being given to the Germans, but there is no proof that this happened. Her other 'information' may also be questionable.

4   They were more than 'a little out of hand': the official report notes that 30 shops were attacked, 37 people arrested and 14 police officers injured.

Some tenements in Whitechapel got badly smashed again. Half London is now suffering from nerves, notwithstanding the papers' statement as to the wonderful absence of panic. People were fainting, screaming and collapsing everywhere. Wid is very shaken up … I am hoping America and her squadrons will be in full play before you take a hand.

Letter from Seton, 11 July 1917
I have my refund papers back again and now they want an army form filled in and certificate from the Air Board to say I am actually accepted … You did not bargain for the 'front' by living in London.

Letter from Seton to Winifred, 11 July 1917
Last Sunday all cadet officers, including me, were late for their company parades, and our OC detachment saw we were pulled up for it. We had our names taken [on Monday] and after 'Swine' had talked to the 'old soldier' we were informed we were not to leave the hutments for four days [confined to barracks or CB]. It is my first military punishment and it will not down my military career at all, cheer up. Last evening I was 'OC very good'. I went to dinner with the vicar of Clendon in the company of Captain Watts and another 'sub'. We played bridge for an hour or two, and we won hands down, but there was no money in it as is invariably the case in any game. Captain Watts broke my CB for me. I could hardly imagine myself in a village vicarage this time a year ago.

From Wednesday 11 July to Sunday 15th Annie and Wid visit Eastbourne, where they are able to see Os and visit Al, looking 'bright and well', at school in nearby St Leonards. Annie mentions the horrible sound of the guns booming away across the Channel in France.

Thursday 12 July 1917
Went to esplanade and sat out watching English crowd holiday making. Bought a couple of newspapers but the news isn't very good today. The air here is simply glorious, bracing, cool and fresh, sunshine bright. The town looks very clean after dear old London. The beach is thronged with people and children paddling and making sand castles everywhere. Plenty of people bathing, both sexes but mostly women. I have never seen such an

ugly collection of people before, not anywhere in England, and goodness knows they are all fairly ugly. But here they are an ugly sunburnt crowd. The band discourses sweet music to the gathering that sits, walks or bathes as its fancy takes it. An airship sails overhead quite low out over the Channel. The destroyers nearby disappear and we know they are scouting for submarines. Crowds of little pleasure boats are out. One can't help compare this English leisure-loving life with our more earnest one. These people don't know what discomfort is; they don't dream of such lives of grind as ours are. But our race is a finer one than theirs – looks, brains, physique and, I believe, self-respect.

Monday 16 July 1917

Went down Moscow Road to hateful German cobblers shop to try to get sprigs for Roger's boots; can't get them anywhere else. Managed to get three small parcels. Just hate going in to the vile place and speaking to the slimy, creepy-looking creature.[5] Wid went to see Dr Groves and he wrote a note for Wid's office to say she was unfit to return for six weeks or so. Wid has to take medicine at night to ensure sleep, also Ovaltine and pills after each meal. The doctor says she has anaemia and debility.

Tuesday 17 July 1917

Wrote a letter to thank hotel manager for sending back the belongings I left behind in Eastbourne: my very best frock and blouse, another blouse and two pairs of stockings – I'm pretty dilly for sure. Went out after lunch to Records Office, saw the colonel, who was very disappointed to get Wid's doctor's note. He said he would have to strike her off strength as he couldn't give her such a long holiday. He didn't think anaemia and debility sufficient cause for an extended one, and said he could easily get another girl to do the work, but she couldn't easily get her strength and health back if she lost it. All the menfolks were very nice and they were all sorry to lose Wid. We went to her old room to see the girls and Mrs Prescott. She leaves for France in a week.

Letter from Seton, 18 July 1917

You and all London have nerves properly … Been reading the *Waitakian* [his old school magazine] and it has made me feel I could face the Hun army but that feeling will soon wear off. We have a Sandhurst cadet here

---

5 Annie was certainly not in the minority in her xenophobia. Anti-German prejudice reached absurd and dangerous heights in both Britain and New Zealand.

from Hampstead. He is gazetted as a regular officer and was styled a 'gentleman cadet'. Poor lookout for your son: he thought he was a gentleman before this …

Annie, letter to Seton, 20 July 1917

I'm afraid you have missed the 'point' about the gentleman cadet, haven't you? They evidently think he is only a 'gentleman' cadet having come through Sandhurst and being a 'regular'. The facts of you being one for a thousand years wouldn't dawn on their weak intellects, as you didn't emerge from the sacred portals of Sandhurst.

Friday 20 July 1917

Mrs Ina Stephens, a guest here, is a bit broken up about her brother and what he has been through and the awfulness of the front. She takes up an attitude of defence for anything our soldiers do. She says we can't criticise or blame their moral standards, that any comfort or pleasure they can screw out of circumstances is their right. That is absolutely the English attitude. The English moral standard is appallingly low, judging by what one sees and hears. Wid, her friend Moira and I fought against such a standard. It's awful.

Sunday 22 July 1917

Wid arranged to go with Moira to the Temple Church in the city this morning.[6] However at 8.30 the guns began to bang and the Sabbath peace was broken. Ina Stephens came running up to our room in her dressing gown so Wid and I in similar attire went downstairs with her. We soon had a goodly sprinkling of similar folks, however the noise only lasted 10 minutes, so we all went back, dressed and had breakfast. This afternoon's paper says 20 enemy planes were on the coast of Sussex but were beaten off and the gunfire here this morning was only a raid warning. So Ina, Wid and I met Moira at Temple Church … The singing was beautiful: it is supposed to be the best choir in London. The pews are old-fashioned with high desks. You can only see the tops of heads and hats when they are sitting down. The master preached a good sermon but I didn't quite agree with him. He made use of some of the fiery psalms as models of our course now!! We saw the crypt at Lincoln's Inn Fields [London's largest public square] as we came home and the marks on its walls of the Zepp bomb that fell there.

6   Sited between Fleet Street and the River Thames, this church, consecrated in 1185, was built by the Knights Templar. It is the church of the two Inns of Court, the Inner and Outer Temple.

Tuesday 24 July 1917

Stayed up last night and let Seton in at about 10 minutes to 12, gave him some wine and held a candle to light him to bed. Ina Stephens had a letter from her mother which said that while lying at the wharf in Wellington last trip the engines of the *Remuera* had been tampered with and officers had to keep a very strict watch all the rest of the time she was there … Oswald's letter says his complaint is neurasthenia. Just exactly what I told him and when he worries it only makes it worse.

Letter from Seton, 22 July 1917

I cease to be a cadet officer on Tuesday, as I have spent eight weeks with the battalion. It has advantages and disadvantages but I am glad to let the 'cadet' go. Our Sandhurst lad is being looked after like an invalid: he is going in the officers' quarters, a junior CO being displaced. I did not get into those exalted quarters till a week ago, but I do not like the company I have in my room.

Letter from Seton, 26 July 1917

St Patrick's Hall, Reading

The people in this hall are mostly equipment officers and the remainder are observers, so few of us that are pilots have interests of our own. I have run into a nest of NZers … There is a very decent Canadian and a Yankee….

Letter from Seton, 28 July 1917

The course is most interesting; the further one gets on the more interesting it gets. By the way, it lasts six weeks, I think. The work is quite simple to understand, but there is such a lot of it that one has to concentrate to keep pace. There is one captain who lectures on theory and rigging, a pre-war bird, whose lectures are most amusing and at the same time highly instructive. He illustrates his work with tales of actual experience.

On their way to Devon on Monday 30 July Annie, Winifred and Al have 'a fairly decent crowd' in their train compartment. 'We ate our fruit and found it very refreshing. The rest of the people had regular feeds, thermos flasks full of tea, sandwiches, hard boiled eggs, tomatoes etc. These English do love their meals.' The three Montgomeries stay with the Reddicliffes at Moortown House, as they will do on many other occasions.

Death from the Sky

Letter from Seton, 1 August 1917

We have had a bit of fun since I last wrote. All of us were paraded last Sunday for church and we marched the half a mile and filed in immediately and eight of our number continued walking and went out the side door. The chaplain noticed it and went looking for OC St Pat's in a very agitated state. This happened to be my friend the Yankee, who gave no satisfaction, and this did not improve the temper of the chaplain. With his temper rising as time went on, the padre appeared and gave out, or shouted out, the hymn and we all thought we were on battalion parade and that the order to come to 'Attention' would follow. He yelled at the top of voice and he had no mean voice. He cooled down slowly as the service went on. Again tonight, guest night we had something very touching. The president, the adjutant in this case, gave the usual 'Mr Vice[-president], the King' and the vice gave 'Gentlemen, the King', and we all rose, and this was followed by a succession of loud bangs as one form after another was pushed back and consequently over by our sudden rising. When this subsided we all carried on with the toast and in the majority of cases the port was blown out of the glasses, and we finished with yells of laughter. I have put down for Hendon and Shoreham as my squadron. Shoreham is in the region of the south coast about Kent or Surrey. I should like Hendon though.

Friday 3 August 1917

Wid and Al had an adventure with some soldiers having a mock battle on the moors just outside our gate. They got right into the centre of the battle and had to fly. They quite enjoyed the episode. After tea went for a walk with Dad; coming home spoke to a woman who lives in a cottage near by. One of her sons is working in the woods and one is in France, aged 19. Poor old thing, mother love is the same everywhere. She says she will show me his photo if I will come along to her cottage some time. She walks about each evening knitting at a sock for her boy and keeping an eye on some ducklings in a creek near the gateway. Her boy is an officer's servant [batman] only, and had been up at the front line for two days, which he said was an experience that shook him up. His officer is in a tank, she thinks. She rambled on about his babyhood of delicacy and what a fine big chap he had grown into and how she sends pasties and sweets to France. No English reserve in that class.

Saturday 4 August 1917

Two letters from Os. His medical board has cleared him 'permanently unfit' for pilot or observer. He has to go back to Eastbourne for another month's treatment. Poor old dear, he will be very disappointed to lose his wings.

Letter from Seton, 4 August 1917

We had our exam this afternoon and it was quite easy, but terribly long. The trouble is they require a good percentage in some subjects, such as 70% in some, so it not altogether easy.

Monday 6 August 1917 A year to the day we arrived in England

Today is the anniversary of our landing in England. Well, it has been a wonderful year and one none of us would have missed. Under ordinary conditions we could never have the insight into places and people we have had, and most marvellous of all is the fact we have been able to keep finances square and yet not deny ourselves anything in reason. I thank God that we came and have been able to keep in touch with our precious boys all the time. I can never be thankful enough. Providence has been wonderfully kind to us all along, and as this new year starts for us, I renew my trust in its guidance. Sometimes I shrink fearfully from the stress ahead, then I think of our wonderful destiny shaping our rough-hewed ends and I trust and carry on. That God may keep my precious boys through this year of stress ahead is my prayer in every moment of thought. The daylight raids worry me because of Wid and Al, but they, too, are in God's care and keeping and nothing can happen if He wills otherwise.

Letter from Seton, 9 August 1917

Had a lecture from an ex-prisoner escaped Scotch [*sic*] Guard officer. He has been a prisoner of war in Germany since September 1914 and escaped a month ago. He came through Holland and altogether had a very rough time, partly owing to the fact he had made two unsuccessful attempts. The Hun has such a hatred of the 'English swine' … I am on engines now and although they are interesting they take a lot of understanding, especially when one is taking four at once. It is similar to learning four languages at once. As Os said we could have done a lot more with the old Krit had we known as much as we do now.

Letter from Seton, 12 August 1917

I saw in the papers where the Foresters were 'at it' [Ypres] but we have about eight battalions in the line and it may not be the one I was in, so you cannot tell. I expect those old houses in Devon are very beautiful but don't get too attached to this country. The best little country in the world is down under. No matter where one goes people say NZ is where they want to go. There is a captain here who spent three years in Taranaki. He has lived in all countries and he said if he made a home he would make it in NZ.

Tuesday 14 August 1917

A thunderstorm and downpour of rain. After we went to bed a violent ringing of door took place. Then Mrs Reddicliffe knocked on the wall between our rooms to inform us that an officer was downstairs: it turned out to be Uncle Jack's friend Lieutenant Stuart from South Africa.[7] I had to get dressed and go down to interview him. We arranged for him to come to lunch tomorrow and meet Roger.

Wednesday 15 August 1917

After breakfast Al set off for the woods to tell Dad about our visitor ... We all like him and he had quite a lot of snaps of the J.E. Montgomeries. After lunch he and Roger went off to the woods on a visit of inspection, coming back in time for late tea. Roger wrote a note of introduction to Jack Tilley for Mr Stuart.

Thursday 16 August 1917

Telegram from Cyril to say he is in London for leave, sent back a wire asking him and Os to come down. Man proposes and God disposes – here I have just sent a letter off to his mother saying that Cyril will be as one of my boys while he is over here on leave and straight away my little plan is knocked on the head.

Letter from Seton, 16 August 1917

The exam on engines is over. The engines really are quite easy but the difficulty lies in the fact that though the principles are similar their design is different and the exam being a sort of record time competition one does not get time to deliberate and the heat caused by the rush is likely to 'seize

---

[7] John Eglinton (Jack) Montgomerie was Roger's younger brother, who fought in the 1899–1902 South African War and settled there.

up' the brain. I am getting quite a few brain waves now that I am initiated in the wonders of electricity … I am certain the car won't be such a mystery to us. I intend to take an interest in the engines and magnetos when I get to my squadron.

Wednesday 22 August 1917

Letter from Oswald, now diagnosed with vertigo, so they are getting closer to the facts. Set off for woods by myself to get some rowan berries and heather to take back to London. Rain came down heavily. Found Roger sitting on the shelter of an engine eating his lunch when I got down to him. Called in at Baileys and said 'Goodbye'. Wrote a cheque for Mrs Reddicliffe, says she is sorry we are going as we have given no trouble and have been so considerate. The maid says the same. It will be strange to go away from the 'to yurrs' and 'to he's' and all the Devon accents. It has been a beautiful holiday and we are sorry it is over.

Letter from Seton, 22 August 1917

Doing all I can to get to Hendon [aerodrome]. We have our artillery observation exam on Saturday so I am busy this week also. I have seen the results of my exams and have got 'good' all through so far.

The family returns to London on Thursday 23 August. The next day there is a note from Lieutenant Stuart to say he has been given an introduction to two admirals: 'Everything went very sweetly until the doctor turned him down because of his eyes. So he has gone into the infantry after all.' There is a visit to the theatre this week, where 'Cyril had some hearty laughs at Leslie Henson.[8] *He is a dear old kid, I wish his mother could have seen him.' Wid and Al go off to stay with the Tilleys in Suffolk. Roger returns to Devon on 1 September. 'Found Seton at home after seeing Roger off. He is not at Hendon as it is over full, but at Acton, which is quite close.'*

Monday 3 September 1917

Wid and Al arrived back at Liverpool station. Jack Tilley was with them. Seton called in the evening as he is so close to the city. He has been up in the air twice today and quite enjoyed it. His pilot is a Frenchman. He thinks flying is a lovely sensation.

---

8 Leslie Henson (1891–1957) was a popular English music hall comedian, actor and film and theatre producer.

Wednesday 5 September 1917

Moonlight raid on London last night. Seventy Gotha machines came over, about 30 of them reached London. About 11.30 the Huns visited us, a strange droning, purring noise coming nearer in the sky. I felt sure it wasn't our planes, I never heard that noise before. Ours make a throbbing sound with a sawmill squeak in it. But those devils seem to fill the air with a droning purring so insistent, so devilish that it held one spellbound. I didn't wake Wid; she woke herself. We put on dressing gowns and went and woke Al. By this time the whole household was on alert, and soon there was a great dressing gown parade on the stairway. The guns opened fire before we left our room, they passed over but then returned closer still. One loud bang turned out to be a bomb torpedo on Edgware Road, about a mile away.[9] Wid got the shakes very badly, no one felt calm or comfortable, it's very unnerving. We returned to our room at 2 a.m. and made Al stay in our room the rest of the night. The guns started booming away after breakfast but nothing more happened. About 11 a.m. we set off for the bank. Going in the tube we saw groups of poor women and children taking refuge there so we got out at Chancery Lane to make inquiries. A girl on the train who had spoken to us (these raids break down all barriers) telephoned from there to St Bart's and got word it was safe. So went to bank, gave some money to poor kiddies in tube there. Seton turned up about 9 p.m., then for an hour we had a great thunderstorm. Seton left again when it was over. He had a bath here as his camp doesn't provide all comforts of a happy home. His pilot had a bleeding nose today and didn't take Seton up, but he had a full day with wireless etc.

Wednesday 6 September 1917

We slept peacefully when Wid discovered a buzzing of engines in the sky but not close enough to tell if it was those droning devils or not. However it was enough to 'put our wind up'. So we put on dressing gowns and Wid began to get the 'shakes' again and we all took sal volatile to buck us up. Later went back to bed …

Friday 7 September 1917

A letter from Grandma with the startling news Barron [the Taukoro manager] has been called up. We all hope her information is incorrect.[10]

---

9 Nineteen people were killed and 71 injured.

10 It was true. Ernest Barron was included in the ninth ballot for the Wanganui Recruiting District at the beginning of July.

Wid's school friend Daphne called. Seton was here and she says the last time she saw him he had just returned from a Kitchener camp seven years ago,[11] and now he is an Imperial officer.

Saturday 8 September 1917

While at the bank we were told a New Zealand soldier had asked for our address this morning. They couldn't tell us his name, but when we got home we found Hugh Anderson here so the mystery is solved. He is looking wonderfully bright and well. Hugh and Al later went out to the Soldiers' Club … Gave Hugh Al's room and loaned him a pair of Roger's pyjamas.

Sunday 9 September 1917

I found Hugh fast asleep when I went up to get him, however he raced the girls down even then. Al and I took Hugh to the Trocadero, sat there and enjoyed the music. Then went off to NZ Soldiers' Club with Hugh to get his shaving things; he was so worried all day because he hadn't had a shave. When we got home we found there had been an air raid warning of which we had been blissfully unaware.

Monday 10 September 1917

After breakfast Hugh came into our room and we sewed on buttons for him: he hadn't *one* on his shirt! Then we went to Kensington and Hugh bought shirt, socks and pants there. He put them on there and it was a great improvement. Later gave his overcoat in and we cleaned the collar with benzine and Al sewed tab on back. Then Hugh went off by train to stay with his aunt. Heard tonight things are fearfully critical about Russia and Sweden, and some man in the smoking room says the war will last another four years.

Sunday 16 September 1917

Hugh back again. We all went for a walk in the Row. Heard that when the raid took place on Chatham and killed all those naval men that the anti-aircraft guns only had blank cartridges to fire at the invaders.[12] They swooped down to one searchlight that was tracking them and just riddled the men with bullets. Hugh went to New Zealand Club to get away early, but before he went he had some of his mother-in-law's cake and some wine, then I lighted him downstairs with a candle. I'm sure he didn't like going back.

---

[11] During his 1910 visit to New Zealand to advise on the country's defence requirements, Field Marshal Lord Kitchener attended military displays and oversaw exercises by cadets and members of the territorial force.

[12] A reference to the 3 September air raid by six German Gothas, which killed 132 people and injured 96, most of them naval ratings.

Letter from Roger to Annie, 17 September 1917

Our mill is not in full swing yet. Matthews's contract is a new one. The ass could not turn in the wood so now I have to put everything in front of the dog kennels on the moor, which means that two full days a week are putting pit wood with six horses in wagons over there. Mr Beauchamp gave me the choice of looking after the mill engine or engine hauling with wire ropes or to continue with the horses. I took the horses as it seemed the easiest work, the most constant work. The hauling engine is not always going … When [it is] not working the men cross cut and stack … With some fine weather Haig could crack the devils in the west.

Tuesday 18 September 1917

Letter from Fergie's brother: he is wounded and in England. Al busy packing up so she set off for Hastings after lunch. One little school girl was in tears at the station and said she just felt like she was nothing. Poor kids, poor mothers, these goings away are just horrid. Wid went off to Taplow to visit family [Thomassetts]. I came home and had a little weep at the loneliness of it all.

Letter from Seton to Roger, 18 September 1917

School of Instructions Royal Flying Corps
London Aerodrome, Acton W3

Dear Dad,

You ask me what it is like up in the air, but before I start I want you to understand that the 50 hp machines here will climb to only 300 feet with two passengers and the 60 hp will only climb to 3,000 with two in them and we can't use these ones solo.

The 50 are used for teaching 'taking off' and landing and one does not go higher than 50 ft for this. When used for solo they will climb to over 2,000 (the 60s are too precious for soloists). I have been up in the 60 to 3,000 twice and right at the beginning so I did not feel then as I do now. I have done three half-hours and of this about 40 minutes above 300 ft, so I want more high work yet.

They are about 1909 model and very unstable when we must fly them, so that the sensations of an aeroplane are yet to come. The difficulty when starting is to know and realise when the ground has been left. One has a sensation of a very strong wind on top of a ridge in NZ and this is continuous. After the first flight this wind does not trouble you at all. When up at 3,000 ft you can imagine yourself on a high hill so I have not lost myself yet. After 1000 feet the difference in the size of things is hard to notice and the same coming down, although you do see how small they look.

You have a look at the wires and smile to yourself and feel as safe as house until the instructor lets go and then, at the beginning, you are frightened to move the controls enough and the old bus is rather cranky and you feel worse than it looks.

If one wing goes down only slightly you feel it and for a start you don't like the feeling at all, but one soon gets over that. It is the same when banking, and your one desire is to level her out. You feel the nose go down, and then the engine is switched off and the wind pressure seems to increase. The ground comes slowly closer, and the air gets warmer on the way down.

Landing is not such a bad sensation as I imagined it would be, and it feels impossible to hit hard as the dense air seems to be holding you back. It is quite surprising how safe you feel up there with the instructor, but I believe solo is a different matter entirely.

The weather last few days has been windy and we have no flying at all. What I said about the Huns was that I thought they would be kind and gentler to the Russians and try to get separate peace that way, but they have taken the other method.

Wednesday 19 September 1917
Seton arrived, very worked up about not being able to get hold of his held-up pay. He had a bath and some supper and went off. He hasn't had any flying for four days, which is all right from my point of view. I don't want him to hurry.

Thursday 20 September 1917
Oswald talking about transferring to the RGA [Royal Garrison Artillery], which is much better.

Saturday 22 September 1917
Seton managed to arrive in time for the theatre at the Playhouse: Gladys Cooper in *The Yellow Ticket*.[13] It was tragic but the acting was good. He put

---

13   This play, written by Michael Morton, concerned a young girl in Tsarist Russia who was forced into prostitution in order to visit her father. (The yellow ticket was the passport that showed she was a prostitute.) *The Yellow Ticket* was made into a film in 1918 and again in 1931.

the wind up his instructor yesterday by turning off switch and turning off his engine, but he soon turned it on again and it was all right. Lex Butler was here today. He said he couldn't express how much it had meant to him coming to us as he had, and I told him I was just trying to keep a little bit of NZ for them in London, and I was glad it was being of use.

Sunday 23 September 1917

Fergie's brother [Jack] arrived a little before lunch; Seton was here till after lunch. While reading the Sunday paper he ate an orange pippin apple, but any of our pippin apples would be ashamed to acknowledge relationship. Mr Fergusson and I went to the Trocadero. I gave him a photo of Fergie: he hadn't one and isn't sure his mother has one either. Seton turned up in evening. One of the fliers had a smash this evening but the machine was the only sufferer, thank goodness. Seton was in the air at the time and didn't see it happen. Fergie's brother and I had quite a good talk today. They have never heard how he died: the officer in charge never answered a letter from their mother when she wrote to inquire. So I will hope on till I have positive proof.

Monday 24 September 1917

Seton arrived just before dinner with news he had booked for *Trelawney of the Wells* tonight.[14] We were just at the door of the theatre when we heard bombs dropping but no one seemed to take any notice and we went to our seats and sat down. Then the stage manager came on front of the stage and said that a raid was on, and as far as they were concerned they were going on with the play. We could sit still or go home as we wished. We sat still, very few walked out, but it was pretty tough work sitting there and trying to take an interest in the play with sound of bombs and gunfire all around us. The actors were magnificent and most of the audience were fine stuff. Just before the last act Dion Boucicault, who was acting with Irene Vanbrugh, came to tell us the 'All clear' had been given.[15] It was a relief. Seton was very practical and calm all the time. I had stupidly forgotten my latch key and when we got home we found four of the guests waiting up for me – decent. Seton had his night cap and hurried off to camp. The dear old kid got his 'shilling' today – he has done!!! his solo flying at Acton. It was a surprise.

14 An 1898 comic play by Arthur Wing Pinero.

15 American-born Dion Boucicault Jr (1859–1929) was an actor and stage director who worked a great deal in the West End and later in Australia. Sir William Gower, in *Trelawney of the Wells*, was one of his most famous roles. His wife, Irene (later Dame Irene) Vanbrugh (1872–1949) had a distinguished acting career for more than half a century.

Tuesday 25 September 1917

The papers say last night's bombardment was the biggest London has had ever.[16] Wid rang up to ask how I had fared, but our three minutes were up before we had half finished. After lunch went to the lounge to hear details of the raid from the 'all knowing ones'. The Bedford Hotel in Southampton Row is one of the places struck in this raid … Seton arrived, set off sharply for the theatre. On the way in tube there were crowds of poor people taking shelter so I asked one if a warning had been given, but it was a dread of last night had caused them to come. Anyhow as soon as we got out of the tube the guns began to bark. Seton thought we could reach the Adelphi but it got too noisy and we ran back to the tube and stayed there till it was over, about 20 minutes. *The Boy* was very good; Seton loved Berry.[17] The paper sellers in tube were selling papers with 'latest news of last night's raid' while the fresh one was in progress.

Wednesday 26 September 1917

After breakfast Seton and I went to Southampton Row to see the damage done to Bedford Hotel. A bomb fell in front of the doorway, making a hole in the street and tearing about the steps of entrance. From corner to corner on each side of the street the windows are smashed; the walls on each side of the road are pitted in holes. Seton rang Hendon for orders and, being allowed to stay tonight, we went off to the Coliseum for matinee, instead of daring the Fates again tonight. It was not a very good programme, but it gave us a few laughs. Have been reading *John Bull* and *London Opinion*.[18] One letter came from Grandma to Roger to say Barron was passed by the doctor. No answer to the cable yet: it's getting very worrying. We met Gordon Pettigrew today. He told us that the only aeroplane brought down by gunfire on Monday night was one of our own, which is simply a tragedy. Some people slept all night in the tubes.

Friday 28 September 1917

Seton came up. He has his orders to go to squadron: he was to go to Narborough near the city of Leicester. He came for afternoon tea, gave him a glass of wine to drink success to the new venture. He leaves by the 5.52 train. He is disappointed not being nearer London. Wid and I left by the 5.20 [for Eastbourne]. I just hated coming away from even a few moments

---

16   Twenty-one people were killed and 70 injured in the raid on London and the south-east coast.

17   English comic actor W.H. Berry (1870–1951) acting as magistrate Mr Meebles in the highly successful musical comedy *The Boy*, based on Arthur Pinero's play *The Magistrate*.

18   *John Bull* was a popular periodical founded in 1820. Under an altered title, it closed in the 1960s. *London Opinion* was an extremely influential magazine for some 50 years before its life ended in 1954. Its most famous cover, drawn by Alfred Leete for the 5 September 1914 issue, showing Kitchener with his pointing finger next to the words 'Your country needs you', was used by the government as the basis for a recruitment campaign that is said to have encouraged three million British men to sign up in the first two years of the war.

with my dear old son. Oswald met us, had dinner together and then went to see a play called *White Heather* at Devonshire Park, a fearful affair after London. Os was not well, tired and fed up. Wrote to Sister Dora asking her if we could have Al out tomorrow.

Letter from Seton, 29 September 1917
Narborough, Swaffam, Norfolk
There are three squadrons here: we are all on the same aerodrome, in the same mess and anteroom. We are 2½ miles from the nearest village and railway and Swaffam, 11 miles, is the nearest place of any size. Kings Lynn is the best place to go I believe but it is worse than Kakatahi [a very small settlement on the Parapara Road]. Tell Os we fly AW [Armstrong Whitworth], 'little' then 'big'. Our machines are very nice to fly and it is hard to kill some of the old ideas and adjust them to these machines. It is very nice to feel you are in a real aeroplane, but this is a great place for minor crashes but no injuries.

Monday 1 October 1917
The papers report they had another raid on London last night. It's jolly well time they gave Berlin a taste of the same medicine. Bought some Phosferine tablets 2/9d for Os.[19] After dinner sat in the moonlight on the esplanade. It was a perfect night but one can't even enjoy such a night now as it only means those Hun devils can come with impunity and drop bombs on London town, or anyone else they like.

Tuesday 2 October 1917
A letter from Seton at last; I am so relieved. The papers report another raid on London, four hours of it. Went to buy fruit and gave a poor woman 6d. Os wrote rough copy of letter to Jack Tilley asking for an introduction to Seton's powerful friend as this morning he received an official document to say he hadn't the qualifications for an artillery officer and recommending him for the infantry. His adjutant told him to write and say as he hadn't been passed fit, so he couldn't be transferred, but it is just as well to have fall back upon in case of accident.

A recent arrival from London made us laugh at teatime about comic happenings during raids. In one bank the manager asked girl clerks to be

19. Phosferine was a tonic said to benefit the nervous system.

sure to cover up their typewriters before they took refuge in the basement during raids. Another was a girl who noticed a baby in a pram on the street and she grabbed it and went for shelter, only to be asked by the mother why she hadn't brought the pram too. But the best one was about an old nurse who, though very brave, confided 'that these raids took the legs from under her'. She had been in the kitchen with a grandson who would talk to her during a raid and she had said, 'For God's sake, stop talking. We might be in heaven in a minute, and I want to think.'

Letter from Seton, 2 October 1917
We have had quite a lot of excitement in this place but we get quite used to it. Yesterday we had three crashes, two very light, but one fatal one: he had four crashes previously and was advised not to go flying, and this was the end of it, worse luck. There are five of us from Acton here now. The time passes very quickly and if you don't get into the anteroom first your chances of an easy chair or a paper are not much. From what I hear I left Acton none too soon as the powers have started some 'frightfulness'; there is a roll call at 9 p.m. every night and if you wish to go after that time you have to get a pass. I should not have got to '40' [Inverness Terrace] so many times at that rate should I?

Friday 5 October 1917
A lovely morning but nippy. Bought papers. Our NZ boys have been in this last 'push' and our bad weather has not been nice to them.[20]

Letter from Seton, 4 October 1917
Sorry to give you all that worry, but I wrote as soon as possible. Now flying AWs. We go out at 30 mile an hour winds, but 'bumps' are the worst things. Our Acton 'buses' would not live five minutes in the 'bumps' we get in the woods in this locality. These machines fly themselves, but of course we have to do quite a lot of work also, or we would never get back to the aerodrome. The elder brothers of these machines, the 'big AWs', are still more stable and object strongly to being manoeuvred and you have to be very careful of them until you understand the nature of the beast.

20   The Battle of Broodseinde on 4 October.

After a few days shopping, taking walks, meeting up with Os and seeing Al, Annie returns to London on Monday the 8th, to find her room very cold and 'the gas stove isn't ready for use yet'. The maid reports that shrapnel and shells were very close in the raids.

Letter from Seton, 7 October 1917

These machines are so easy to fly that I have started flying solo, worse luck, but it can't be helped. In some other squadrons, especially 64, they have about three weeks before they start flying at all … I should be very glad if you would buy some White Rose brilliantine.[21] One fellow that was at Acton with me had joked about my reference to being Scotch has the idea that all colonials are after the escaped convict type … I showed him my tartan handkerchief and he asked what tartan it was and asked if one could design a tartan that way. I said it was only about 900 years old and he shut up like an oyster with the exclamation, 'Some Scotsman.' Not a word has passed his lips since.

Friday 12 October 1917

Got a letter from Seton. He has flown over Sandringham while the King was in residence. It is 20 miles from their aerodrome. Page brought me a telegram at dinner to say he was coming at 9 p.m. for weekend leave. Hurrah. Asked waiter to keep him some dinner. Seton's nice friend Wood is in the casualty list today, killed. It's just too awful, these lists. He was such a fine fellow, and left a wife, child and mother. It's just tragic.

Saturday 13 October 1917

Os and I went along to Dr Groves who says Os has a dilated heart, with the apex out of place and some more technical stuff. Anyway Os has his letter to produce now, and can demand some definite attention to his case. It's been a mockery of treatment. Dr Groves says it's enough to have caused chronic trouble and render him an invalid for life. Boys shared a room, number 15. It's lovely having them together. Pity their leave is so short.

Wednesday 17 October 1917

Received a letter from Os saying the officials down there had ignored Dr Groves' letter and had given him more to do, and he didn't know how he

---

21 Brilliantine was an oily, perfumed hair grooming product intended to soften men's hair and give it shine. Invented in 1900, it was very popular during the first half of the 20th century. One captain in the trenches reported in his diary that he had to give up wearing brilliantine because rats were licking it from his head.

could stand it. I felt quite murderous and Wid and I went straight to Dr Groves. He was also annoyed and will do what he can, but he doesn't think he can interfere too much. He comforted me by saying there is no danger for Os but still it is very wrong that he should be doing these things, and it is bound to make him feel all used up. He says it takes some years to make it chronic. I would like to screw their necks then, pig-headed, ignorant muddlers. They're typically English.

Thursday 18 October 1917

Letter from Seton: he hasn't done any flying for a week, which is good news for me. Also one from Cyril. Poor boy has had some bad luck – was kicked by a horse on the face. It knocked out four teeth and made a hole in his face. The blow knocked him senseless … On the way to the bank heard a whistle from a taxi, then it stopped and a boy from Wanganui jumped out, a boy I have never spoken to in my life and Wid hasn't either for years. This war 'don't 'alf level things'. He is a second lieutenant and quite chirpy about everything. Wid and I were quite tickled over the meeting. Heard that Wid is still in demand at Records. They told her her place is still open for her.

Friday 19 October 1917

In the evening we heard that an air raid warning had been given, so went down to the lounge and sat by the fire until 11 p.m. As we undressed we heard two guns go off and we kept our clothes on and put on fire coats ready for emergency. A waiter came home from the theatre saying that a fresh warning had been given, then we heard that the trains were running with no lights, so knew the brutes were somewhere about.

Letter from Seton, 19 October 1917

I had a little diversion from the ordinary this evening. It was a calm evening, absolutely splendid for the first solo, so I took one of the large AWs up. I got on quite all right and landed it, but being so calm I had no head wind to stop me running and I ended up in the hedge at the far end of the 'drome. I went up on my nose a bit and it was quite a pretty sight. I didn't get a bump at all, and when I wasn't cursing for having smashed it up, I was laughing at the pretty sight it presented. I shall know better next time and shan't curse my old friend the wind. Fate seems to will it I should get through in a hurry, as the authorities want 13 turned out by the end of the month, and there are only 11 of us in the running so far. The flight commander didn't curse me, he cursed the people that want to get us through.

Saturday 20 October 1917 Roger's 51st birthday

There was a Zepp raid last night, went to Piccadilly Circus to see the damage near Swan & Edgar. The windows all round had shattered and they say 30 lives were lost.[22] The two reports we'd heard were these bombs. The brutes dropped bombs on South London and Cricklewood; they have improved their engines so they don't make a noise. Went down to Walton to visit George Lethbridge. He is safely out of France for the winter. Were back in London by 7 p.m. and already people sheltering in the tubes but no warning had been given. When we got in Ernie Butler was here, just over from France, but he brought very sad news. Poor Lex was killed just a few days after he went back.[23]

Sunday 21 October 1917

Ernie Butler came about 11 a.m. and we went to the park. As usual the riding was atrocious. Ernie has a fearful cold so I gave him a dose of cinnamon before he went off to the [Soldiers'] Club. Before he went he thanked us for what we had done for him and said we helped him a lot. Poor boy, we are only to glad to help him in his misery. The sight of the frivolous empty-headed crowd in the Row today made him very bitter, just as it does me.

Monday 22 October 1917

Seton's letter contains worrying news. The authorities want to get him through by the end of the month, which is not far at all. He can't possibly have command of his plane and himself in such a short time … Ernie Butler came to lunch and then he and Wid went to *Zig-Zag!*[24] Ernie went to an evening show, *Romance*, by himself; Wid isn't keen on night performances while the raid season is on.[25]

Letter from Roger to Annie, 22 October 1917

Thank you for the birthday greetings and Wid also. You had better send Al a two-bladed pen knife for her birthday, nice and sharp. I could not see any selection in this little town. Mind that you do not spend too freely as we

22 In fact 36 were killed and 55 injured in this 13-Zeppelin raid (larger airships were used) on east and north-east England and London. Five enemy craft were brought down.

23 Lance-Corporal Ernest Edward Butler, 3/2156, Lex's younger brother, left New Zealand on 27 May 1916 with the New Zealand Medical Corps. Twenty-five-year-old Lex Butler died of wounds on 5 October 1917. He is buried in White House Cemetery, Ieper, West-Vlaanderen, Belgium.

24 *Zig-Zag!* was a revue at the Hippodrome. Among the cast was the great English music hall comedian George Robey.

25 It was indeed air raid season: another big Gotha raid on Kent, Essex and London on the night of 31 October would kill 10 and injure 22.

have no idea what the harvest will bring next year and we ought to carry a surplus for this year.

Letter from Seton, 23 October 1917
You seem to have misunderstood me and my crash. It was not my nose that I stood on, but my machine stood on its nose. It was quite a scientific crash as the whole machine is useless, written off and I received nothing whatever … Today I got my own back by taking a machine up for under an hour and I landed it quite safely this time. Don't think I am missing my Winchester course – that has to come when I leave here – but I will be finished here by the end of the month. It is a pity I didn't hurt myself in the crash as it would have meant leave.

Thursday 25 October 1917
Letter from Seton with good news he is going to Winchester when he finishes at Narborough at the end of the month. Later Ernie came with me and we went to the Tower of London … One of the Beefeaters took us. Ernie enjoyed it immensely … He left me his mother's address and said all sorts of nice things about how much it had meant to him to have me along. He is a very nice boy with lots in him.

Monday 29 October 1917
Letter from Seton. He only has to do four more hours to graduate. Heard about a Canadian boy who has been gassed but not too badly. He says it is fearful over there: God help the boys who are in it. A letter from Fergie's brother with an enclosure from an officer who knew him and says he was killed instantly with a shell and never suffered. He is buried near Farbus Wood [near Vimy Ridge in France]. Al has a letter from Cousin Allie Tripe to be bridesmaid at his wedding to Ethel Dampier Atkinson; she is very excited. Heard that they are erecting a huge aircraft factory near Croydon. It will cover 8 acres; it is going up like magic.[26] It is an Anglo-American affair. This lady thinks we will be living in 'dugouts' next year. The war news is awful today: Germany is gobbling up Italy now.

Tuesday 30 October 1917
Letter from Mrs Barron. It is very disquieting so telegraphed to Roger to

---

26 The Ministry of Munitions commissioned three national aircraft factories in 1917: this one at Waddon (Croydon), one at Aintree (Liverpool) and one at Heaton Chapel (Stockport).

come up and interview the high commissioner. Jim Watt didn't try to get an exemption and was putting Joe Salt in as manager – such a cheek. Seton has four days leave, but his Winchester course will only take a fortnight, then he only gets 24 hours before going to France. It is heart-breaking. Roger to arrive tomorrow.

There is great family indignation and much correspondence when farm manager Ernest Barron is conscripted and the manager appointed by the lawyer, Watt, proves a bad choice. On 1 November Annie and Roger visit the high commission, where a 'not very sympathetic' Mr Rowe sends a cable to Prime Minister Massey. The drama continues over the next few weeks and is not resolved until after the war.

Friday 2 November 1917
Seton bought a beaver fur collar for his flying coat 30/-, also some triplex [kind of safety glass] for himself. He has had his watch engraved and bought some warm gloves. Also had his photograph taken for his RFC certificate. It has been a muggy day and we are all very tired; I have had my flatulent heart pain all day. A newspaper man was calling out that 'Russia has given in', which upset me very much, but it isn't so after all. Goodness knows their chaos and helplessness is bad enough.

Saturday 3 November 1917
Letter from high commissioner to give text of cable: 'Mr R.A. Montgomerie from Makirikiri extremely concerned at calling up of his farm manager, A.E. Barron. States that came to England to be near his son in RFC and is doing war work. As no capable man available to take Barron's place he fears financial disaster. Asks for extension if exemption not possible. Message sent at request and cost of Montgomerie, who is anxious for early reply.' Cost £4 5s 3d. Roger returned to Devon.

Seton continues to buy military necessities – long boots, a pair of leggings, a face mask ('didn't fit too well so I tried to fix it up') – and then packs. Annie wears her new velvet frock to dinner 'for Seton's benefit'. Os rings about the Barron problem and reports that what Annie calls 'the medical creatures down there' say he has nothing wrong with his heart: 'there is another tangle to unweave'.

Sunday 4 November 1917

Seton went off to Winchester from Waterloo. Heard that Os can insist on having his case taken to a Higher Authority. Any soldier can if he is not satisfied. After dinner came back upstairs on my own and lit gas. Feel tired and depressed with all the war news.

Wednesday 7 November 1917

When maid Daisy brought me my hot water this morning she said, 'So you have got your son again, madam', and I said I expected him last night and he didn't come. She said, 'I got Number 22 ready for him and there is a gentleman in it this morning, and a khaki tunic hanging up.' Got dressed quickly and the waiter told me my son had arrived at 11.30 last night. Later on he appeared. He tried on his flying collar but it wasn't quite long enough so we decided to go to the Angel to get it fixed properly ... The page got a patent gas lighter for me which cost 1/7d. It's really a wonderful affair if it lasts. Seton left at 9.10 p.m. He told me that nice bright laddie Alan Payling died of wounds; he saw it in the *Times*.[27] It's all tragedy, this hateful war.

Thursday 8 November 1917

Went to Walton to see George Lethbridge, who said he is boarded for NZ but expects to be there two or three months and then back again. When returning on the train a lady in the same carriage said her mother was from there and that several places are named after their family. She oozed money. The skunk muff was the biggest I've ever seen. She lives at 13 Marble Arch.

Friday 9 November 1917

Read the paper after breakfast, was feeling vicious about the Lord Mayor's Show. Such mumming tomfoolery is jolly bad taste in the present state of affairs. These people will never learn a war is on, never. It would have been over now if they dropped their stuffy antediluvian methods and got to work properly. It's all eating and drinking and pomposity with them.

Saturday 10 November 1917

The news in the paper about General Sir Henry Wilson, Foch and Cadorna being chosen to control the war fronts is exceedingly hopeful.[28] General Wilson should have been in charge long ago.

---

27 Alan Payling was just 22 when he died on 11 October 1917 in Belgium.

28 Field Marshal Sir Henry Wilson (1864–1922), General (later Marshal) Ferdinand Foch (1851–1929), French Chief of General Staff, General Luigi Cadorna (1850–1928), Italian Chief of Staff. The reference is to the setting up of the Allied Supreme War Council. Wilson was the British representative.

Letter from Seton, 11 November 1917

[The inoculation] has affected me differently this time. My arm isn't half as stiff but it has gone to my head, making it a little sore. We 'big Ack merchants' will have to fly another type of machine on leaving here as the demand is for them and not our friends.[29]

Monday 12 November 1917

Wid returned from Eastbourne and we went to the Records Office to look up Cyril and Roy but couldn't find anything so that was a relief. Poor Alan Payling was shot in the leg on 11th October and died the same day. Os had his [medical] board this morning and managed to get his three weeks' leave. Dr Groves said his heart was from 2½ to 3 inches out of place but five doctors meeting at Eastbourne said there is nothing the matter. Anyhow he has a chance now to get away from the muddlers. Jim Montgomerie came to stay.[30]

Tuesday 13 November 1917

Oswald came up from Eastbourne. Jim came with me to the bank; he is very taken with the tubes. Later he and Os went to see *Zig-Zag!*, which they enjoyed very much. Had a visit after dinner from Allie Tripe and Ethel. Their bridesmaids have let them down at the eleventh hour and Ethel asked Wid if she would fill her gap. So Wid is to be ready at quarter to nine tomorrow morning, to be picked up by taxi and taken to the shop where the bridesmaids' things are on hand and see if something can be fixed up for Wid. Later Seton turned up with his 'wings up'; Os pretended to be very jealous.

Letter from Roger, 13 November 1917

The war news is no doubt very bad but the Italian traitors will be sorry they surrendered when their stomachs are empty.[31] The chances of invasion are very small as our navy would be there in time and transports cannot carry big guns for defence – one hit would settle any transport.

Friday 16 November 1917

Os went to Air Board and Wid and Jim went to Records Office. Wid looked up Alan Payling and received the extraordinary news that he had a wife as well as mother for next of kin. I don't believe it; I think he has been mixed up with someone else.[32] Os found the Air Board very frigid. They didn't

---

29 No. 2 Squadron at the time was equipped with the Armstrong Whitworth FK8 'Big Acks' crewed by a pilot and an observer/gunner.

30 Alexander James (Jim) Montgomerie, 46058, was Willie's older brother. He left New Zealand on 9 June 1917.

31 At the Battle of Caporetto 24 October–19 November 1917 near the town of Kobarid on the Italian-Austro-Hungarian border the Italians were routed by the Germans. Young German officer Erwin Rommel took 9000 prisoners and was awarded the Pour la Mérite.

32 They did make a mistake: Alan Payling was single.

hold out many hopes of him getting a transfer. After tea we concocted a letter to Cousin Jack telling him Os hadn't much chance of a transfer without some push and asking for an interview with Colonel More. Received a letter from Hugh this afternoon with half of it commandeered by censor. They are pretty smart in this country censoring harmless and loyal people's letters and they leave rotters and aliens to flourish everywhere. I'm glad Lord Northcliffe gave them a hard knock in the paper this morning but I don't expect even his plain speech will pierce their tough hides.[33] Os overhauled his box tonight and got out his warm undies. Gave him £1, also 10/- for a bottle of whisky when he goes to Tavistock to see Roger.

Sunday 18 November 1917
Daisy the maid told us there was a flare of a big fire in the sky. We put on our coats and went along the end of the street and the flame was almost terrifying. Made me think of the Great Fire of London. There are all sorts of rumours as to where or what it was but time will tell. We heard the fire engines rattling around ringing their bells. The papers are very vague about everything today.

Letter from Seton, 18 November 1917
It is very different flying these light machines, especially when one has a lot of work to do as well as fly. If I had been up much longer today I should have been able to fly in my sleep.

Thursday 22 November 1917
Letter from Sister Dora to say there was a measles scare on and asking if I wish to have Al at home in case she developed symptoms, otherwise she would be there for part of the holidays … We showed Mrs Harris [next-door neighbour] how our gas lighter works. She finds the noisy crowd here a bit of a hurdle. She is an Australian and is a brick the way she has soldiers here to dinner. Often men she doesn't know simply because she wants to help them along if they are friendless and lonely. Her husband is a major in France. She canteens and VADs most of the time.

Letter from Roger to Annie, 22 November 1917
Haig has done well today and I hope the Allies got a big blow to the devils

---

33 British newspaper and publishing magnate Lord Northcliffe (1865–1922) – the *Daily Mail*, the *Daily Mirror* and the *Times* were all his – had enormous (and alarming) influence over British public opinion during the war. He helped to make Lloyd George Prime Minister in 1916; the latter appointed him Director of Propaganda

in Italy close to Venice. Would like to see someone slate Lord Hugh Cecil in the papers re conscientious objectors, which he rightly deserves.[34] I am seriously thinking of returning to NZ if Watt's letter and manager are not satisfactory, in the autumn … you can all manage without me as long as there is plenty of boodle [money] for you to remain in wet and dirty old England. She seems to be wet and dirty all over. Of course I would return as soon as possible. Would like to go to NZ on a troopship … Lloyd George seems to have boasted too soon in submarines. It seems England has plenty of food but has to help France and Italy.

Friday 23 November 1917

Os interviewed Colonel More and then got passed on to an unsatisfactory creature, Major Dawson. Os went back to see Colonel More … He seemed quite interested till he heard Os was from NZ. Then his interest faded away. He said there were 1800 people waiting to go into RGA and he wouldn't hold out any hopes at all. Mrs Harris came to see Wid [in bed with flu] before lunch. She, like me, very decided about the swollen-headed inefficiency of the English. Her husband told her the Australians were let down by the English troops not long ago in France. The best stunt he had been in was when the Australians, NZers and Scotch were together and everything went like clockwork. An NZ soldier, Flac Homersham, came.[35] I made coffee in our room. Wid was in bed but it didn't matter. Flac is not a bit keen to go back to France. He has a month's leave to do farm work at his Aunt Dot's.

Letter from Seton, 23 November 1917

I told them to send the [graduation] certificate to you; you had better keep it. I had a little air experience today. Just after I took off my engine turned 'dud', so went round the 'drome so I could land and had just done so when my engine seized up altogether and I landed right where I started from. The prop could be turned when I got down.

Saturday 24 November 1917

Letter from Mrs Watson, was considerably censored, written from Plymouth. Colonel More has told Os to go and see him again if at any time he could do anything for him. He advised to get an equipment officer's job in

---

34 Lord Hugh Cecil (1869–1956), Conservative British politician, who campaigned on behalf of conscientious objectors. In the House of Commons on the day Roger wrote to Annie Cecil eloquently opposed an amendment to disenfranchise conscientious objectors, arguing that a large number of them refused to serve on religious grounds. Roger's attitude was typical of a great many people in those blindly patriotic times.

35 Private Flacton Charles French Homersham, 10350, from Otorohanga, left New Zealand on 6 May 1916 with the Wellington Infantry Battalion.

the meantime, until he gets strong again when Os told him about his unfitness for the infantry. I made a cup of tea this morning, the first I have made in England. Wid had café au lait as she couldn't face dried milk.

Sunday 25 November 1917
Went to the Trocadero in the afternoon. It was crushed but we waited because Os wanted to see Gordon Pettigrew. Caught him as he was going out. He says if you are on the general list they can pretty well do as they like with you, and Os is on the general list. It is worrying. He expected so much from the AMS and he doesn't seem to be at all powerful in this case. Felt tired and depressed. Shall insist on Os seeing a specialist if they want to force him into the infantry. I'm sick of their high-handedness over the bodies and spirits of our boys. It's a pity they can't use their powers to make their own people face their obligations. It's just rotten. They have queer ideas of British liberty.

Letter from Seton, 25 November 1917
We are all going to the 'pool'. We finished our course on Friday and we got our report on our course yesterday. I got 'very good' as a general remark, 'good' for other items. With luck I may stay in the pool. They are getting five new AWs from Newcastle and I am hoping they will allow we 'big A merchants' to do a bit more flying on them instead of switching to the RE8.[36]

Monday 26 November 1917
Letter from Mrs Thomassett; it had sad news of Roy's death in Palestine.[37] He died of wounds on the 14th of the month. It's too dreadful to realise that dear patient Dave's boys are both sacrificed in this fearful hateful war. The only comfort is that he has them now, but poor Jessie and Gran will be desolate. It certainly doesn't help me to hear the English muddling with COs [conscientious objectors] and such trash. Felt too seedy to do anything all morning. Os left tonight to go to Kilmarnock to stay with Great Aunt Bettie.

Letter from Roger to Annie, 26 November 1917
It is very sad to hear of Roy's death. It has been on my mind he would be spared to return to his mother ... The saw bench is a fine easy job compared to the wood work but of course Beauchamp may ask me to take over the

36 Although less popular with pilots than the FK8, the Armstrong Whitworth RE8 was the standard British reconnaissance and artillery spotting aircraft from mid-1917 to 1918.

37 Roy Mason is buried in Ramleh War Cemetery, Israel. He was on the list for a commission.

horses again. There is no doubt the bench is the place for the winter. Rain half the time, I am under the roof and the engine is a fine thing to dry one or one's clothes a bit at 12 o'clock. Just about one hour with the truck on the rails we get through enough logs to last the day.

Tuesday 27 November 1917
Wire came from Seton to say he would be here at 2 o'clock: he has two days leave. Wid and I went with him to the Troc. There seemed no earthly reason to make him miserable, but it's all very sad and Seton was very upset to hear of Roy's death.

Letter from Seton, 30 November 1917
I was told today I should be attached to the squadron here for a month for the purpose of taking up observers. Picture me waiting to go for a joy ride preparatory to going up solo on an RE8 and answering a call from the flight commander to get that thrown at me. I must say I am quite pleased … so there is a possibility I will be in Blighty [England] for Christmas.

Sunday 2 December 1917
Up first and went to the doorstep to get my papers. It was bitterly cold so gave the little paper girl 2d. After lunch went off to Romford, we walked to Hornchurch, 3 miles.[38] The Mahutonga Hut where Moira works is very jolly indeed, crowded with boys. We also looked at Grey Towers and its garden. Saw Jack Fergusson today.

Monday 3 December 1917
Os went to see Sir James McKenzie, heart specialist, at 9.30 and had complete satisfaction from him. He gave him a letter to use, saying he had gone to camp too soon after the operation, and was unfit for work for some months. He charged £3.

Letters from Auntie Jen and then Mrs Barron on 5 and 6 December confirm the family's worst fears about how Taukoro is being neglected and mismanaged, and leads to another visit to the high commission. There is also a letter from lawyer Jim Watt: 'an oily plausible epistle, might easily mislead us if we hadn't had the truth from Jen'.

38 The New Zealand Convalescent Hospital at Grey Towers, Hornchurch, some 20 miles north-east of London, in Essex, could take 1900 (ultimately 2500) patients. It specialised in massage and electrical treatment. The Mahutonga Hut Annie mentions was in fact the Mahutonga Club, run by the War Contingent Association.

Thursday 6 December 1917

There was an air raid between 4 and 6 a.m. this morning – guns began about ¼ to 5. We stayed in Mrs Abraham's room; Mrs Matthews and little Bobbie joined us. She had her gas fire alight and it was quite cosy. The bombs did some damage again but luckily they got two planes down this time and caught the crews alive.[39] Bobbie came in after tea to get some chocs and a 'teeny piece of cake'.

Saturday 8 December 1917

Al's letter was a sad little one. She is so distressed that measles should stop her seeing Seton before he goes off to France. We hope Seton will still be here at Christmas. Took train to Tavistock to see Roger … He isn't as excited over [the letters] as the rest of us, but even he is pretty wild.

---

[39] The raid on London and the south-east counties by 25 planes killed eight people and injured 28.

SETON GOES TO FRANCE

CHAPTER SEVEN

By the time Seton leaves for France in December 1917, the British have had some success in the Battle of Cambrai, using tanks for the first time, and Jerusalem has been captured from the Turks, but the Germans are not held back for long. From March they push hard against the Allies, and Seton is in the thick of it, at Hesdigneul, near Lille. His letters and diary entries give a vivid picture of life at the front as Annie describes life in London.

Monday 10 December 1917
There was a very nice English girl in the carriage [on the train back to London] that I talked to a lot. Her brother had just been killed and had won the VC. Even she acknowledged that England wasn't awake yet and didn't know there was a war on in lots of ways. Back at '40' darling old Seton's luggage was in the hall and he under orders for France perhaps on Wednesday. It just stuns me because I didn't expect it after his being told he was attached to squadron for a month. The sneaks have some friends at squadron who have superseded Seton. He went to St Leonards to see Al today: she is in a room by herself and he was allowed to see her for ¼ hour. He says she is unhappy, poor little kid. Talked till about midnight, he had his night cap and went off to his room on top of the other house laden with personal belongings. He is very bright about it all.

Tuesday 11 December 1917
Os turned up, he managed to get leave to say 'goodbye' to Seton. He had to go to headquarters to get his orders, he leaves for France tomorrow, has to be at Victoria at 7.35 a.m. It was a blow: we had been hoping against hope all the time. He wanted to stay the night at the Grosvenor, as it was handy for the station but it was full up, but managed to leave his heavy luggage there. So he decided to stay here and travel early by the Metropolitan line; the porter has been asked to call him at quarter to six. Seton went to bed without a night

cap, although he was tired enough to sleep without. My precious baby boy going to France tomorrow. I'm just stupid and headachy and stunned.

Wednesday 12 December 1917
Porter woke me at quarter to six and I got up and lit gas and boiled kettle to make a cup of coffee for Seton, He and Os had a drink and biscuits before starting off. Seton was looking a bit shaken. God knows it is a wrench and we said 'goodbye' here. Os went off with him to the Grosvenor where they had breakfast together and collected the luggage. I wasn't very fit to go down so had breakfast in bed, so did Wid.

Letter from Seton, 12 December 1917
Royal Pavilion, Brighton
Waiting to embark this afternoon about three. On our trip here not a word was spoken; there were five of us. I don't know what happened to my kit this end. It may be in France by now.

Second letter, RFC Officers' Rest House and Mess
Going to No. 2 Squadron,[1] but of course I don't know and I can't tell you the locality. Just put after my name No. 2 Sqdn, RFC, BEF [British Expeditionary Force]. I am going on my own as far as friends are concerned.

Thursday 13 December 1917
Had letter from Seton from Folkestone. He was to leave there at 3 p.m. and would be in France last night. Such a dear brave letter and it was very comforting to get it. I thank God for giving me two such dear good sons. Feel very unstrung. Ordered two bottles of wine at Whiteley's.

Letter from Seton, 13 December 1917
I have arrived here late at night. The one I'm in tonight is a real home away from home. I am seeing quite a lot of life. The French really are too funny for words. I pity anyone who takes themselves seriously.

Friday 14 December 1917
Jim can't get away for Christmas unless he is invited somewhere, so he asks me to come to the rescue; wrote to him after breakfast. Wid and I went to

---

[1] No. 2 Squadron was formed in 1912 and is now the world's oldest fixed wing flying squadron. At the start of the First World War, it was the first squadron to leave Britain; it was known for reconnaissance.

the Records Office to interview Colonel FitzHerbert about her going back, but he says the office is full to the brim. He rang up the Pay Department so Wid and I went round there for an interview and it is arranged she starts there Monday. Oswald has applied to go in the Gunnery and offered to forgo his light duty if they would let him go. The poor old kid is far too keen. Letter to say Seton's Aero certificate number is 5405. Got letter from him, written just after he got to France, giving us his address. The letter doesn't say much but to me it sounds lonely and lost.

Letter from Seton, 14 December 1917
I have seen the aerodrome and then the rest of the place in daylight and satisfied my curiosity. You may not believe me but it would be hard to make ourselves more comfortable. We have a fair bit to do with the French people so that with a little study and work on my part I should pick up some French. Don't worry about Christmas, we shall have a 'bon' time here.

Each flight has its own mess, so that we could be separate squadrons for all we see of other flights. Ours is a good mess and there is a good cook. Colonials are known as 'coloured troops' out this way. The Canadians earned it and I have great pleasure in joining them. I hope you are not too worried about me because I am perfectly happy and this is certainly one of the most amusing and useful episodes of my life. This will broaden a man's outlook more than anything else. Just think of me sleeping between sheets in a comfortable billet.

Letter to Roger from Seton, 14 December 1917
I am doing my best to convince Mother that I am quite settled down, more than comfortable, but of course one cannot get this comfort outside the RFC. I have a deep respect for those French in the war zone. I don't think the people in England have a great deal to complain about. It will be some time before I start flying.

Sunday 16 December 1917
After breakfast sat in lounge a while and blew up a mine there by telling them that Lord Lansdowne represented a good number of the English who would face an inconclusive peace rather than give in to the fact that England couldn't win on her own bat and had to acknowledge that America was

going to save civilisation.[2] I don't care if they were wild. I'm too sore and bitter just now to care in the least what they think. The war would be over now if England had gone to work like America is doing.

Letter from Seton, 16 December 1917

So that we shall know the country without having to keep continually looking at our maps, we have to copy out the map of our area. I started mine today and it is very interesting if tiring.[3] Some of the products are splendid, but others are awful, and I should imagine they show the efficiency of the officer … Flying coats out here are issued in addition to our other kit. Very nice too! We get leave about every three months.

Letter from Seton, 17 December 1917

I had better economise in ink and write in pencil in future. I think tonight will be exceedingly cold. I notice the moon is young again. He is used out here for night raiding by the Huns and us.

Tuesday 18 December 1917

A letter came from Sister Dora which was very upsetting as she said Al had a thorough measles rash out, which showed it had been suppressed all these weeks. I was so anxious I set off for Hastings as soon as I could get ready, scribbled a note to Wid first. Arrived Hastings 3 p.m. and got a taxi, saw the sisters, they all said Al was well and promised to take good care of her. Al sent a message to say she would get well as soon as possible. I wanted to have a peep at her but couldn't. I kept the taxi waiting and went straight to the station. All the train blinds were drawn and a woman said a raid warning had come through, which sounded anything but cheerful but it was quite true.[4] When we got to a place called Batham all lights in train were put out and we went on to London in darkness. When we got to Victoria the train stopped at the entrance to platform and it was queer plodding all the way along platform in dusky darkness. I went down to the underground to get my train and was held up for some two and a half hours, got home at 11 p.m. Wid had been very worried.

Letter from Seton, 19 December 1917

I could have been in this place for years. My flight commander is going

---

2 Lord Lansdowne (1845–1927), former Conservative foreign secretary who, in November 1917, campaigned for a negotiated peace with Germany.

3 Seton's map is now in the Whanganui Regional Museum.

4 Fourteen were killed and 85 injured in the raid on London, Essex and Kent.

home soon. He is a very fine fellow even though he is mad at times, and he will be missed by all, but he has finished his time out here and he deserves it.

Thursday 20 December 1917

Letter came from Mrs Thomassett asking about Maori words for a New Zealander's wreath. Telegram from Os to say he is 'Coming Sunday till Thursday'. Thick fog all day; thanks to the fog the Huns haven't repeated their visit.

Letter from Seton, 20 December 1917

Parcel arrived today. I believe Os has found out from his people where I am. I could not have gone to a better part of the front or better squadron. This is a peace front and I hope it remains so; I think my luck came with me when I came here. I have spent quite a lot of time on my map: you have no idea what a long job it is. Had a hair cut in a town today nearby.

Friday 21 December 1917

Went to Buzzards to order Christmas cake but they are not taking any more orders.[5] Bought two tins of café au lait and one of condensed milk 4/6-. Roger arrived from Devon. Funny old Dad wanted to stay in his crumpled up clothes but we made him change. Wid has holidays till Thursday, thank goodness.

Letter from Seton, 21 December 1917

I find I will not be spending Christmas with the squadron. My flight commander told me today I shall be going to batteries tomorrow for 'liaison'. Artillery and infantry come here on the same job for days and we go to them so that we understand them better and we can see their difficulties for ourselves … like a Cook's tour.[6] I have finished my map. I am in neither of the places I spoke of … Please send some Wrights coal tar soap and two Eveready dry batteries No. 1689. I use my light quite a lot.

    PS. Please include some Cadronas [pine tablets], Bournemouth Breezes in a small tin. They are for colds. I have not got one but they prevent them.

Saturday 22 December 1917

Pc from Sister Dora to say Al's temperature is normal … Felt uneasy about my dear old Seton this morning, couldn't understand the feeling. Then my confidence in God's care helped me shake it off.

---

5 Buzzards was a posh cake shop in London's West End.

6 Reasonably brief guided tour of a place, referring to pioneering British travel agent Thomas Cook.

Letter from Seton, 22 December 1917

I am still here as the battery I had to go to just shifted and did not want to be troubled by 'liaison' officers. I did my practice landings and my flight commander was quite bucked with the exhibition. The next item on the programme is to look at the line with an old observer. I shall be in no greater danger than before. My introduction to France was a bombed town, and I may say that town gets bombed very frequently as well as shelled, and still people live there. It is only about half an hour since it was heavily bombed as well as many places round about, and up to the present we have missed that pleasure. In return we do the same to the Hun.

Sunday 23 December 1917

Mrs Watts rang up from Paddington canteen and asked Wid to go round and help them as they had a rush on, so Wid went off. Os arrived. He isn't looking quite so bright. These cold winters don't agree with him and Aldershot is a bleak old hole. Wid got back at 3.30 tired out. Mrs Harris had an Australian colonel visiting. He told great stories; one was about a soldier's will: 'If I get knocked out [killed] in this leap over [going over the top in the trenches] I leave my gilt [money] to my tart' and he was knocked out. They were trying to prove his will and find his tart.

Letter from Seton, 23 December 1917

I had a look at the line today and it seems funny to say so but you don't realise there is any trouble on and those people down here are very keen to have your life. The thought of Archie watching keeps you employed.[7] You look over the side and see a ruin. That same ruin is as historical as London.

Monday 24 December 1917

Pc about Al to say she is doing well and getting up today. Os and Wid gave me a snapshot album and Wid spent most of the evening arranging snapshots in it. Letter arrived from Seton. He seems very glad he joined the 2nd Squadron and he likes the locality where he is at present. Darling old son, God shield and keep him is my constant prayer. He went over the German lines again.

---

7   Archie was slang for an anti-aircraft gun or shell, or a member of an anti-aircraft force, in this case the Germans.

Tuesday 25 December 1917

After breakfast Bobbie Matthews came upstairs with me to get his book and grapes and for me to see his presents. At 10.30 went to Bobbie's party, met Mrs Binnie. Her flying son has been a prisoner in Germany and expected home soon. A note arrived from Mrs Tilley asking us to tea this afternoon. When we arrived found the children round a very small Christmas tree, but all very happy. Back home had awfully nice dinner, turkey and sausage, cauliflower and potatoes, also roast beef, sherry jelly, mince pies and plum pudding, cheese and coffee. Tips 24/- for Christmas.

Letter from Seton, 25 December 1917

I did a bit of proper work today, but it was not successful as the weather turned 'dud'. We had quite a good time flying round in the mist at about 400 feet. My observer, being an old one did not lose us, but I should have most certainly if I had been alone. He is a captain and bears the same name as your manager at Taukoro [Barron]. It is a funny feeling to realise you are part of the war machine and it gives you some satisfaction … I don't mind flying round there at least: you have no sense of immediate danger as you may imagine with no actual experience. The country looked like a dream with all the trees and everything standing was covered with whiskers of frost. It was like that for two days. It is pretty but 'très froid' while it lasts.

Letter from Seton, 26 December 1917

Christmas is over. It was 'some night' and things went just as I expected. We have a room to live in now – minus all its windows, several pictures and two broken-hearted armchairs. One of the other flights came along to do the dirty work for us, but they found it all done and were heavily defeated – the snow that nearly prevented us from going to dinner came in very handy on that occasion. Our major – who by the way is an Australian – came out of his reserve and was the leading spirit. There were many laughable incidents, especially when the other flight attacked: there were six casualties in less than five minutes and we suffered more though they were not serious. I don't think they will attempt another raid without considering the cost …
It would have been a 'loss' to lose that Xmas dinner with the RFC in France in 1917. I had rather a shock during the dinner because I was told I was to liaise with infantry four days from today, but as before, it collapsed this

morning. I am looking forward to that visit because I shall have opportunities of trench life without participating.

Thursday 27 December 1917

Went to bank to see about our finances: £100 sent to me from NZ has arrived. Cable arrived from Barron: 'Leave granted till 30th April'. We were very excited; it is a beginning. Anyway it means those Salt creatures have got their marching orders.

Letter from Seton, 27 December 1917

I don't know what your danger instinct recorded on 22 December: I can't recollect any extra danger I was in at that time ... I would not place too much faith in that instinct. You will find a town called Béthune on the map – well, I am about 3 miles in a westerly direction from that.[8] I don't think anyone could take offence at that information as they don't know me or what I'm in.

In letters over the last few days of December Seton reports on his first shoot – he runs out of petrol and has to return – and notes that 'you can get a better afternoon tea than you can in London: as many cakes as you like and best French pastry'. He is enjoying living in the cellars of a 'one time nice house ... I can see this [the liaison] is going to be a top hole experience.' He describes looking at 'the spot where Sergeant Michael O'Leary won the VC early in the war',[9] and reassures Annie: 'Don't think this tour is dangerous, the difference is you hear what's coming and you don't in the air till it has arrived and it is a blessing.'

Monday 31 December 1917

The last day of 1917, God grant that 1918's last day may find us all well.

---

8 Seton was at Hesdigneul, near Béthune, in the Pas-de-Calais region of Northern France.

9 Irishman Michael John O'Leary (1890–1961) won the Victoria Cross in February 1915 for single-handedly destroying two machine gun-defended German barricades near the French village of Cuinchy.

1918

CHAPTER EIGHT

Tuesday 1 January 1918
A nice big NZ mail, including one to say Gran has a septic throat and is not a bit well. Os arrived. He has been sent to a gunnery officers' course at North Weald, Essex and so his French draft is a washout. However he is pleased to be doing something definite again. He took the 3.30 train from Liverpool Street. He had a new cane from Southampton Row. He took a lovely eider and waterproof quilt with him as he feels the cold so much. I'm feeling much better tonight, though troubled by not hearing from Seton today.

Letter from Seton, 1 January 1918
The new year has arrived and we sat it in last night – needless to say we drank it in too, in the popular style headed by the CO. It is a good sport watching our planes buzzing round and Archie following up, and you see the Bosch planes also – a thing that the pilot has not time to see in the air unless the Huns get in front of him. Trenches are all very interesting but those four days will have me bored to death. You wander round and come back through very similar trenches, squinting out at very similar places and moving on again to keep your feet warm and return to your HQ, in this case a cellar. I have seen a real live Hun, in full view about 800 yards off, and watched a fellow put a bullet after him. It was too misty to see without glasses, so he was not hit. Our people played the dirty on the Hun on Christmas Eve, so last night we half expected they would return the compliment but they did not … but listening to the shells and other flying missiles and you have to satisfy yourself what they are and whose they are. I have seen a sight that has not greeted my eyes for 18 months – a few bottles of 'Bulldog' beer and it is quite like old times.

Letter from Seton, 2 January 1918
Last night of trench life … There is a small country cemetery and the

Bosche gas shells and other ones have been blowing the crosses and ground about … Just on top of the graves of the 'unknown' soldier. There have been some fine new houses actually built recently but at present they are proper has beens. The usual French habitat is a bad erection of mud and timber and I wouldn't care to stable a horse in them.

In a second letter the same day he thanks his mother for 'farm news and parcels': soap, pudding, toffee, dates and three copies of the Auckland Weekly News.

People have me a hero out here now but you are mistaken: I have not done half of what the majority in the squadron have done … Don't enjoy going about my work but I know it is my duty so I don't mind. I had one of the best sights of my life today as I left battalion HQ. The Bosche shelled about 100 yards away from a bridge we crossed and when we had him at a respectable distance we watched this exhibition. Shells, unlike bombs, fall in a restricted area, so 100 yards is a long way. I hope you will see that in shelling you try for a point whereas in bombing they tumble down in any old spot.

Seton, diary, 2 January 1918

Had a look at gas shelling and picked up three souvenirs. Shells had a very musty odour and several officers and men were slightly gassed. Orchard Keep cookhouse was hit and the small cemetery just opposite. Did nothing in the afternoon.

Seton, diary, 4 January 1918

Tried to shoot in the morning with Heney … Went up again … Visibility was not good … Archie holed my leading edge in one place.

Friday 4 January 1918

Read my paper as usual, then came downstairs and wrote a letter to the *Daily Mail* about the criticism of Mr Jamieson's speech in NZ on the London street evil.[1] Showed Mrs Harris and she was very pleased about it. After tea Al and I went to see Wid as I wanted to see the *DM* letter before I posted it. She was a little dubious about one sentence, but I ended up posting it, then as soon as I did I was sorry so went to a little shop and bought pcs and envelopes and went back to Wid's office and scribbled a note to

---

1 Back in November W.G. Jamieson, the commissioner for the New Zealand YMCA, had told the association's annual conference in Christchurch that 'absolutely nothing' was being done to prevent the New Zealand troops arriving in London from 'getting into mischief' (i.e. sleeping with prostitutes). Annie was not the only one to object: the YMCA in London explained that 'every opportunity was taken to occupy the men's leisure hours' (*Ashburton Guardian*, 6 November 1917). Prime Minister Massey, as the *Evening Post* reported on 6 November 1917, spoke of 'marvellous work' being done by New Zealanders in Britain and in January 1918 the four principal chaplains to the New Zealand Expeditionary Force asked Defence Minister James Allen to assure the public that the New Zealand civilian and military groups in Britain were 'doing all in their power to protect our boys' (*Press*, 3 January 1918).

editor *DM* asking him to take out two words from sentence in letter which would make it quite unassailable.

Seton, diary, 5 January 1918
Art[illery] patrol in morning with Heney. Archie got us in about eight places …

Letter from Seton, 6 January 1918
Saw a primeval sight in the form of a French marriage ceremony – the couple walk at the head of a procession, which in this case was about 50 yards long, and consisted of couples holding each other's hands and a whole lot of kids paired off. They march around the village. Today I did a successful shoot, but I did not do it in the manner appointed by the CO. He issued a pamphlet of advice as to the best heights for working in the air. I did not abide by it so he wanted to know the reason why and I informed him it was only advice and not an order, and that the machine I was flying was painful, like a dying horse, and I had to get on with the work somewhere. I was quite ready for him and I argued as usual, and I think held my end up even if I did not win; I think I did. I don't know how he will take it and I don't greatly care. I am not going to be ticked off by any Australian when I did my work successfully and that is all that is required. He was up at the shoot and made a bad attempt the other day and from what I hear he was not too successful. But that does not mean that it was a difficult shoot. In any case I am going to be guarded with him now, and will endeavour to hold what I have already gained and to take advantage when possible. [The CO's advice became an order a day or two later.]

Letter from Seton, 8 January 1918
[Other pilots flying in a snowstorm landed at an aerodrome 20 miles south.] Lucky to find it as snowstorm blots out the ground even 100 feet. The thaw yesterday turned the 'drome into a sheet of water – when it froze last night it was like a sheet of glass. Now it's covered with, or was till the wind got up, about six inches of snow.

During the week Annie has the diary she has bought for Seton initialled and sent off. On the Monday Mrs Binnie's pilot son, who has been a prisoner in Germany for nine months, arrives for dinner: his mother is 'beaming with happiness'. He was only one month in France when he was shot through the arm and fainted in his plane, which crashed to pieces when it fell. He was then captured. Nephew Jim arrives on the Saturday and they show him the sights of London, including St Paul's with 'its dear old pidgies', and he visits the theatre. A very worrying letter is received about Gran, who has been having fainting fits.

Letter from Seton, 10 January 1918

I was on early show this morning and we had nothing exciting. The weather was pretty 'dud' and windy and we had the line to ourselves for over two hours. It was fairly lonely with no other machines about, you have no definite work to do. My personal contribution to the National Day of Prayer [4 January] was a successful shoot on a Hun battery. At the time Jim was watching the crowd at St Paul's I was being chased around the heavens by Archie, and at the same time doing my best – through the battery – to blow a few Huns and their guns out of position. Archie does not worry one all the time; he looks you up when he has nothing better on, and that is usually once an hour with luck. I must say the mere thought of <u>you</u> gives me a great deal more confidence, so you are indirectly having an active part in the war.

Letter from Seton, 11 January 1918

You have the impression that a war in any particular spot affects the whole line, but believe me it affects only those immediately in the vicinity and no others. The battalion HQ I was in was hit, damaged – only a few more bricks knocked down is about all.

Saturday 12 January 1918

Al, Jim and I went off to Westminster to see the Houses of Parliament. It was all very impressive … Quite the conventional setting for pomp and ceremony so dear to these English people. The House of Commons just made me feel cramped, English cramped – no wonder we get cramped legislation. Heard a story about an old woman in the last raid sheltering under basement steps, who was worrying to go home as she had an iron cot there that she used to cover her head in raids. Some times she placed it resting on two tables and sat between them with her head encased and nursing her cat.

Letter from Seton, 12 January 1918

I am rather late tonight as the major has been aviating with an RFC general to satisfy their curiosity about some new flares. It is night flying of course and they require ground lights to take 'off' by and for a while I was in charge of them but I got out as soon as possible. Since then I have been watching the display and they certainly make good fireworks if nothing else … I am not surprised about Os being sick in the air: it is not an uncommon occurrence out here amongst 'fit' specimens, though it is usually the observer. You seem quite perturbed about those broken windows and my welfare but I am still living and we are not frozen yet. We can't procure the glass – that was known beforehand so it will remain so until the war is over. We will use that mess for many more years as they are putting up huts for us, so they turn us out of our comfortable billets. The army is taking back some of its stuff so that in future we will have to use our own. They are giving us something in exchange but is not serviceable except for its <u>proper</u> job and the old issue was useful at any time.

Sunday 13 January 1918

Mrs Harris, Al and I went with Jim to Petticoat Lane. I have never dreamed of any thing so dreadful: it's a blot on civilisation and a disgrace to England. Some of the men and women look more like animals than human beings and their 'wares' are as horrid as themselves. The 'crush' was fearful and the crowd most unsavoury; I was very glad to get away from the place. Jim and Al went off to see Tommie Parker at the Alexandra Hospital [Queen Alexandra's Hospital for Officers] in Highgate. They found him looking bright. His left arm was shot in the socket but he can use his fingers and is talking of joining the RFC when he is better. He was wounded at Cambrai. The patients have electrophones and can listen to concerts and theatres as they lie in bed.[2]

Letter from Seton, 13 January 1918

I have just received Al's beautiful little diary: my trouble is to do it justice. Out of my window I can see two of our planes practising fighting. One of our old buses is doing its best to throw off one of our scouts and it is like a flea and an elephant. The little scout has twice the speed and manoeuvring ability and catches up and does what it likes, but of course that is practice and in the real

2 The electrophone was a British telephone-operated audio system that relayed live performances, and such things as church sermons, through a special headset. This hospital saved the limbs of many who would otherwise have faced amputation.

thing the old slow bus's observer is a nasty mouthful for the scout. You will be very pleased that America's entry into the war has been quite a tonic and from what I hear the old Hun will be getting a nasty time in the future.

Letter from Seton, 14 January 1918
I received your letter, not at all cheering. It [Roy Mason's death] must have been a stunning blow for Aunt Jessie and we think of her, but there are the girls to be considered too … It is three years since they saw Roy so that time must soften the tragedy. Gran is getting too old to stand a breakdown in health and we must expect the inevitable – I look at it this way, that she is living a life of sorrow now … This morning it snowed for a long time, and after staying foggy cleared up slightly about three and put the wind up us as we detest nothing more on principle than having suddenly to go up for an hour [when the fog clears]. It is a useless inconvenience at that time of day.

Letter from Seton, 15 January 1918
I have spent the afternoon reading one of William Le Queux's all-engrossing criminal tales,[3] or if the electric light hadn't failed I might still be reading … *Punch* has a cartoon of a farm scene that are actual conditions here. In the farmyard where our mess is, is also the residence of the mayor. Some residence – the stable is in one corner and in the vicinity I often see this 'witch' attending two old white draught horses. It is hard to believe it is a woman – accent on the man. She stands more rough weather and long hours than the majority of men, though she must be at least 60.

Letter from Seton, 16 January 1918
There is one fellow in this Squadron who will get the MC, VC, or Wooden C [wooden cross or grave] in the near future. He should be dead or a prisoner already, but his number is not yet up it seems. On four occasions now, one was this afternoon. He has done some marvellous things, especially for these machines … he is a Canadian, and has only been out a short time and is keen, and foolish, though fearless.[4]

Letter from Seton, 17 January 1918
Don't know how people live in places they do. These people build their farms in a square about 40 yards and in the centre is a square excavation

[3] Anglo-French journalist and writer William Tufnell Le Queux (1864–1927) was best known for his 150 mystery, thriller and espionage novels, particularly the bestselling 1906 anti-German invasion fantasy, *The Invasion of 1910*.

[4] Seton is referring to Second Lieutenant Alan McLeod. See p. 159.

about 4 feet deep. This is filled with straw and all winter the sheep are penned up in it, fresh straw being added every morning. I leave it to you to imagine the perfumes that proceed from it and still the home is on one side and the other farm buildings on the other sides. How plague doesn't sweep the country I don't know.

Right through January Seton is reporting in his diary on air attacks, which he does not mention in his letters. On the 18th, for example, he writes in his diary: 'Fenn-Smith and Cornforth shot down at 10.25 near Hullock [Hulluch] but in our lines. Both killed, probably a shot from the ground or may have been two Huns – fire broke out, and bombs went off.' Second Lieutenant Norman Leslie Cornforth, aged 28, and Second Lieutenant Warren Kemp Fenn-Smith, aged 18, who was South African, are buried at Chocques Military Cemetery. Seton's letter, written on the same day, talks of his 'successful shoot', the weather ('The trenches must be in a fearful condition now as it has been raining and drizzling about the last week') and a change in mess arrangements that will mean 'losing our only pianist'.

Letter from Seton, 19 January 1918

Rise in pay, I benefit by it to the extent of about £4 10/- as I claim for October when I was not a flying officer. The battalion fairly pounded the Hun position, and it gives one great joy to see it … Australia has thrown out conscription by a vast majority, haven't they?[5] I hear half the trouble is the failure to grant leave to the original force.

Letter from Seton, 21 January 1918

Our electric light has the little habit of going out about 10 minutes at a time some days. When I was in the trenches the power station used to run down for hours on end, very inconvenient in the cellars. Just as well to state the Australians ran it. You will remember I mentioned a general going up with CO to play with flares, well, the poor twit has gone west and I attended his funeral today. Even if you are a general that doesn't escape you from death, as he broke his neck in an aeroplane. How he managed it no one knows as he was a splendid pilot.[6]

Tuesday 22 January 1918

Read paper. My friend Sir Edward Carson has resigned from Cabinet.[7] This

5 It was not a 'vast majority'. A first referendum, on 28 October 1916, asking Australians if they were in favour of conscription, had failed: 51.2 per cent were opposed. In a second referendum, held on 20 December 1917, 53.3 per cent had been against the idea.

6 Brigadier-General Gordon Strachey Shephard, aged 32, was killed near Auchel on January 1918 when his aircraft spun into the ground. Seton attended his funeral on 21 January: 'Many "brass hats" present and a large collection of motor vehicles'. Shephard, who was mentioned in dispatches six times and was a Chevalier of the Legion of Honour, is buried in Lapugnoy Military Cemetery.

7 Sir Edward Carson (1854–1935) was an Irish barrister (he represented the Marquess of Queensberry in the Oscar Wilde trial), judge and unionist politician, who opposed Home Rule for Ireland.

Irish question is a shameful thing and I just hope they won't do anything to try and force his decent loyalty to bend to the treacherous wants of enemies. It would be quite an English idea of justice. Os is quite stiff today through getting his legs chilled while up on planes yesterday; he was up 11,000 feet.

Wednesday 23 January 1918

A boy named C. Bluett called while I was at tea.[8] He came with a note from Hugh asking me to give him £3, which I did. I asked him to come and see me again. He seemed a little 'oiled up' [drunk] but it may have been nervousness. He promised to come again before he goes back to France. He says Hugh is a very fine fellow and liked by everyone and that he went into the line the day he came out … Wid wrote out her resignation to Pay Office tonight; her head is 'dud' again. Jim didn't come to dinner tonight; he took a WAAC to the pictures.[9]

Friday 25 January 1918

After breakfast I read my paper and then got ready to go and see Jim off at Paddington. He had a cup of coffee and then we set off, got there half an hour too early. It always gives me the jim jams to sit about in these stations because in case of raids, but nothing happened. Jim thanked me very nicely for having me; he really is a dear old thing. And his seeing life hasn't done him any harm, I'm sure of that. He is just a dare-devil Dick and full of adventure. His fussy old manager at Manhattan Hotel gave him £1 note instead of his receipt and I promised to fix it up for him. Came back from station and tallied up my bank book. Then page came up to say wanted on the phone and when I got down I found it was Mrs Whiteman and she wanted me to go to lunch with her at Norfolk House, the Duchess of Norfolk's town house, but lent by her as a club for Overseas Ladies. I took a taxi from Whiteley's but the old donkey took me to a ladies' club in Piccadilly. However I asked a policeman and he got me another taxi and I got there (2/-) and so I crossed the ducal portals. The rooms are very handsome and are supposed to be furnished just as the Norfolks used them – maybe, maybe not. Still it is a magnificent gift, and a great boon. We had a very nice lunch and sat in the lounge until afternoon tea time just gossiping. Had tea and departed our several ways. The drawing room upstairs and the ballroom and writing room are all very grand and the stairway is such an easy grade for

---

8 Possibly Private Charles Bluett, 31942, from Whakatane, fighting with the New Zealand Rifle Brigade. If it was this man, he did not have long to live: he was killed on the Somme on 27 March 1918.

9 A member of the Women's Army Auxiliary Corps, founded in Britain in July 1917 in answer to pressure for women to have some role in the army, doing tasks that would release men for front-line service. The organisation was divided into four sections – cookery, mechanical, clerical and miscellaneous – and women performed a variety of roles, in Britain and at the front. More than 55,000 women served in the WAAC from January 1917 to November 1918.

walking up and down. One can feel quite graceful! Mrs Harris came in for a chat, she and I both think Wid should take up motoring.

Letter from Seton, 25 January 1918

Although I admire that Canadian's daring I have no desire whatever to follow suit. I am not built that way and the rest of the squadron are similar. On early show, the trouble will be when daylight comes about three in the morning and lasts till nine at night. Not much time to sleep then.

Second letter from Seton, 25 January 1918

I was up this morning and had one of the most perculiar [sic] experiences of my life, I had just left the 'drome when I ran into mist, so I proceeded to try to see through it, but the only ground I could see was the clear patch which I took good care I didn't lose, which kept under me. The mist was just up to the top of the chimney stacks and it was funny to see the black streaks in the white blanket mist. I climbed up about 7,000 and stayed there for two and a half hours before the whole country cleared. It was very nice up there in the sun and I took sights of the clear space and went away over to Hunland with the intention of dropping my bombs but I found I could see nothing – afterwards I found I had none [bombs] on. It is peculiar to see the white below and know that Archie is cheated out of a shot. I'll bet he heard me. I have just had a short stop to listen to Brother Bosche droning overhead on a bomb raid, and he has just this minute left here.

Letter from Seton, 26 January 1918

There is this man called Nissen somewhere in the Allied countries,[10] and he has patented a hut, which is all very well if it is decently lined, but when these heathen Chinese you mentioned put them up with the working ability of a young elephant,[11] the resultant so-called huts are not all that could be desired. When completed the whole squadron will rush from their billets and make themselves at home in them. Billets were wanted in the village so the last joined in each flight had to go the completed huts and I have dodged it by coming to this billet. I am afraid our equipment officer is not becoming popular over it and I think that in the winter a dugout would be better than those huts. I have secured a real bed to take with me ... I went the highest I have ever been today.

10 Mining engineer and inventor Major Peter Norman Nissen, of the Royal Engineers, designed the prefabricated half-cylindrical corrugated iron hut in 1916. Easily transported and assembled, it was widely used, particularly in the Second World War.

11 To fill the manpower shortage caused by war casualties, Chinese labourers were recruited to perform non-military tasks on the Western Front: 140,000 worked there during and after the war. Of these, 100,000 were part of the British Chinese Labour Corps, members of which would have erected the Nissen huts. These workers were treated harshly and a large number died, mostly of influenza but also as a result of enemy fire.

Letter from Seton, 27 January 1918

Today we amused ourselves by firing through the mist to Hunland, and dropped our bombs as near as we could judge where we wanted to. The Hun machines couldn't leave the ground because they couldn't see to land again. I have done just over 50 hours' flying out here now. Glad to see it mounting up.

Monday 28 January 1918

After dinner had just written a little more in Seton's letter when the maroons [rockets] sounded an air raid warning and Wid and I got into our coats and went downstairs. We went to smoking room and had some coffee and then Mrs Abercrombie, Mrs Harris, Wid and I sat together. One new woman, Mrs Bailey, was shockingly nervous, also Mrs Jardine, who came in the smoking room also. The raiders were very persistent and there was a lot of grim fire. At 10.30 we thought it was over (it began about 8 o'clock) and we all came upstairs. I finished Seton's letters and found the post was gone so Wid and I went out to the Met post box and posted it. Then Mrs Harris had some coffee with us and we went to bed. And the brutes were back again at 12.30, for a short spin. We jumped into dressing gowns and coats again and took our rugs and went down to the drawing room, presently we had Mrs Glasgow, Mrs Harris, Mrs Matthews and Bobbie and a Miss Cowlishaw with us – all Australasians – and we waited there till the all clear went at 1.30.[12] Then went to bed tired out.

Tuesday 29 January 1918

When I got back found telephone message from Wid asking me to go and have lunch with her. Got fearfully shaky for fear it meant something wrong with Hugh and had to take whisky to pull myself together. When I got there I found it was because the raiders had done so much damage roundabout Russell Square that she had sent for me to see it with her. We had lunch at her little restaurant and then went to Endell Street and saw the devastation: one home just struck flat and the rest of the buildings had caught on fire and numbers were burnt. *John Bull's* offices were destroyed and numbers of people were caught in basement and drowned because the water main was cut. One bomb fell in the old street, Bedford Place, and made a great hole of pavement and basement. Ever so many more places I did not see – Ah

---

12 By this point all clears were being given by bugle calls from Boy Scouts or men in cars.

me, it's too fearful. Came home and Os rang up immediately after, He can't come to dinner tonight. He was up most of the night, poor old kid, and his head felt dud. He is coming to lunch tomorrow instead. One fight took place just over their aerodrome. Rested on chair until afternoon tea time and read paper; my flatulence is bothering me today. Allie and Ethel Tripe called and while we were talking to them in the smoking room the maroons went for another raid. They didn't know whether to try and get home or stay here, it ended in their staying for nearly an hour. Then as nothing happened they set off. Allie borrowed £5 from me. They hadn't been gone long when the guns started and the raid went on for about an hour.

Thursday 31 January 1918
Wid came rushing up this morning with a letter from the War Office. It was to say Seton has the mumps in France and is in No. 12 Stationary Hospital, St Pol.[13] Wid got the worst shock as she had to open the letter and it was a relief to find it was the mumps, although that is horrid enough. Went out and sent a tele-cablegram 6/6d to Seton, reply paid. Then went to Selfridges and ordered grapes and oranges 17/6d for him. After tea got a letter from Seton, quite bright. Went to bed early and while I was in my bath Wid came up and rushed me out in a hurry because she thought she heard guns beginning, but it turned out to be fog signals as it has been very foggy all day. Wid left the Pay Office today.

Letter from Seton, 2 February 1918
Mumps have slid across to the left side of my face. I am worse than 'fed up' as I had safely finished with the right side and had hopes of getting up today. We have a good selection of sisters, English, Scotch and Irish – one is green down to her handkerchief. They have a lot to look after and we don't see much of them.

Monday 4 February 1918
Mrs Bennett says that a majority of censors in her department are Belgian. To me that sounds awful. How can they trust Belgians to do such work? They censor German, Dutch, Spanish and Italian correspondence. No wonder things go wrong very often.[14]

13 Despite its name, a stationary hospital was actually reasonably mobile and could be moved from place to place. In the British Expeditionary Force there were two stationary hospitals per division. No. 12 Stationary Hospital was at Rouen and, when Seton was a patient, at St Pol.

14 This is perhaps a curious reaction, considering that neutral Belgium had been invaded by Germany in 1914 to the accompaniment of often hysterical anti-German propaganda. There were some 250,000 Belgian refugees in London during the war. But the suspicion of 'aliens', wherever they were from, was very strong in these years.

Tuesday 5 February 1918

Had a little strife with Miss Gaines this morning ... She must have heard something I was saying as she came in about England always being too late and as she is staunchly English she got nasty and suggested I should go back to NZ. I hadn't the sense to tell her I had just the same right to be here as she had and that I also had a right to criticise their muddles when I had to risk my own precious boys in their defence. 'Say now,' a Canadian said to Ina's bank manager, 'I think you people are too shut in. You put hedges round your fields and brick walls round your streets.'

Wednesday 6 February 1918

We took a bus to Southampton Row, we saw a lot of fresh NZ boys tramping round to the [Soldiers'] Club and to the Shakespeare Hut.[15] We spoke to some of them. They are 30th Reinforcements.[16] When we got home to lunch we found old Os here; it was such a lovely surprise. In *Daily Mail* today it came out that 1200 farmers' sons in Kent alone have exemption vouchers. The cases were to be scrutinised – this country is supposed to have conscription.

The fruit sent to Seton was not a success: only the oranges and one grape survived. In letters he assures his mother that she must not worry about 'the wants of the inner man – the meals are splendid'. He also explains that he will have to fly for three weeks before he will be due for any more leave: 'sorry, but you have to face the facts'.

Friday 8 February 1918

We went in bus and the girl conductress told us she had been working for a year, 20 years old, a nice-looking girl whose country parents are scared of her living in London because of raids etc. She lives with the bus driver's wife, but gets very lonely and can't sleep at nights. Another case of raid mares. She seemed glad to talk to us.

Sunday 10 February 1918

Page got our papers. It is a new page now, a very nervous lost-looking boy. I went up to enquire for Laurie Watts. I told him I was taking him under my wing as his mother was absent, that I was a foster mother for stray boys ... Overheard a guest of the Abercrombies saying that some woman in the bus

---

15 A YMCA hut used for rest and recreation.

16 The 30th Reinforcements had left New Zealand on the *Corinthic* and *Arawa* on 13 October 1917.

had prophesied that the war would be over on 28th February or beginning of March and would end in a snowstorm. She had previously informed the people sitting near her how much they had in their purses and she was right in each case.

Letter from Seton, 10 February 1918
This hospital, like all others, possesses a library and I have samples of about 10 books already and there are plenty more still. Is Tiny considering any stunt such as dancing at the Coliseum or amusing the wounded troops that she could suddenly desire to go to 'foxtrot'?[17] I shall look for her photo in the *Tatler* [a society magazine].

17 The foxtrot, introduced in 1914, looked rather like a waltz but was danced to 4/4 time – originally ragtime. Its heyday came in the 1930s.

Monday 11 February 1918
Got letter from Os by evening post and was so glad because my last letter to him was returned from his squadron this morning, so I knew he had moved somewhere and it is worrying not to know just exactly where they are. Later on he rang up from his new place of abode, Hainault Farm, but he is only to be there three days. He will come up on Thursday for a few days' leave.

Letter from Seton, 12 February 1918
I spent a little time revising my French today. Matthews has a book that will teach French in three months and I am using that. Russia has pulled out of the war altogether now but she has been practically that since the revolution. It is not very nice to contemplate but I don't think it will make much difference now that America is going to start.

Wednesday 13 February 1918
Wid helped Miss Thorne entertain two blind Australians in smoking room. They were very bright and very pleased about Wid being an NZer, said that would do them next best to an Australian and told her a story about two Yanks and an NZer travelling in a train. One Yank was from New York and the other from Chicago and when the NZer said he came from New Zealand they asked, 'Where's that?' On being shown it on the map they said, 'Say now, where do you go when the tide comes in?'

Letter from Seton, 13 February 1918

We [he and Annie] do nothing but talk about when I will get my leave … You must be having a trying time with rationing just starting and nobody knowing what they are doing.[18] You need not worry about me, I have all the papers. You can see from the papers we have a terrific 'gust-up' on the Western Front about a German offensive,[19] and I only hope if it does mature it will take place elsewhere than on our front. This is not very excellent weather for making an offensive.

Letter from Seton, 14 February 1918

I'm afraid I have a bombshell for you – on making inquiries I leave here on the 19th, Tuesday, so switch over your address to the squadron. Have heard there is a possibility I will not get 2 [Squadron] again. Now I know the day I leave I am writing to the squadron, so they can, if they want, wrangle me back … I am pretty sure they will, but you must understand that after 14 days we are struck off strength … In the question of flying, I would rather fly than lose my squadron.

Friday 15 February 1918

Os and I walked to Piccadilly and bought Seton a pair of wings at Andre's. Os says all the fliers say it is luckier to have 'wings' given you than to buy your own, so we are sending them to him – for luck.

Letter from Seton, 16 February 1918

I can see Paris is no place for me if everything is so expensive. The people in this village seem to be even poorer than the ones where I have been living. There are plenty of decaying farm buildings; the houses are about in the same condition.

PS You always mention flying at high altitudes, but 7,000 to 8,000 is not considered high. Add 10,000 to them and you are high, compris?

Sunday 17 February 1918

The page got our papers. They contained the good news that Sir Harry Wilson is Chief of Staff now in place of Sir W. Robertson – Hurrah.[20] Last night's raider dropped a bomb in Sloane Square and buried an invalid officer, his wife and the children. One enemy airplane was brought down.[21]

---

18 Rationing on basic foodstuffs such as sugar, meat and butter was introduced at the beginning of 1918. Coupons were required. Sugar and butter continued to be rationed until 1920.

19 This is the Spring Offensive, launched on 21 March 1918.

20 This was Field Marshal Sir Henry Wilson (see footnote p. 122). He replaced Field Marshal Sir William ('Wully') Robertson as Chief of Imperial General Staff after the latter was pushed out of the job.

21 Six were injured and 12 killed in this raid on London and Dover.

After dinner came upstairs and rested till maroon went at 10.15, then got coat and rug each and went down to drawing room. Found Mrs Matthews had Bobbie there and Mrs Bremner was there too. So we made up the fire and settled ourselves down. Later on Laurie Watts came in and joined us. We got our kettle down, cups etc and had café au lait. Afterwards Laurie showed Mr Matthews the steps he had learned at Bournemouth and they kept us interested while the firing was on. Towards 12 o/c everything was quiet and we all came upstairs and got into bed. The all clear went about quarter to one. They were more persistent tonight and got closer.[22]

22 This raid on London killed 21 and injured 32.

Letter from Seton, 17 February 1918

There are rumours that the Hun advance has started and from the sounds that drift even this far back I can quite credit it.[23] I have a good idea where it is … I have spent an hour looking at a *Waitakian* and it has some very sad news: two brothers, and I think the only ones [children]. It is very hard on old people. Roll of Waitaki Old Boys serving 600.

23 What Seton probably heard was the ton of bombs dropped on Metz, in Lorraine, in north-eastern France.

Seton, diary, 17 February 1918

Went for two walks. Bristol fighter landed here lost. Gothas came over bombing, we think stunt has started.

Monday 18 February 1918

After breakfast sat a short time in lounge and then Wid got ready to go to her fox-trotting lesson. She is very tired as her sleeplessness is troubling her again. She simply cannot stand the raids. Afterwards went to Madame Felicia's to look at evening frocks. She tried two on a model for us and quite killed our fancy for them. The 'model' was a very uncouth specimen. 9.30 when the maroon went again. It was some time before the gunfire began – Wid and I went down to the drawing room.

Letter from Seton, 18 February 1918

I am supposed to be a nice clean boy now and not possess any germs as my clothes have been disinfected and I have had a disinfectant bath, but you will be amused when you hear I am in the same old bed and in same company.

Letter from Seton, 19 February 1918

I have been doing my duty today by lending my trench coat to a sister to parade in the rain before the Surgeon General to be presented with her Mons ribbon, in company with four sisters and some officers and men.[24] You will see that few 'originals' are surviving … Unless the unexpected happens, meanwhile I shall proceed to No. 2 and find the lay of the land. I shall make every endeavour to get back to 2.

Letter from Seton, 20 February 1918

Pleased to know I am in 'A' flight, No. 2 Squadron as before. I humbly apologise for not writing last night but considering I was some where in Northern France when I should not have been through no fault of my own … you will excuse me. I had no place or light to write. I shall tell you on leave about my wanderings and they were not altogether unpleasant, and I can't mention places names in this letter. I am in a billet with that other fellow and not in a Nissen hut. I find a few changes in the squadron – new pilots etc and many crashes, my old 'dud' has gone during my absence. I have quite settled myself down.

Seton had taken the wrong train from St Pol on 19 February and ended up in Hazebrouck, where he stayed the night. When he returned to his squadron at Béthune he discovered that Captain Sydney Broadbent, aged 33, and 25-year-old Lieutenant Alfred Jones Homersham ('Hom') had been killed on 18 February in an air fight. Both men are buried in the Gorre British and Indian cemetery, Pas de Calais. Captain J.M. Allport and Lieutenant A.W. Hammond were later awarded the Military Cross for shooting down two German planes in the confrontation that killed Broadbent and Homersham. There were more deaths on 9 March when, as Seton's diary notes, 'Collins and Heney killed and burnt just after taking off the 'drome. Collins turned when nearly stalled and spun from about 300 feet. Caught fire and the bombs went up.' Second Lieutenant R.S. Collins and Lieutenant John Bower Lewis Heney, of the Canadian Field Artillery, are buried at Choques Military Cemetery.

Thursday 21 February 1918

In Eileen's letter to Wid she says Aunt Jessie was alone in the house when the wire came about Robin's [Roy's] death and her screams brought the

---

24 The 1914 Star, known as the Mons Star, and ribbon was given to members of the British forces who served in France or Belgium between 5 August and midnight on 22–23 November 1914. The colloquial name arose because most recipients took part in the retreat from Mons. The ribbon is the red, white and blue of the French tricolour.

neighbours in. Poor, poor Jessie – it's too awful. Auntie Jen's letter has sad news of poor old Gran. The doctor isn't satisfied about her throat and seems to think there is suffering ahead … It's all very sad, and I hope he is wrong in his diagnosis.

Throughout the rest of February Seton writes of his shoots. On 27 February, for example, he describes going 'for a trip over Hunland', flying above thick cloud: 'It was very pretty up there in the sunlight looking over the oceans of white, but it was not advisable to stay long as they threatened to cut us off and make us come down through them, which is not a pleasant experience when they are so thick. It is similar to losing yourself under water, but in this case you go down and don't know how you are going.' At one point he apologises for 'the worry over my welfare. I did not like the outlook myself but worrying would do no good.' He also tells his mother that the Christmas cake from Buzzards has 'never been seen'. By 1 March he is only two off the leave roll.

Saturday 2 March 1918
I am all on edge today – tonight's papers say those devils have been raiding Béthune, which is just quite close to Seton. Finished Seton's letter and filled hot water bags, then wrote this. It is very blowy tonight. Cecil Watts wrote to his mother today to say he doesn't expect the big push for a year. It seems to me things are fairly lively already.

Letter from Seton, 2 March 1918
Two parcels of sweets arrived today, thank you: I thought there was a war on and sweets were scarce. I have not had time to eat any but the chocolate yet as I am orderly officer today. The CO does go up and he went up today, and I am glad to say had to come down again. In regard to his knowledge, although I, like all the others, hate him, I will give him credit for knowing his work. I should not be surprised if he were the most efficient squadron leader in France, and with that he has a fearless disposition. But with regard to his ways and habits I have no respect whatsoever. He expects us to know as much as himself and is very hard on some … From what I have seen of the way women drivers are worked in the RFC I am not surprised Mrs Watts had to give it up.

Letter from Seton, 3 March 1918

It is the first day for some time now that has been unfit for flying. The usual 'dud' day we have to sit about with one eye on the clouds and one on the clock to see who is going to reach night first and it is a rotten game crawling up in the late afternoon to see the day out … You have misunderstood me about those huts. I am officially in one but I am still in my billet. Nearly all the squadron are in them now, and it will be a matter of days now before I move. We are painting it inside and buying mats and things so to make our lives more comfortable as possible and after we have been in a day or two it ought to be presentable.

Monday 4 March 1918

At the bank we saw the Lord Mayor setting off in state to open one of the banks operating in war bonds this week.[25] These state displays always seem utter tomfoolery to me – and anything but winning the war efforts.

25 War bonds were government-issued savings bonds used to raise funds for the war effort.

Wednesday 6 March 1918

About 12 o/c old Os came on a surprise visit – it was lovely to see him. There was a little difficulty at lunch about giving him meat [owing to rationing] and I asked waiter to give him mine but Miss Ibbotson managed to give Os some but at dinner time she couldn't so I had gravy and waiter brought Wid a good helping and asked her to share it with me!!

Monday 11 March 1918

Found some NZ mail at the bank and found a letter from Barron – which we opened and read on the spot. Absolutely appalling account of the house and farm when they took it over after those Salt creatures – who dug up and took away the potatoes, and shook all the Irish peaches off trees and carted them off too. Auntie Jen went up with the Barrons so they have a witness to show how things were left. Mrs Harris came in to supper and Mrs Binnie and Matthews came in later to tell us about the English element blowing off again about our being here and eating their food. They didn't like it when Mrs Binnie said she would gladly go home if she could take her boys. They said her boys had a right to stay and fight, they were fighting for themselves. Last raid night Moira Gaines said to Mrs Watts that she didn't come down on the raid nights as she was too tired of her twang. Oh, these

English rotters – they wouldn't have a blessed country to exist in by now if her colonies hadn't saved them.

Seton, diary, 11 March 1918

I did early morning patrol. Went down to Vimy and saw the memorial and crosses on ridge. Saw 7 Hun Albatrosses D3 who attacked us at 3,500 feet and followed us to 400 behind the line. Jenkinson's [his observer Lieutenant R.A. Jenkinson] gun did not fire well so I spiralled all the way down. Nothing hit at all.

Two days later Seton is on photography duties with Lieutenant W.H. Wardrope over La Bassée at 9000 ft when a German plane dives on their tail. He puts the aircraft into a spiral descent and the observer fires 20 rounds from a range of 25 yards. Bullets are seen to go through the engine and into the enemy pilot's seat, and Seton and his observer watch the aircraft stall and spin down to 3000 ft before they are attacked again by another enemy aircraft. The observer fires 10 rounds and it turns away. They recross the lines while the remaining German planes are attacked by Sopwith Camels from another squadron. The next day Seton does not fly but while he is visiting batteries 'shells fell about 50 yards off and were too close at that but the "strafe" soon stopped'.

Friday 15 March 1918

Letter from Seton but he didn't get here last night. I waited up till 12 o/c and then crawled to bed. Since had word that the boats didn't leave Le Havre yesterday – it's a very worrying world.

Sunday 17 March 1918

Went down for a while and stirred things up with my views on 'heel clicking' and sloping arms 'stunt'. Laurie Watts argues that unless men are disciplined like that they can't be good soldiers. We can understand now why it was so usual before the war to speak of the spineless wasters as 'old soldiers'. Is it any wonder they are spineless when their spirit and self-respect are broken by this ceaseless drill and discipline? I contend that our undisciplined boys are the best 'fighters' in the world – and they don't 'run' like these well-drilled machines. Clicking heels isn't going to win this war. Grit initiative is.

Seton, diary, 17 March 1918

Early show and tried to shoot but battery did not fire because of Hun planes. Quite a lot of Huns about. Fired on aerial range and did practice bombing.

Monday 18 March 1918

Ian [soldier friend] had to go off very soon after coffee. I gave him this mascot before dinner – he is a nice kid. It's a loathsome horrible war and I hate it more fiercely every day. I kissed Ian goodbye as he sets off for France. It's the least one can do and it's very little after all. These boys are all so brave about setting out on this great adventure.

Wednesday 20 March 1918

Had letter from Seton at lunchtime and he expects to be here at lunchtime tomorrow! I hope it's true this time, but I'm afraid to place too much hope on it.

Thursday 21 March 1918

Just when we were almost finished afternoon tea Seton arrived, and it was a real joy to see him again. He is looking not a day different to when he left. I ordered tea for him in the smoking room – and afterwards Roger and I went along to Food Controllers with him to get a food card for him. Then Seton came up and read NZ letters etc and then dressed for dinner. Sat in smoking room afterwards. Wid is having a stretcher in Mrs Harris' room tonight – so we are all under one roof, which is a great comfort. I shall not need to 'grouse' now for a whole fortnight – Oh, the joy of it. German offensive began on the Western Front.

Friday 22 March 1918

After lunch we dressed and Wid and Seton went out shopping together and Dad, Al and I went to Grafton Galleries to see the war pictures. Then we met Wid and Seton at Troc and had tea there. Afterwards walked up Regent Street and then Seton and Dad came home together. Gave Roger 10/- to shout the Grafton Galleries and he lost it. Then Seton, Dad and I drank 'Good luck' to Seton and we went to bed.

Winifred kept quite a few photos of the young soldiers she met but not all are named. This is identified as 'Les Hill on the left and Gerrie Barton'.

Left: One of the pendants that Annie had made as mascots for her boys in April 1917. The four-leafed clover pattern was in fact a natural formation in the moss agate stone that was used. Talismans like these were very popular during the war, given by families hoping to keep their loved ones safe in battle.

Far left: The bullet extracted from Seton's leg.

An April 1918 letter to Annie from the New Zealand High Commissioner's office, after Seton was wounded, explaining how next of kin were advised of such events.

DOMINION OF NEW ZEALAND.

C.J.W.

TELEGRAPHIC ADDRESS.
"DEPUTY, WESTRAND, LONDON."
TELEPHONE NUMBERS.
GERRARD 840
841
842
843
ALL COMMUNICATIONS
TO BE ADDRESSED TO
THE HIGH COMMISSIONER
FOR NEW ZEALAND.

IN YOUR REPLY PLEASE
REFER A/B.

NEW ZEALAND GOVERNMENT OFFICES,
STRAND,
LONDON, W.C. 2.

24th April, 1918.

Dear Madam,

I am requested by the High Commissioner to acknowledge the receipt of your enquiry dated the 18th of April and, in reply, to state that New Zealand casualties in Imperial Units are always cabled by the War Office to the Dominion when the next-of-kin is resident there, but when the registered next-of-kin is resident in this country, the War Office notifies them and does not cable to the Dominion. In the latter cases a cable is sent to the Dominion by the High Commissioner and this has been done in your son's case. Sir Thomas Mackenzie desires me to say that he is very sorry to hear that your son has been wounded and he trusts that he will make rapid progress towards recovery.

Yours faithfully,

Mrs. Montgomerie,
40, Inverness Terrace,
London, W.2.

Secretary to the Department.

xviii

A button from Oswald's and Seton's uniforms, together with the badge of the Notts and Derby Regiment (known in the family as the 'Crusader's Cross'). According to a note left by Winifred, Annie wore these, and a small tiki, on a fine gold chain around her neck for the duration of the war.

Annie on her way to Pew Tor in Dartmoor, very near Moortown House where the family stayed for summer holidays in Devon when Roger was doing wartime forestry work.

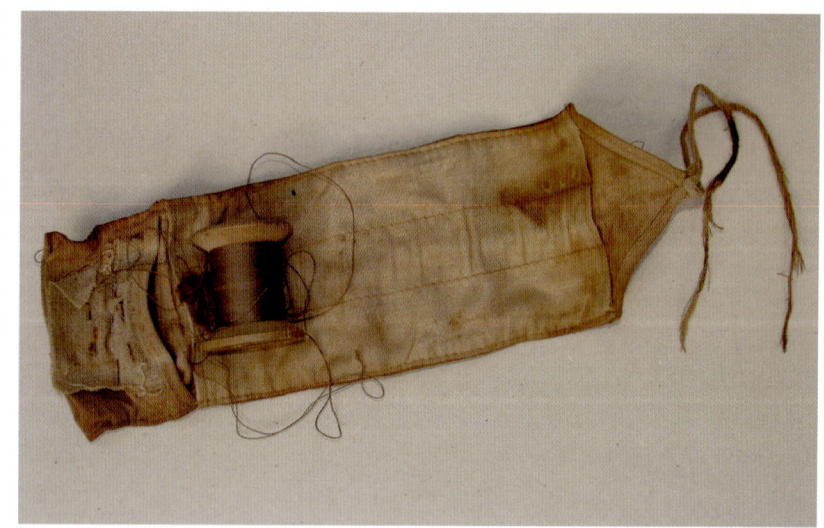

Above: Moortown House near Tavistock in Devon was the scene of very happy summer holidays with the Reddicliffe family.

Right: A sewing kit, known as a housewife, or hussif, was standard issue for men at the front. This one belonged to Os.

Above: Seton and Os, brothers at war.

Left: The Armstrong Whitworth 160 crashed in heavy fog by Lieutenant Thomson at Hesdigneul air base, northern France, in February 1918.

Pilot W.S. Wyborn and Lieutenant Lyell Spence of the Canadian Field Artillery. Spence, who was Seton's observer in France, was killed in action in May 1918, aged only 22.

Lieutenant W.H. Wardrope of the Royal Canadian Dragoons, who served with Seton in Squadron 2 at Hesdigneul, photographed in his flying suit in March 1918. Shortly afterwards Wardrope was severely wounded in a bombing raid over the Somme.

Above: Os on a Lewis gun at Uxbridge, 1918.

Left: Winifred, left, and an unknown friend at Hornchurch in the spring of 1919.

Right and opposite page: A letter from Roger to Seton, in June 1917, signed by 'your loving Dad'.

Hecklake
June 17th 1917

Dear Seton

Very pleased to receive your letter. Was not surprised to hear of your marching orders as it had to come some time, and you have been in the army a long time. It is very hard to write this letter. It is a pity I'm so far away. Was looking at the map the other day & this place is some distance from London. However I know when you are called to do your bit it will be nobly done. If you go to France now tell Wid that mother ought to come down here for a week or two or more. She could go from here to St Leonards when Al gets her holidays. The heat is very trying here. It is a worse heat than we get in N.Z. There were plenty of strawberries in Tavistock yesterday at /4½ a box.

That was a splendid letter Jim Mason wrote to the Taukoros. Waimangu geyser has been blowing things about a bit in his letter. The hole got bunged up a year or two ago & I suppose it had to blow up again to make another shaft. Did you read Barrow's letter. It is a pitty he held the cattle so long as the drought may reduce the price. Well Seton old boy I will say good bye hoping to get another letter soon.

    From your
     loving Dad

You did not mention whether you received my postcard of Calstock.

Winifred in London, 1917. Note the fur wrap and muff.

Above: Annie and Winifred in Hyde Park, 1918.

Left: Annie and her boys, most likely in 1918. Her face shows the strain: she was only 51 when this photo was taken.

Above: Os, Annie and Seton in Hyde Park.

A services banknote used while Os was serving in Egypt and Palestine.

The London crowds on Armistice Day, 1918.

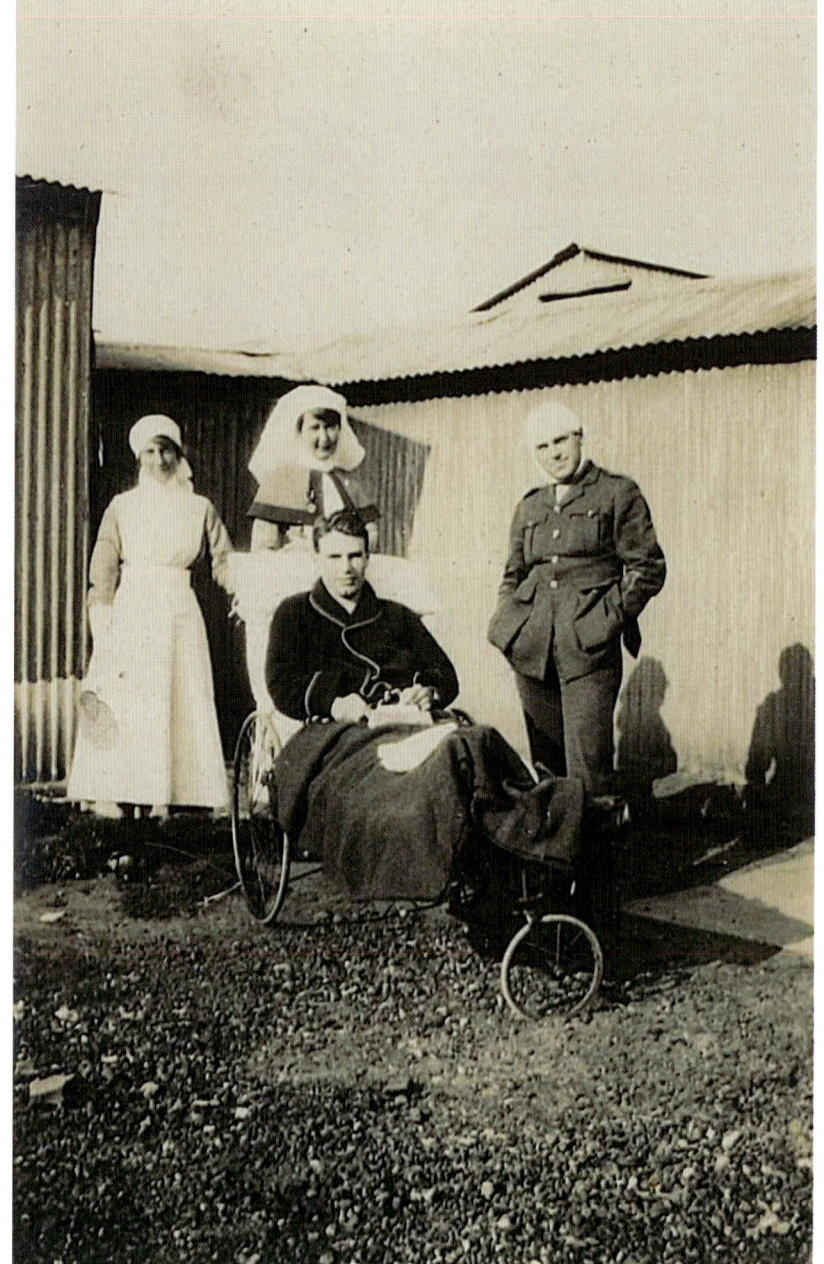

Seton, in the bath chair, at Belton Park Military Hospital, Grantham, in May–June 1919 after the removal of his appendix.

Above: RMS *Remuera*, which took the Montgomerie family to England in June 1916. Built by Denny & Bros in 1911, she operated on the round-the-world New Zealand–Britain route. She was acting as a troop and frozen food carrier when she was sunk off the north-east coast of Scotland on 26 August 1940 after being bombed by German aircraft and then hit by a torpedo. All 93 crew and one gunner escaped in lifeboats and were saved.

Left: A family photo taken at Taukoro, Parapara Road, Wanganui, in the early to mid-1930s, before the brothers were married. Roger would die in 1936. The adults, from left, are Annie, Roger, Winifred, Alex, Seton and Os. The two children are Alex's daughter Priscilla and her son David.

Roger and Annie's grave in the Aramoho Cemetery, Wanganui. Winifred's name appears below theirs. Those of Os, his wife Beryl and their daughter Helen are on the other side of the stone.

Saturday 23 March 1918

After lunch we all went to see *Flora*; it was quite good. Gertie Millar was Flora.[26] When we came out Wid went home as she felt sick and we went to the Troc, found it crowded so went to Fullers for tea. Os turned up unexpectedly and could stay the night. With Al home yesterday we had a complete Taukoro family for dinner. I always thank God when I have us all together under one roof. First complete family gathering since Christmas 1916. Seton's shout all day.

Monday 25 March 1918

Seton went off to catch train to visit Os at Hainault Farm. He was back in time for us to go to *The Bing Boys on Broadway*. George Robey was practically the whole show and we were glad to have seen him.[27] Got a taxi and were home by 11.30. The war news this morning was cruelly depressing and I am intensely thankful Seton is here. Leave has been stopped now.

Thursday 28 March 1918

The war news is very bad. Mrs Glasgow and I had a war talk and she thinks things are not as critical as I imagine, but to me they are appallingly so. The papers make sorry reading. At lunchtime a cable came from D'Arcy to say 'Doing utmost to keep Barron' and that Taukoro had escaped the bush fires …[28] We were a happy crowd for dinner. Wid went off to the foxtrot after dinner; Os, Seton, Dad and Al went off to see the show *Pamela*. I had seen the show so didn't go and sewed Seton's new wings on. Had the kettle boiling for the giddy throng, six 'Taukoro' and two guests till 12.30 p.m., then Os went off to train. Heard tonight the New Zealanders and Australians are in the fighting. It's all too hideous.

Good Friday 29 March 1918

Oswald's *New Zealander* [small paper with New Zealand news] came and we saw about the bush and grass fires in NZ; it has been very serious. There was a heavy thunderstorm last night but I was so tired I slept through it. Some people thought it was the German long-range gun firing on London like they are doing on Paris. War news is very critical. Seton's friend Mr McLachlan came to dinner. He has been Seton's observer a lot in France and

---

26 Gertie Millar (1879–1952) was an actress and singer in Edwardian musical comedies. After her first husband, composer Lionel Monckton, died in 1924, she married the 2nd Earl of Dudley. Annie was perhaps right to be lukewarm about *Flora*: the show was not a success and Millar retired from the stage soon afterwards.

27 George Robey (1869–1954), known as the 'Prime Minister of Mirth', rose to fame in the predecessor to this show, *The Bing Boys are Here*, in 1916.

28 William Alexander D'Arcy was the manager of the New Zealand Loan & Mercantile Co. Ltd, the family's stock and station agent. Disastrous bush fires on 19 March had wiped out the settlement of Raetihi. In the 1970s Alex added a footnote commenting that when the family received the cable saying Taukoro was saved, for a while they concluded it had been a bad earthquake. They later found it referred to the Raetihi fire, which came so close to Taukoro that the windows and doors blew out, and then the rain fell and stopped the blaze.

is very interesting. He spoke awfully nicely about him and said he was about their best pilot. Personally he said he was the best pilot in their flight.

Monday 1 April 1918

In the papers this morning Lloyd George is appealing to the dominions for more men, which is an outrage, with things as they are both here and Ireland. According to present rumours the colonies have saved the Empire again in France this week or two and have paid the cost very heavily.[29] They say NZers were put in [at Albert] against the Prussian Guards. The Australian have been cut up [two divisions over the Ancre] and the Canadians are holding at Arras. If only the English troops could have done the same thing for just two days this terrible position would have never come about.

Wednesday 3 April 1918

Seton and Oswald went off to Kilmarnock by train, 9 p.m. from St Pancras on Easter Sunday, to stay with Aunt Betty and arrived back Wednesday. She took them to Eglinton Castle but the family were not at home so they left cards. Driving back they met the earl and had a talk to him; the boys thought he was the gamekeeper or some such thing when they saw him first. After lunch went to see *Pigeon Post*, which was quite good. Seton is looking better for his holiday and is quite bright about going back but I am just sore, sore, sore. It isn't fair when all those crawling _____ are shirking. My darling boy gave me a lovely RFC brooch this morning.[30] God has given me two precious sons. He sets off in the morning early; Os goes as far as the train station.

Thursday 4 April 1918

Seton woke me up early and I got up and boiled the kettle. Took him down some hot water and then boiled it again for coffee – then both boys came for coffee. Darling old boy was very bright and kept up very bravely but I knew the strain was there. God knows it's hard. Then my baby boy set off again for France. It was such a comfort to have Os here and go with him to the station. There were several boys they knew going back so it will not be quite the acute misery of last time. Os came back for breakfast and afterwards he and I went out … Later went to the Troc with Jack Fergusson. Said 'Goodbye' to Jack – he leaves for France tomorrow.

---

29 The successful attack by the New Zealand Division on 30 March, in what became known as the First Battle of Arras, was decisive and significant. As Glyn Harper points out, in *Spring Offensive*, it 'stunned the Germans and provided considerable encouragement to the soldiers of the Third Army'.

30 It was gold and diamonds.

Letter from Seton, 4 April 1918
Hotel Folkestone, Boulogne-sur-Mer
Got this far safely, calm crossing. Officers' Club full up so staying here the night. Hope to find squadron where I left it, but one cannot be sure of anything these days.

Friday 5 April 1918
Mrs Watts has had a letter from Cecil in which he says that she needn't worry as we have the situation in France well in hand – that the Germans have done more for us than we have done for ourselves. Rubbish – complacent English twaddle. If the colonials had not held the Germans they would have been about in London now.

When Seton returns to his squadron on 5 April he finds that, in two bombing trips to the Somme, 'Chisnall was wounded in the foot the first time, second time Smart and Barford were missing. Dunkerley and Wardrope, McLeod and Hammond were all severely wounded. Hammond got three Huns and Spence one.' Lieutenants Edward Treloar Smart and Keith Purnell Barford were both killed on 27 March and are remembered on the Arras memorial. In September McLeod was awarded the Victoria Cross for piloting his and Hammond's burning aircraft into no man's land while standing on the wing, and while badly injured. McLeod pulled Hammond from the wreckage and dragged him to the British front lines. McLeod died of influenza the following November while recovering from his wounds. When there is another 'fight with the Huns' on 6 April, during which Lieutenant C.F.G. Doran is wounded, and a German triplane is shot down, Seton notes: 'This makes nine Huns to the squadron in three months.'

Saturday 6 April 1918
Os came … He and Wid lunched together and Al and I set off for Walton. It was pouring with rain when we got there but cleared up afterwards. We found Hugh looking quite bright and well, although his wound is not as slight as he had led us to think. The bullet hit his shoulder and ran down his side exploding inwards and scattering some shrapnel about and just grazing his lung. Dr Andy Wilson told him he had a very close shave. It happened at Serre; he had his Lewis gun shot out of his hands and several narrow shaves. The doctor told him he would be sent back to NZ and so Hugh is very pleased.

Sunday 7 April 1918

In the afternoon went to Mile End Military Hospital [in Bancroft Road, London] to see three wounded NZers. One said that when our boys got down to Albert there was an 8-mile front without a soul in charge and the Tommies who had been running for three days were being rounded up by sergeants and officers and driven back to their lines. Got back and found Os struggling among the old hens for his tea. He doesn't like his new quarters a bit: the mess is very bad, the accommodation rough and he is going to hire some furniture to try and make things more comfortable. I am longing to get a letter from Seton to hear if he is back at his old squadron and if they are still in the same place.

Monday 8 April 1918

Letter from Roger with a copy of one from Watt, a weak unsatisfactory epistle. Also got a small parcel containing our photos which I gave to Fergie. It is just six days off a year since he died, poor dear boy, and it was sad to get it this morning. His brother Jack found it in his kit and thought I would like to have it. Tonight's paper says those Hun devils are bombarding La Bassée, which is Seton's front line. I wonder if those English muddlers will hold this time. Got a letter from Seton by evening mail – a great relief. It seems ages since he left last Thursday morning

Tuesday 9 April 1918

Went to the Mercantile to see Mr Brander about the chances of being caught for tax by transferring money from his office to the bank. He rang his solicitor who assured me it was no more of a risk than with the bank. I am doubtful. We had a heated argument about the iniquity of it. Of course he, like the rest of the people here, pities himself because tax is slightly higher than NZ but they forget that we have our produce commandeered, which is very much our loss and their gain. I told him that if we were enough belonging to the Empire and having our boys taken, then our meat and wool commandeered, then we ought to be assured that we were not treated as outsiders and aliens. That a double tax on a British subject is a mocking of justice and I would like to know if we are aliens. Mr B. advised removal from town for a few months as they are scraping everyone into the net. I was too tired and miserable to do very much tonight.

Letter from Seton, 9 April 1918

Hugh is very lucky getting to Walton and if you get rooms down that way it will be very nice for all parties. This nasty war has started today to the north of us, cannot say anything about this situation. I don't want you to worry about me. You can say what you think about the situation, but don't drag me into it. If we fall back I shall be quite safe as we don't have a panic like the ground people. It does not take long to move. The trouble is that you will have all the news in the paper before you get this.

Wednesday 10 April 1918

The war news is very bad this morning [a new German offensive on the Lys had begun the previous day]: the Hun devils have gained 3 miles between La Bassée and Armentières. The bulge is just north of Seton's part but there was hard fighting at Givenchy, which I know is on his part, and I am just fierce with worry. It is Mrs Harris's wedding anniversary; her husband is in the struggles near Seton. She is fearfully worried so we can feel for each other. I have been very depressed all day. I feel all sore and fierce.

Seton, diary, 10 April 1918

Went up on patrol. Cloud and mist 1,000. Got lost over Hunland and machine was badly holed by MG [machine gun] bullets. Climbed into the clouds and came out of them over Béthune. Hun line much the same as yesterday. Armentières reported taken by Huns. Spence was my observer.[31]

Thursday 11 April 1918

A letter arrived from Seton, the evening before the fight at Givenchy. Visited Hugh at Walton. A boy in the next bed, an American who went to NZ to join up, gives a description that staggers one. He says that 25,000 English troops practically laid down their arms and ran. He says they aren't worth feeding. News tonight Armentières is evacuated.

Letter from Seton, 11 April 1918

Managed to get a very good sleep, judge present situation from that. As you have noticed in the papers of our gallant Allies the 'Pork and Beans' and seen they were in it.[32] I hope you will duly note how our front line is at the present. The future is not in my hands.

---

31 Lieutenant Lyell Campbell Spence of the Canadian Field Artillery.

32 The Pork and Beans were the Portuguese, so called because military rations contained very little pork and there were said to be few Portuguese troops on the Western Front, though there were in fact two divisions, under British command. They suffered many casualties during the German Spring Offensive.

Saturday 13 April 1918

The news is very depressing and on top of it the Zepps were over the coast and Midlands last night, and Gothas over Paris. Seton's first letter said there was a nasty war going on to the north of them but doesn't tell me much. He is afraid of me getting too worried. God keep my boy from danger is my constant prayer. Second letter said he had been low flying that day and assures me it's least dangerous. Got a cable from Archie [Annie's brother, Archibald Mason] to say to say poor frail, suffering Gran died this morning. It was a shock even though I knew to expect it, and know it is the kindest happening for her. It has been too cruel to think of her suffering. Saw Os; he says I look 80 today. I have been fearfully depressed. The world is a sad war-torn spot these days.

Sunday 14 April 1918

Wid got up early and went canteening with Mrs Harris. After breakfast Al and I went to Spring St PO, Paddington and sent a cable to Auntie: 'Get wreath for me. Thank Archie for cabling me. Much love.' The news is still very bad; they seem to be fighting closer to Béthune.

SETON GETS A 'BLIGHTY'[1]

CHAPTER NINE

[1] A wound severe enough to require convalescence away from the front line and possibly get a man sent back to England.

While Seton is recovering from a flesh wound received during a bombing raid on 14 April 1918, the Germans are attacking along the Lys River to the north of Hesdigneul. Their objective is Hazebrouck, south-west of Ypres. Haig calls on the Allies to fight to the end. In later years Seton talked of Manfred von Richtofen, the German fighter pilot known as the Red Baron, credited with 80 'kills', who is shot down and killed near Amiens on 21 April. In the third German offensive launched on 27 May the Americans come to the aid of the British and French.

Seton, diary, 14 April 1918
Successful shoot on 4 Field Artillery battery near Richebourg … When dropping a bomb I got hit above the right knee with a MG bullet. Finished shoot and dropped another bomb by Pacaut Wood [north of Hinges] … Went to 33 FA [Field Ambulance] at Fouquières and was sent to CCS [casualty clearing station]. McLachlan was wounded with Rathbone and went to 2 2CCS.

Letter from Seton, 14 April 1918
You will be pleased and surprised to hear I got a slight flesh wound under the right leg this afternoon. I am pretty sure to go to England. Believe me it is quite slight.

Monday 15 April 1918
Two letters from Seton, one for me and one for Oswald. I opened his letter and found that Seton's 'low flying' that he told me about had been quite dangerous and his machine had been hit. He had been lost in the mist over Hunland and only his common sense had helped get safely back. Of course I have always known his work is dangerous each day, but it seemed appalling to read the dear kid's letter. Of course I was not supposed to read it.

Seton, diary, 15 April 1918

Saw McLachlan in 2 2CCS. Left Lazinghen for hospital train at Lapugnoy after lunch. Arrived at Étaples in morning. Went to No. 1 Red Cross Hospital [known as the Duchess of Westminster's Hospital, in the casino at Le Touquet].

Tuesday 16 April 1918

Mrs Watts came in after lunch and we sat mending, sewing and talking when page brought me a letter from Seton to say he was wounded in the right leg on the 14th and he thinks he will be sent to England. It made me shake like an air raid but we were all thankful to know he is out of that fearfulness for a time anyhow. So wrote a note to Roger and Oswald. Later had a letter from Roger to say he is thinking of going into transport again but I am going to write to tell him he mustn't. It's just too bad to think about such a thing while all these brutes, conchies and ASEs are still at large.[2]

Letter from Seton, 16 April 1918
No. 1 Red Cross Hospital

This is where I have landed and I am afraid I shall stop here too and not get to England. Everyone assured me I should. I knew it was very light, lighter than I first thought. It was a machine gun bullet that got me, the only one that entered the machine – some luck, eh! It hit just under my right knee from the right side and came out about an inch and a half from where it entered, so you see it is nothing. I have the bullet and it shall be a treasured possession. I shall not be here long … Don't write until I know where I am going. Going to try to get back to the squadron …

Thursday 18 April 1918

Letter from Seton … He says the hospital is splendid, and is very fit. Dear old son is worrying about getting back to his squadron, and I hope he can too.

Seton, diary, 18 April 1918

Left Étaples early morning in hospital train for Calais, arrived 12.30. Crossed in *Princess Elizabeth* to Dover. Arrived at Charing Cross and sent to RFC Hospital, 82 Eaton Square, London SW, arriving there about 10.30. I was carried by German stretcher bearers at Calais and Dover.

---

2 The ASE was the Amalgamated Society of Engineers, a large and militant British union founded in 1851.

Friday 19 April 1918

At lunchtime found a letter and a wire from Seton, to say he is in London at 82 Eaton Square and was going to ring later. So we waited for a message but it didn't come so we dressed and set off. Sent a wire to Roger on the way to tell him to come up for the weekend. It was snowing and sleeting and we couldn't get a taxi so went by Met to Sloane Square. Found Seton asleep and looking quite bonny in his smart blue pyjama suit. After he was hit he went on with his 'shoot', then went back and got a fresh supply of bombs and went back to find them! Then came down and got his wound examined. The nose of the bullet was just sticking out of the skin and an orderly had to cut it out. Everything seems very nice at this hospital … Os and Wid let out tonight that Seton had brought a plane down on March 13th before he came on leave. It was one of the Hun's newest type of plane. They never let me know in case I got 'windy' [afraid, nervous].

Saturday 27 April 1918

Seton's wound is healing very fast, was hoping to be able to visit '40'. But it means France too soon again; we don't want him better too quickly.

While he is at Eaton Square Seton's diary entries record two squadron deaths on 22 April and the other wounded pilots he encounters, especially Dunkerley, who has a very bad septic wound. Lyell Spence is on leave and they meet at least five times. Getting together and sharing their experiences is very important to these young men.

Friday 3 May 1918

After lunch went to an RAC [Royal Automobile Club] concert,[3] had tea at a standing counter place and got good seats. The first item was a wonderful woman who whistled like a skylark or thrush. Marie Dainton gave very good imitations of George Robey.[4] A blind boy sang; it was sad to see him. Came back and after dinner but didn't have any coffee because we are supposed not to light gas on a Friday, even boil a kettle. Mrs Harris reminded us, we forgot!! Mrs Watts got news from her boy Cecil that he was 'gassed slightly, mustard'.

On 10 May Seton goes to Chalfont Park Convalescent Hospital at Gerards Cross, where he remains until 12 June. While there he makes frequent trips to London.

---

3 As the *Wanganui Herald* reported on 5 April 1918, 'the Royal Automobile Club, the largest Social Club in London, has been given for the use of our soldiers, and is now known as the Royal Overseas Officers' Club'.

4 Marie Dainton (1881–1938) was an actress in both music hall and conventional theatre who was renowned for her gift of mimicking famous theatre people.

Saturday 11 May 1918

The American soldiers marched through London this morning and were received by the king at Buckingham Palace gates. Seton came before lunch. He is delighted with Chalfont Park. It's a lovely home with beautiful grounds, butler, footman and every comfort, perfect meals.

Monday 20 May 1918

Was up till after 1 am with an air raid. Read today that we got four Gothas last night, but the bombs did a lot of damage again. Mrs Glasgow and Wid went off to Hampstead to see the 'Arrys and 'Arriets on their bank holiday. They both enjoyed 'Appy 'Amstead. Cyril arrived on leave before joining flying and he said it's all true about the English troops running and the general warned them before they came over that they were not to talk about it as there was a lot of bitterness already.

Thursday 23 May 1918

Seton is very undecided as to whether to take home service for a time or go back to France and he expected Pole [a fellow pilot who crashed in France and is in hospital in Hampstead] to help him decide. Most of Seton's chums from 2 Squadron have gone and the CO … is very unpopular. Seton has been very lucky so far, so I hope his luck will hold and that his way is made clear. The observer that was flying with Seton when he was wounded has since been killed. Both he and the pilot were shot down in flames. There have been a lot of casualties lately.

Wednesday 29 May to 2 June 1918

Met Mrs Whiteman who told me that a major friend said the 'Tommies' ran again this week, but when they got to the colonials they turned their guns on them and threatened to shoot if they didn't go back, but it's all so hateful. How can we ever make any headway when such rotters let us down? Seton went to see his friend Pole from No. 2 Squadron and he came back prepared to accept home service, for which I am very thankful.

On 1 June Seton hears of Lyell Spence's death. He had returned to France on 10 May; he was shot in the stomach when attacked by five German aircraft over La Bassée and died a few days later, on 25 May. He was 22 years old.

Monday 3 June 1918

Yesterday went to see Australian war pictures at the Grafton Galleries, some of them very vivid pictures of war.[5] It makes one wonder more than ever that such things are possible in our 20th century of Christianity. The war news is still very bad.[6] Wid and I went to 33 Cornhill and arranged with agents of Lloyd's Insurance to insure our personal effects for £500 and our lives for £500.

After a successful medical board on 11 June, Seton is given three weeks' leave on the 12th. That afternoon Annie and her two boys have a delightful summer picnic by the Thames.

Thursday 13 June 1918

Letter from Dad, he has been kicked by a horse on his leg but expected to work again the next day. Seton here. I sewed his lieutenant stars on this morning: he was ticked off for not wearing his extra 'pip' at the board, so he has them all on. Bought Seton a signet ring at Packers in Regent Street – it is his [20th] birthday on the 25th – and we have left it to get the crest engraved. Os and Seton went to see *Going Up*, which was very good; both boys enjoyed it as it is a flying play.[7] Oswald got his orders for Egypt, a wire to say he is to report on Sunday and leave on Monday … Have chosen a cigarette case for Roger for a silver wedding present: Oswald suggests the engraving '1893 R A M 1918'.

Sunday 16 June 1918

Oswald had to report for orders: he has to leave Waterloo at 11 a.m. tomorrow for Southampton. They go from there to Le Havre and train there to Marseilles, along the coast of France into Italy, embark from Brindisi, I think. I sewed some press studs inside his inside pocket because I want to prevent his mascots from falling out. Gave Os Aspirin, quinine, castor oil capsules, chlorodyne and pills to take with him.

Monday 17 June 1918

Went to Waterloo with Oswald, an hour too soon so went to a restaurant and Os and his friend had a poached egg and purchased sandwiches for consumption on the way. Three RFC boys had a carriage to themselves. Os

---

[5] This was the Australian Art Exhibition at Grafton Galleries, London, which opened on 25 May 1918. Included were six photos by Australian Imperial Force (AIF) official photographer Frank Hurley. As he had done in the Antarctic, he often created 'composites' of more than one photo. One of his images in the exhibition was a 20 x 15 ft image of action near the Belgian village of Zonnebeke.

[6] The third German offensive of 1918 had begun on 27 May.

[7] Set in the United States at the end of the war, *Going Up* was a very popular musical comedy written by Louis Hirsch, Otto Harbach and James Montgomery. It had a successful Broadway run in 1917–18 and echoed this achievement at London's Gaiety Theatre from 22 May 1918.

went off happy but it is a fearful wrench to see that train steaming away. I pray God will shield him and guard him and bring him back to us.

Seton, diary, 19 June 1918

Went to *Fair and Warmer* with Tiny and Mrs Harris. Went and saw A.W. Hammond.[8] Went to *Chu Chin Chow* in the evening.

---

[8] Hammond, McLeod's co-pilot, was badly wounded and lost part of a leg. Seton later noted McLeod's death under this diary entry, adding that the Canadian was 'braver than I thought'.

HOLIDAY IN DEVON

CHAPTER TEN

The Germans launch the fourth stage of their spring offensive, Operation Gneisenau, on 9 June; the final phase, the Second Battle of the Marne, begins on 15 July. The day after, deposed Tsar Nicholas II of Russia and his family are murdered by the Bolsheviks. On Thursday 20 June Annie, Winifred and Seton head off to Devon, with extra rations of tea and sugar, which they have saved up. They will stay with Mrs Reddicliffe and then at Moor Cottage. Roger joins them on their first night.

Friday 28 June 1918
Letter from Os. He is finding his railway journey pretty monotonous, but says he is seeing quite a lot. Caught the train, crowds of marketing people and their conversation was illuminating, mainly the price of eggs and poultry. They see a paper about once a week. Got to Dolforgan about 6 p.m. and went straight to school to see Al for a few minutes. Went for dinner, Seton was very tickled with all the old feminine wrecks that collect in such places as this. Goodness knows where these ugly washouts come from, with their peroxide hair and made-up skins.

Tuesday 2 July 1918
A card arrived from Os from Italy: they were having some funny incidents in their endeavours to buy additions to their food supplies. Seton was most matter of fact and cheerful going off, been posted to Leamington. After he had gone I bought a book, *Germany and the Germans* by Price Collier 3/6d.[1] Did shopping and tramped back home. The day was dull and overcast and so was I. If all the mothers of the Empire feel as bitter and sore as I do, there is a day of reckoning coming for all muddlers, and may I live to see it.

1 The full title was *Germany and the Germans from an American Point of View*. The book was published in 1913. As the *New York Times* noted when Collier died, the book aroused resentment in Germany owing to its 'uncomplimentary views'.

Letter from Seton, 4 July 1918
Hucknall [Nottinghamshire]

Arrived at this place … no further forward than I was last night in respect of what I am going to do. Have not seen OC yet. This is an absolutely new aerodrome – not got anywhere near half its complement of men, officers, machines … 117 is the only squadron that exists. Want to see if I can get an AW squadron as I can't see the use of instructing on work I have not done myself. Just before I left Leamington I saw an NZ chaplain and I asked where he came from. He had been in Wango [Wanganui] with a parish. He asked my name and he remembered seeing in the papers about some family that had all gone to war work, sisters, everyone.[2] I knew what he meant but I kept quiet, but it was rather a funny incident. All I said was that I had a cousin [Willie] in the CMR [Canterbury Mounted Rifles].

Friday 5 July 1918
Letter from Seton written from Rugby, a place that he says the song 'Tipperary' reached just last week.[3] He was very fed up with his journeying in the Midlands. He was to go to Hucknall next day, near Nottingham and go through a bombing course on DH4s [De Havillands] there. What is bothering him is whether they are trying to put him in a bombing squadron, which will be the dizzy limit of stupidity when he is such an excellent and reliable artillery observer pilot. The blithering old major at Leamington said the AWs and other two-seater squadrons had sufficient reliable pilots for their art obs [artillery observation] work. Spence wouldn't be dead if they had, or many others. The English don't seem to like any kind of efficiency. Seton says he can't understand the drift of Providence this time, but I tell him I'm sure it still had its hand on the helm and things will come right.

It is decided that Seton is to do a two-week instructors' course at the School of Special Flying at the village of Lilbourne, near Rugby in Northamptonshire. He hopes to return to his old squadron. As he explains in a letter on 10 July, 'Messing is very good and altogether this is a "posh" place.'

Thursday 11 July 1918
Letter from Os today dated the 1st. He is still in the same place and sounds a bit 'fed up'. He says they purchase books by the dozen from the YMCA

---

2 In June 1916 the *Wanganui Herald*, and other newspapers, had reported on the Montgomeries' departure: 'an instance of practically a whole family volunteering for service in the war'.

3 'It's a Long Way to Tipperary', said to have been written for a bet in 1912, became extremely popular after 1914 and throughout the war. Rugby must have been very behind the times.

and spend their time devouring cheap novels. He is regretting not having his bathing costume as he can only bathe when some one lends him one instead of twice daily if he had his own.

Letter from Seton, 12 July 1918
Haven't flown for two days. My idea of flying got set in France – these people don't come anywhere near it, and considering their work they are right … unless one flies there is nothing to do. Rugby is about as lively as Tavistock. We had a great hero while at Chalfont Park with the MC, and I had the impression he had 11 Huns to his credit, six for himself and five for his observer. I disliked him from the first glimpse I got of his face. There is a man from his squadron here [who says] it is an undisputed fact that he has only two Huns, and those his obs got for him, and that is what he got his MC for. Pity he made such a fool of himself; he was not liked by anyone. Makes one wary.

Letter from Seton, 14 July
I did about 45 minutes solo yesterday afternoon; instructors are continually taking us up to see if we are developing bad habits. Seeing that I have not won the admiration of my instructor he won't let me loose for long. When I learned to fly I practically taught myself. Consequently I didn't do the job well and the RAF saw this about a year ago and are now trying to turn out people who really do instruct. You can fly for years quite successfully, but may be violating laws of flying constantly … Newspapers say the Yanks have over a million men in France now.

Tuesday 16 July 1918
Letter and pc from Os dated 7th, so he is having a long delay in Italy. He sounds much cheerier and is learning 'how to amuse himself'. Seton has been flying solo and finding rather funny at first but is getting to 'feel at home' again. He wrote on the 14th, three months since he was wounded and it seems like three years. I tell him he can't live through crowded hours without feeling like that. After afternoon tea packed up ready for tomorrow's change to cottage. About 11 o'clock when the house was all quiet a most awful screaming and banging started, and later on footsteps tramping round the house. Then a flickering light in the passage worried me so much that

I got up to investigate and found it came from Wid's room, where she was enjoying a read in bed.

Letter from Seton, 16 July 1918
We were flying yesterday and today and I still have to make a great improvement to my flying. I have lost the art of making soft landings, much to the dismay of the instructors here. That will go against me more than anything else in this course. Today I did some startling turns, one effort being an attempt to bring a machine gun range along to the hangar with me. I did not do any damage, but it was very nearly a broken wing.

Wednesday 17 July 1918
The screaming and noise of last night turns out to have been that poor kitchen maid, Beatrice, who had just been dismissed from here, who had run away from her home, and was trying to get in. Her father had followed her and tracked her, and thrashed her. Oh dear. What a hopelessly awful life for a human being. But from what Mrs Reddicliffe tells me she is not good and is a danger to the young boys about the place. Poor wretched girl, she can't be judged by our standards; she hasn't a chance. After breakfast read my *Times*. The offensive has started again, but the papers don't give much of an insight into the situation yet.[4] After dinner took some odds and ends down to the cottage, while there made 1½ lbs of raspberries into nice jam, cooked on a kerosene lamp affair. Opened up Seton's cake [from New Zealand] and found 1½ lbs of sugar, which is very acceptable. The cake looks A1. It has 'Kia Ora Seton with love' on it on the icing. Dear little Auntie.

Friday 19 July 1918
Mrs Jeffrey told me tonight that Beatrice hadn't been home since Tuesday night and she thinks she sleeps out. No wonder she haunted me last night. It seems that she has a stepmother and sisters at home, which makes her case harder than ever. Sleeping out in this wet weather will soon make her ill. She told Mrs J. she was too afraid to go home.

Sunday 21 July 1918
Reggie was here with the milk before I was dressed this morning, I find it a fearful fag getting breakfast. I always did and it seems I always will. Wid said

[4] The fifth and final phase of the German Spring Offensive.

it was quite successful when I do it so that's something anyhow. It really is nice having nicely cooked food again.

Seton leaves Lilbourne on 19 July for London, where he reports to Waddington 27th Wing on the 22nd, only to find that he has been turned down as an instructor: 'I didn't think I was as bad as that ... would like a decent job – instructing is a very boring game at the most. I shall have to run around the country and find some other occupation now, but here is not a great deal outside ferry pilot. It may make it possible to return to France just when I [and you] like, and not stay here when they want pilots next spring and rush in to the heat of it.' On 24 July he is posted to 24th Wing with a CO he admires. The next day he is made 'OC formation flying, the duty being to gather what machines and pilots there are available and put them into the atmosphere, then have to observe the said formation and by means of ground strips communicate my ideas of success they are having, and if thoroughly satisfied, say so and let them depart from the vicinity of the 'drome. If they do not satisfy me I should recall them ... So far not had to use my powers.'

Monday 22 July 1918

Oswald's cable arrived this morning. It said 'Arrived safely', which means those submarine devils did chase them. Now we must wait for his letter but thank God he is safe. It has been such a long wait, I feel limp after such a long strain.

Tuesday 23 July 1918

A letter from Oswald and I think it was written in Brindisi. Anyhow he was in Alexandria on the 18th. He mentions there is no war news whatsoever where he is; I expect it is because he can't read foreign papers.

Wednesday 24 July 1918

Seton's letter was rather worrying as they turned him down as an instructor ... He tells me I must have been mistaken about his flying and I tell him he is much mistaken if he thinks I would change my mind about his capabilities because of some muddling mandarins in the air service haven't got the brains to recognise it. I only think they are bigger fools than ever.

Monday 29 July 1918

Letter from Seton from Spittlegate, Grantham. He is temporarily attached to 27 Squadron and is going to try to stay in it as 50 is removed to the north of Scotland, and he wants to stay near London and us. 37 Squadron has 'Big AWs'. Al has been reposing under a peach tree writing poetry.

Tuesday and Wednesday, 30 and 31 July 1918

Seton's news was that he had passed the wing examiner quite satisfactorily and after a few days now will begin instructing. He finds he can't throw the Big AWs as easily now as he used to in France. So he was aviating the last two days [joy rides] and taking up Huns as ballast. Seton seems pleased with war news but I tell him although the Americans and French have been doing good work we have no guarantee the English regiments won't lose it all again.

Thursday 1 August 1918

In yesterday's *Times* I see our 'Bill' [Massey] has been speaking about Britain's great war effort and how the 'proverbial modesty' of these people might lead one to suppose they were not pulling their weight and he goes on to show England has contributed 60% and the colonies 12%. If so, I would like him to explain when they have pulled their weight. I think our little 12% is right on top. In the ship building the *Times* acknowledges they are still being beaten in their contest with submarines and that the American yards are doing far better. In the munitions last week the display of ASE strikers shows this.[5] This speechifying is all hogwash.

Letter from Seton, 2 August 1918

We are getting Bristol freighters ... altogether we are most fortunate. They will put the wind up Fritz when he finds every machine he meets can look after itself and at the same time devote quite a lot of attention to him. ... I don't altogether agree about our Bill [Massey] myself, but you must not forget there is a war on and that he cannot show any ill feeling towards England, as it is not only likely to delay the above mentioned war, but it would give the other Bill [German Kaiser Wilhelm II, often known as Kaiser Bill] something to feed his family on. I am sure all this soft soap will be discussed at the end of the war, and nobody will be more pleased than I to have these statements of 'fact' properly cleared up.

---

5 Annie is referring to the recent strike by munitions workers – thousands of them in Coventry and Birmingham – demanding that the Ministry of Munitions withdraw its embargo on the employment of skilled workers. The majority of the population, including Annie and Seton, who said it would give him 'great joy' to bomb 'our "loyal" munitions workers', took the view that the strike was insupportable, but the workers had a valid point.

Saturday 3 August 1918

NZ mail. A letter from Cissie Duncan says that she doesn't like to think of us being here without 'proper food' – surely all those who have returned could tell them we have plenty to eat. Hugh Anderson was to arrive any day and Nell was going to Auckland to meet him. Mr Watson says he finds NZ very quiet after England and easily understands how men enlist again. He enclosed a paper cutting to show Agricultural Unions demand for more wages. We set off for town in the jingle [horse-drawn carriage] in the afternoon but hadn't gone a hundred yards when Spider [the horse] stumbled and fell, both shafts snapped like carrots and we were all thrown out. Spider didn't kick so we were not damaged, though Wid has a very sore arm.

Sunday 4 August 1918

Wid's arm is still stiff and sore but it was a wonderful escape for us all … Dad spoke to some American soldiers on leave and they said that the Americans are confident they can beat the Bosche by October.

Seton, diary, 4 August 1918

Went to Stamford 'drome with Captain George and met J. Sloss who I went to school with at Waitaki.[6]

Tuesday 6 August 1918

The post woman told me this morning that she had just taken some awfully bad news to the housekeeper at Langstone: both her boys were killed by one shell. It's too dreadful.

Friday 9 and Saturday 10 August 1918

Arrived at Waterloo on 12.25 train from Devon. Saturday went to meeting and talked over [Barron] situation with Mr Brander. His face was a picture while reading our letter to Mr Massey. In the end it was arranged to ring up and see if we could interview Mr Massey before going any further, so … a meeting arranged for Wednesday. Wire came from Seton and he arrived before dinner looking much thinner but very bonny. He went to the theatre with Colin Fyffe.[7]

---

6 Second Lieutenant James Duncan Sloss from Cheviot, who flew with 108 Squadron of the Royal Air Force, died on 23 November 1918, aged 21, of wounds received on 9 November. He is buried at Terlincthun British Cemetery, Wimille, Pas-de-Calais.

7 Second Lieutenant Colin Henry Fyffe, 22563, from Silverstream, left New Zealand on 13 February 1917 with the 22nd Reinforcements.

Sunday 11 August 1918

Seton told me last night he has written to arrange for his return to France. I was rather unhappy about him giving up his rightful time here, but from his point of view he is right in a way and I can't go against him, the dear kid. Colin came for lunch and then we went to the Troc. He finds the Troc and theatres a bit hard to understand in these days of war. The levity of London strikes all newcomers. He is staying at the Shakespeare Hut. The girls will arrive by train tomorrow.

Tuesday 13 August 1918

Got a letter from Oswald. He has been posted straight away to a squadron in Palestine, which pleases him very much as he says everywhere else is so expensive. He says he should thrive there from what he can see of the country and is pleased because he has lost 9lbs in weight, lives in shorts and shirts and he will get so sun tanned we won't know him.

Wednesday 14 August 1918

Took a taxi so I was at the Savoy in good time, sat in Mr Thompson's [private secretary's] room till Mr Massey was ready and was exceedingly nice. He said I could get a letter from the Board of Trade to him on the same lines as the one they sent last April [that they would refuse consent to Roger's return unless absolutely necessary]. That would be sufficient. When he said 'goodbye' to me he expected it would be all right and that there was not the same shortage of men and more concessions were being made. He says the Military Board has supreme power in NZ but exceptions of course could be made in cases of real hardship such as ours.

In 'intensely hot' weather Annie returns to Devon on 15 August 1918: 'the country looked beautiful all the way down with its fields of grain in every phase of harvest.'

Saturday 17 August 1918

I feel collar proud [restless in harness] after my week's spell. Heard that Seton will arrive today and am in a fever in case it means France and my heart will be full of thanksgiving if I find it is just this six days leave from Grantham and it is a real joy to find my fears were miscalled for. He travelled all night, left London at midnight, he left Grantham at 8 o/c. Dad came and we all walked into Tavistock, bought groceries and came back in taxi.

Wednesday 21 August 1918

Blackberrying, shopping, making jam, visiting Langstone. Seton's leave finished and he set off on night train, in the afternoon we all went to Pew Tor for a walk and sat on top of its rocky battlements and enjoyed the glorious breeze, Seton quite revelled in it. He has enjoyed his few days in this primitive place, and he loved the cream. My heart is achy tonight for both my precious sons. God keep them is my constant thought and prayer.

Letter from Seton, 25 August 1918

There is an observer here from 2 [Squadron]. He left a month after I did and he has given me quite a lot of news. I can hardly credit it but I believe Snow came back about three weeks ago suffering from <u>nerves</u>. What hopes has an ordinary mortal got when a man like that falls victim to the worries of the war, but I am afraid he overdid things and I am glad he has gone. Yesterday I went with Steele to a Hun's crash. He made an unsuccessful landing, and I had to use my influence to stop Steele from flying the machine back, a distance of about 20 miles.

Tuesday 27 August 1918

Got two letters and pc from Os, of 30th and 31st July and 4th August. On the 30th the dear old kid had just recovered from another attack of sandfly fever,[8] but he was feeling fit again when he wrote on the 4th August. Even on the 4th he hadn't received quarter of his letters. The Egyptian mail seems very erratic.

The next two days are spent picking blackberries and crabapples, then making jam.

Sunday 1 September 1918

Roger stayed the night, had nasty palpitations last night when he went to bed, blames the bacon stuff he ate for upsetting his digestion. Then he got toothache so it was a restless night. I got up for some chlorodyne but it didn't do much good, then he tried a plug of tobacco.

---

8 Sandfly fever, common in the Middle East, is a virus caused by the bite of female *Phlebotomus papataci* midge. Symptoms include a high temperature, headaches, sore eyes and lack of appetite.

Letter from Seton, 1 September 1918

I am afraid I have dropped in for some work now – I was told I am being transferred to another group. They are short of instructors and they are a decent lot but I do dislike the idea of work as it will make it more difficult to go to France. I have visions of myself now with a flock of pupils and more work than I know what to do with. I have written to another fellow in '2' and I expect an answer in a day or two. Then I hope to start my offensive …

At the beginning of September there is more upsetting news about the Barron problem. Annie writes: 'Roger isn't helpful at these times and my head was buzzing like a beehive. I went up and got myself a little brandy and that steadied me a bit.'

Letter from Seton, 3 September 1918

I started work on my new flight this morning. I have four pupils so far and I have only taken one up. This afternoon I ought to take up the other three and see what they are like … I don't believe in working all day and getting little thanks for it … France – I must get there this month if I want to be back for spring … I would much rather get the worst over straight away and settle down for the winter than go out late and look forward to the hot time that was to come.

Annie is very concerned about Seton's keenness to return to France: 'I knew it must come but it always worries me to think of it. I daren't interfere, I must leave it in God's hands.'

Saturday 7 September 1918

Had early dinner and went to town in the jingle, went straight to Dr Hillyer and found him in. He says Al is very anaemic and she has a large goitre. He didn't say what caused the lumps on the glands, gave her a tonic and wants to see her next Friday. Roger came after supper and we talked all evening.

Letter from Seton, 9 September 1918

There certainly is a war in France at the present time but it is vastly different when we are attacking. If our bombing people wipe out any 'dromes the Huns will have no place to keep their machines … Don't be surprised if I grow a large pair of wings on my back in the near future – it won't be the

RAF's fault if we are not all angels soon. The Air Ministry have instituted prayers at am daily and it matters not whether you are in the mess, ante-room, office or hangar etc the senior present takes a short prayer. I presume those in the air are excused on account of advisability of not stopping. It proves, as does the uniform, who runs the ministry.

Tuesday 10 September 1918
Did some mending, got six warm stockings refooted ready to run round with the machine, and darned a dozen pairs of summer ones. The boys brought the paper: the NZers have been in the fighting again.

Wednesday 11 September 1918
Seton hasn't heard from France yet, and I am glad … Gerry Barton's letter to Wid says they have been over the top four times and would have got further only the Tommies seemed to have got held up every time and they couldn't go on without them. He says, 'I bet Mother is worth listening to now. I could tell her some tales about the Tommies now that would make her jump.'

Friday 13 September 1918
In Seton's letter he says he has had no word from France yet and Snow has written to say he has no power in the squadron now. Took Al to the doctor and he gave quite a good report of her. Although he says she needs great care he thinks more exercise and riding would be excellent.

Saturday 14 September 1918
Got a letter from Oswald to say he was in hospital with malaria, dated 18th August. Wrote to Air Ministry asking to know his present condition and whereabouts. Sent a cable to Os 'Anxious for news, much love', addressed to Lieutenant Oswald Montgomerie, Cox's Bank, Alexandria. Cable cost 12/-.

Sunday 15 September 1918
My head is buzzing away all day. Have been hunting in a cupboard for a medical book so I can look up malaria, but couldn't find one.

Letter from Seton, 15 September 1918
I am thoroughly fed up with the old RFC that they should let the Naval

element please themselves in the Air Ministry. The Yanks have at last put their weight in the war as a unit and they have gained great success. The haul of prisoners seems to have exceeded expectations. My old friend La Bassée has come into the limelight. I hope Auchy is not taken as we would have no place to drop our bombs.

Tuesday 17 September 1918
After dinner Al finished up her box packing, then we walked to town and were rewarded by several letters from Os. He was much improved but had lost a stone in weight: that is 2 stone since he left here.

Wednesday 18 September 1918
Al went back to school today. Asked for the taxi to come at 2.30 so that Al could catch the train and go up with the girls from Plymouth. Then Al and I walked over to Dad's abode to get some of his throat lozenges as she had a sore throat. We found a letter from Aunt Bettie there and took it down to the woods only to find Dad had gone into town to the dentist. After tea he arrived in a miserable state with toothache. Tried everything we could find – brandy, painkiller, chlorodyne-turpentine, hot water bag, cotton wool and flannel – but it still kept on. Made him drink hot milk and brandy, and then a mouthful of supper and then bed.

Letter from Seton, 19 September 1918
I saw a flight commander from 2 who left there only a week ago and he brings very bad news from poor old 2. The new CO is one of the outside 'outsiders' and it looks as if he's going to spoil it and this has damped my enthusiasm … I am at an absolute loose end now to know what to do …

Friday 20 September 1918
Mrs Reddicliffe put black cotton on the machine and I stitched round half a dozen pairs of refooted stockings and put an elastic top on my bloomers. Dad turned up after dinner; he had just come in a taxi from town and had his tooth drawn. The poor old dear was nearly mad with pain last night. There was an abscess at the root and they seem to think it couldn't be saved but I feel quite grieved it had to be pulled out.

Sunday 22 September 1918

Wid gave me a scare by saying she thought she had appendicitis. I got some turpentine from Mrs Reddicliffe and sprinkled some thermogene wool for her to put on … The doctor came later and Wid had to go to bed for an examination and he thinks she has a touch of it. She must stay in bed a few days and see how she gets on. He thinks she has had it in chronic form for a long time and that is why she has been in such unsatisfactory health. He says she will be subject to these attacks now most likely.

Tuesday 24 September 1918

Wid is much the same this morning, if anything brighter; she has been very moody most of the time. I brought her things from the little room after breakfast as she is now in one of the sunny front rooms. The doctor arrived about 11 a.m., found her much better but still insists on the necessity for an operation – says it will make another woman of her. She is perfectly healthy in every organ and this trouble is the cause of her ill health. He wants to operate in about 10 days' time, but says she is not in any present danger but it must come in time. Tried to write some letters after he had gone but my head was buzzing away and making me perfectly stupid. It has been a wet, cold miserable day. Roger came over this evening and sat with Wid, he stayed the night.

Letter from Seton, 26 September 1918

It seems there is a successful war in Palestine and Salonika.[9] It will be a great blow to the central powers if the Bulgarian army gets cut off. I hope you are not getting concerned about Os now that Palestine is the centre of interest, as it makes no difference with his job whether peace or war.

Sunday 29 September 1918

Wid was meant to get up today, but as it was wet and cold decided to stay where she was. Roger spent most of the day reading an *Auckland Weekly* and after supper set off for his dugout, a cold walk with a blustery wind blowing. Had to alter our watches to 'winter time' tonight. Roger is always very indignant about their 'summer time'. He says it's 'bally rot' and will ruin the health of all the children as it only gives them a longer day and less sleep.

---

9   British forces had occupied a number of areas of Palestine in the last few days.

Tuesday 1 October 1918

Bulgaria is out of the war, thank goodness.[10] The news is very good now.

Wednesday 2 October 1918

Letter from Os, snaps of his dear old self. He says his health is OK again and no after effects from the malaria. He says he is going to get sheets for his bed as he can't see the spiders and centipedes easily enough on an army blanket. Wid is just a little touchy on her side so is staying in bed reading *Nicholas Nickleby*.

After a second opinion, it is decided that Wid's operation will go ahead: 'Wid seems quite anxious to have it done. The doctor says if she was his daughter she would have been done and nearly well again by this time.' Roger is to go to a new wood at Lifden, on the boundary of west Devon, not far from the east Cornish town of Launceston.

Monday 7 October 1918

At the hospital Wid's room is cheerful and nice, a fire and an easy chair. The nurse brought us a cup of tea. Had to come away so as to catch the boys with the jingle. I just hated leaving her there, but the nurses are cheery and kind. Came home feeling very lonely, tired and worried. May God bless and keep guard of my dear big girl. It's a big ordeal for her, I'm sure, as well as a worry for me.

Letter from Seton, 7 October 1918

Startling news this morning: the Germans forced to abandon the Hindenburg Line on October 4th and other German forces in retreat.[11] But I am not one who thinks the Huns mean anything but breathing space in which to organise to oppose us. I don't think Foch will give him the desired time but will keep hammering on … but the end is near.

Tuesday 8 October 1918

Walked into town. Got Richard Dehan's book, *That Which Hath Wings*, for Wid, 7/-.[12] She was looking quite bright and enjoyed her letters. One was from Gerry Barton: he has the MC since he went back.[13] The nurse says Wid's operation is to be on Thursday morning at 9 o'clock. I stayed at the hospital until about 5 o/c, started to walk home. I was so tired I hardly got

---

10 Hostilities between Bulgaria and the Allies ended on 30 September.

11 The Hindenburg Line was a German defensive position that ran through France from Arras to Laffaux.

12 Richard Dehan was the pseudonym of eccentric Irish author Clotilde Graves (1863–1932), who also wrote successful plays under her own name. Her first novel was published in 1911 when she was 46. *That Which Hath Wings* appeared in 1918.

13 As the *Evening Post* would report under the heading 'Battle Honours' on 11 February 1919, Barton 'was in command of his company at a spot where the attack was held up in a wood. He pushed on, however, with great vigour and determination, and cleared the section in front of his company, capturing a machine-gun and 26 prisoners. He led his men with conspicuous gallantry and energy.'

there. My left foot has been very sore all day; it feels as if the bottom has dropped down. When I got to the gate Roger came along, and when he saw me he said, 'Oh, you poor old thing', and I was.

Wednesday 9 October 1918
In the mail was Oswald's commission paper with George RI signature.[14] Inquiry about Harry Bruce Lethbridge's number.[15] Had a very miserable night with my old heart flatulence. After dinner went to town, called at the Bedford and managed to get a room for the night, so left suitcase and went on to the hospital and stayed till about quarter to seven. Wid was very bright and the matron and nurses over ruled me about going up tomorrow morning. They are going to phone me when it is all over and I may go and have a look at her about 12 o/c and after lunch sit with her a while. Then went to the Bedford. The Goose Fair crowd is simply horrible.[16] The crowd kept up their 'Orgy Gorgy', as Mrs Reddicliffe called it, for hours.

Thursday 10 October 1918
Hardly slept last night. Went down to breakfast and was just about finished when Dr Hillyer came in to say the operation was all over and all had gone well. He said Wid was very good and bright; I was so thankful to get the news. Later saw Wid. The poor old thing was looking pretty wretched; she wanted to sleep but couldn't. After lunch at the hotel bought some eau de Cologne 4/6 to dab on her forehead and kill the smell of the chloroform. They had given her a powder to make her sleep, but she was sick after it. I tried to soothe her forehead but it does not work like with Os and Roger. Matron gave her some hot water, which made her sick too. It hurts her to be sick. I sat by her until 5 o/c reading most of the time.

Friday 11 October 1918
Went in by jingle and found Wid propped up and looking much better but not bright. After lunch sat with Wid until 3.30 but she wasn't a bit bright or pleased. Don't even know if she likes me to be there. It's a rotten feeling and I don't know what to do for the best. Later a wire came from Seton, he will be in Tavistock at 9.30 tonight so that's a comfort … When Seton arrived he had some café au lait and some supper; hadn't had anything to eat since breakfast. He is looking so well.

---

14 The 'RI' after George V's signature stood for 'Rex Imperator', King and Emperor.

15 Gunner Harry Bruce Lethbridge, 50883, from Wanganui, left New Zealand as a member of the Field Artillery on 21 November 1917.

16 The Tavistock Goose Fair has been held annually on the second Wednesday in October since 1823.

Saturday 12 October 1918

Visited Wid in hospital [with Roger]. She wasn't very cheerful, but the doctor came while we were there and said she was doing splendidly. Talked until after 11. Wild rumours are going around about the German surrender, but I'm afraid it's too good to be true.

Monday 14 October 1918

Found Wid getting on well. Got a letter from Al which wasn't too cheering: she sounds as if she is getting that horrid Spanish flu.[17] Met Mrs Doidge, who told us about her sons who are away. She says farmers should be called up before working people as they have more to fight for. Dad came. He is great on the German peace stunt; he won't believe it's only a trap to gain time.[18]

Wednesday 16 October 1918

Letter from Miss Fearon to say Al has that horrid flu. She says the doctor expressed himself satisfied it is a straightforward case. I wish I had the confidence in him like she has. The poor kid had a high temperature and was feeling wretched. Wrote to Al and enclosed 10/- for grapes. Went into town in the jingle, bought some grapes for Wid, 5/6d, but they were beauties. Wid is still going on well.

Thursday 17 October 1918

Al is having a wretched time with sickness, nose bleeding and temperature. They managed to get some ice to stop the nose bleeding. The school bill also came. After breakfast I read newspapers and then did some mending. It was fearfully cold and I just felt all miserable and lonely. It was as much as I could do to tackle my dinner. Had a good cry, which did me good. It looks as if Germany is really going to give in.

Seton, diary, 17 October 1918

Arrived London 6.45 a.m. and called at Inverness Tce for a raincoat to fly in. Arrived back at Spittlegate at 11.30 and went up for flight in evening but engine was 'dud'. Heard that Flight Sergeant Warne has been killed by an Avro propeller. Also that Lieutenant Morgan had been killed at Cranwell [airfield in Lincolnshire] in a Camel – machine collapsed.[19]

---

17 The 1918 Spanish influenza pandemic killed an estimated 20 to 50 million people worldwide. The name originated in newspaper reports, made possible because Spain was neutral, of the disease's progress in that country. The King of Spain was an early victim. There are a number of theories about its source, but the extensive troop movements of the war may have helped the virulent disease to spread.

18 On 3 and 4 October Austria and Germany sent letters to US President Woodrow Wilson requesting an armistice.

19 Twenty-three-year-old Albert Edgar Warne of the Royal Air Force was killed on 13 October 1918; he is buried in Ugborough (St Peter) churchyard. The second man was almost certainly Lieutenant Bertram Morgan DCM, RAF, who was killed on 16 October; he is buried in Cathcart Cemetery in Renfrewshire, Scotland.

Friday 18 October 1918

Five letters from Os. He is back with his squadron again and sounds very happy. He says he is taking the liquid phospherine and feels better than he has for the last two years. Pc to say Al is much brighter. Went to town and read a paper and found it all rubbish about Germany capitulating. It's a shame to put so many lies in the papers. It only makes me restless and doesn't help one to 'stick to it'.

Letter from Seton, 19 October 1918

The news these last few days has been very good … the Germans must be retiring on a shorter line which presumably runs from Antwerp through Brussels, Namur etc. I do hope to get one or two of my pupils solo in near future. I am tired of giving them dual and getting no further.

Sunday 20 October 1918 Roger is 52 today

Roger here, found the fire alight when we came down, not cheerful weather. After dinner Roger went over to Baileys to do his packing and I went in to hospital, drove in alone. Asked Sister if I ought to see Wid as I had come from an influenza household – Mrs Reddicliffe and Jack are getting it now – but Sister said as I hadn't had it she thought it was all right. However I didn't kiss Wid or go close. Spider stayed quite good while I was in the hospital. Roger was here when I got back. Asked Mrs Reddicliffe if she would like me to go to Tavistock while she was on the sick list but she said she wouldn't.

Monday 21 October 1918

Had a cup of tea at a café and then said 'Goodbye' as Roger didn't want me to go the station. He had about eight or nine men going with him. Roger was very important with his batch of men. He had his tent and saw and all sorts of 'bushman' outfit with him. I do hope he gets good lodgings there. Didn't enjoy my walk back one little bit, felt all depressed and horrid, and the sight of old Pew Tor with Roger on the other side just made me feel as lonely as could be. My bag grew very heavy and I was very tired.

Seton, diary, 22 October 1918

Woke up feeling very bad, in head and all over my body. Misty all day.

20 Belton Park was a military camp that included a hospital.

Reported to MO [medical officer] after lunch and he sent me with Captain Woodward to Belton Park Military Hospital – near Grantham.[20] My temperature was 103.6 degrees. We are in Ward 9.

Seton, diary, 23 October 1918
My temp was 104 degrees F this morning. We find that this is the most ungodly hospital that one could possibly get in to. The food and cooking is appalling. I am feeling very sore and aching all over. Milk is hardly ever seen in this hospital.

Seton, dairy, 24 October 1918
My temp is still up and I am aching all over especially my back. The only meal we get is at midday and that is insufficient. Other meals are not worth touching. I am very thirsty at nights.

Friday 25 October 1918
Letter from Seton to say he has the wretched flu and has been sent to hospital. I am thankful for that as they will take care of him, but I have been fearing he would get it. Went in to the hospital: Wid had been up and taken a few steps. The doctor forbids her to go back to Moortown. She will be ready to go to Exmouth next Thursday if I can get rooms. I saw her wound today, quite a big cut … Wrote my usuals and then as I felt a bit queer and in case I am getting the flu I packed up my goods and chattels so there won't be any muddle if I had to go to hospital.

Letter from Seton, 25 October 1918
I feel more like writing today, but we are still handicapped. Broken backs are quite common and I possess about as much strength as a kitten. I didn't realise how quickly a man in the best of health could lose control of himself. My legs don't support me, all our muscles are similarly affected. I shall not be surprised if Spittlegate has to shut up for some weeks. All the instructors are coming here; without them the war cannot possibly proceed satisfactorily. I don't yet know how long we will be here – but as soon as one's temperature comes down they don't waste any time on one. The war news is very good.

Seton, diary, 25 October 1918

My nose bled this morning and did not stop for about ten minutes. In the end I nearly fainted but I got over it all right. A bad patient was taken from the ward today.

Seton, diary, 26 October 1918

I am feeling a bit better today but my temp is still up and the food is unbearable. The bacon and tea are atrocious and the bread is not too appetising.

Letter from Seton, 27 October 1918

I am still in bed and my temp has not yet come down to normal. There are 30 of us in the ward and it took exactly 24 hours to fill up. The majority of them belong to the MGC [Machine Gun Corps], which covers the country round here.[21] Our great joy in life is taking powders – it is stated they reduce the temp but in our estimation they are sufficient to kill anyone. You will be pleased to hear that grapes can be procured here and I did not take long to secure some. They are nice big black ones and they taste good.

Letter from Seton, 29 October 1918

Before I forget, you can hang onto those quinine capsules till they will be some use. I hope you haven't got the flu as it is not very pleasant in its early stages, and it takes all the vitality out of you … My temperature is right down today and I am feeling quite OK while in bed, but outside it is different. I am very fortunately situated right by the fire. We don't get any leave from this place when we leave but have to rely on the generosity of our units. I don't think we shall get more than a week, but we are going to agitate for a fortnight.

Wednesday 30 October 1918

Coming back from the hospital set off home. It was drizzling hard and rather late and I had to work hard to get Spider along, I hate coming home late. The lanes are dark and creepy, cows and horses seem to loom up in dark masses and people passing like some grotesque figure approaching. However after much scolding and pleading and jerking and whipping I got the little crab home again but I always feel used up after my effort. Mrs Barkall in

---

21 There was a Machine Gun Training Centre at Grantham.

Barratt's told me today that of all the ladies coming in and out of the shop I was the nicest! – poor thing. She said I would be a pleasant memory. The matron wanted to get a victoria and send Wid out to Moortown for a drive but couldn't get one.[22] War shortage and so many funerals with this wretched flu, they said.

22 A victoria was a horse-drawn carriage.

Wid leaves hospital on 30 October and she and Annie travel to Exmouth. The next day Seton sits up for a short time: 'I am not looking for a relapse,' he tells his mother. 'Once is quite sufficient.'

ARMISTICE

CHAPTER ELEVEN

As the news improves, and the end of the war seems imminent, even cautious Annie becomes optimistic. A convalescent Seton returns to London in time to celebrate the Armistice.

Friday 1 November 1918
Wid had breakfast in bed through the agency of the maid and waiter who is a good old thing. He brought me a *Western News* to read at breakfast and it contains the good news that Turkey has given in.[1] It's great news and I wonder how it will affect old Os and whether we get him back here or he will be sent to some other theatre of war. After lunch we rang up Southlands and they said I could go at any time to see Al. Found her looking quite herself again.

Seton, diary, 1 November 1918
I got up for the first time and dressed today. It is very bad weather, raining all day and I could not go out for a walk. I feel very weak and my puttees go about twice around my legs. An NZer named Lester from Christchurch arrived today.

Saturday 2 November 1918
Letter from Miss Ibbotson saying she is trying to give us our room from next Thursday but has raised the price to £5 5s. Seton's letter says he hopes to get away on leave on Sunday or Monday but that sounds far too soon for me. Roger's letter is a very happy one; he has struck very good quarters indeed. Wid and I have decided to write to Miss Ibbotson and say we wanted the room but were sorry she had raised the price. We won't stay long in London unless I take up censor work or something like that. Al came out for the day. The paper says the war news is still good.

---

[1] The Turks surrendered to the British in Mesopotamia on 30 October and then signed an armistice with the Allies.

Letter from Seton, 2 November 1918

Moving round a little today – fraternising with some 'Pig Islanders' [New Zealanders].[2] Only three of us originals left now and we are getting not a little 'fed up' but I realise I am still unfit to travel.

Sunday 3 November 1918

Delighted to find a letter from Os, a very bright one. He had been riding on mules and doing some shooting instead of constant work. He is sending me a card case made from olive wood from the slopes of Nazareth.

Monday 4 November 1918

Seton thinks he will be here about Tuesday; I have arranged a room for him. Great news today: Austria [Austria-Hungary] has signed the Armistice. So the end of this hateful war is in sight. Everything depends on how Germany will knuckle under. Her army is still unbeaten, but for all that she has lost the war.

Tuesday 5 November 1918

Seton arrived before we were up this morning. He is looking pulled down and is quite weak yet. He needs feeding up: the meals here are excellent though quantity is not too strong a point. Belton Park Hospital seems to have been a place of horror – food bad, attendance also no comfort. The morning Seton left the temperature in the ward was about 43 degrees and no fire at all. One man in his ward died and each day the Union Jack was brought in and a dead body taken out from another ward. His one thought was to get away from the place.

Letter from Os dated 8th October. He had been to Jerusalem and was very puzzled with the filth and ignorance which was so much in evidence. He says it's like listening to dogs and jackals howling hearing the Mohammedans chanting their midday prayers. Went up to school to get Al. On our return found the mother of one of the girls here. They are very anxious to get to New Zealand and wanted to hear from us what is was like. After dinner Seton felt very tired. I got him a hot water bottle and put two rugs on him. He has had a big shake-up.

Thursday 7 November 1918

Yesterday's paper has some quite good news: the Germans have to apply to

---

2   Slang expression for New Zealanders dating from late nineteenth century, presumably owing to the country's large number of wild pigs.

Foch.³ Heard this afternoon that the news has come through that 'Germany is done in', but it is only rumour. Anyhow we are full of high hopes. Took the train to Exeter and went to the Royal Clarendon for lunch, then went to see Raleigh, Frobisher and Drake's meeting room in the little shop in the cathedral close. Seton and I went to the Guildhall to see the NZ flag hanging there, also Australian and South African ... Took train to Paddington, arrived at '40'. Saw Rita Harris. She is bubbling with joy over the thought of peace.

3   Between 7 and 11 November a German delegation met General Foch in his railway carriage HQ at Compiègne near Paris to discuss the terms of an armistice with the Allies.

Friday 8 November 1918
In the afternoon went to the RAC, the lady who receives is always Lady Dunmore, had afternoon tea and a good concert. Dressed for dinner and then went to see Doris Keane in *Roxanna*; I liked her best in *Romance*.⁴

4   Doris Keane (1881–1945) was an American actress who worked on both sides of the Atlantic. She played the part of Margherita Cavallini in Edward Sheldon's *Romance* both on stage and in a silent film made in 1920.

Saturday 9 November 1918
Went into see the bank manager: I am allowed to overdraw from £50 to £100 this next month. People were waiting to see the Lord Mayor's Show; it took a long time to go past. It was the first time Seton had seen one. The rush in the tube was awful but we managed to squeeze through. Then Seton, Wid and I went to see *The Law Divine*, one of the best shows I've seen. We taxied there after having waffles and maple syrup at Fuller's. Found Cyril here when we came back, so he and Seton went to the theatre together in the evening.

Sunday 10 November 1918
The papers have the news of the Kaiser's abdication as official. Also the Crown Prince [Wilhelm] renounces his right to the throne. We are all on edge with expectation that the Armistice will be signed or not tomorrow. Wid met a friend who said no passage back to NZ can be booked in the next 12 months as the space is wanted for soldiers and their wives.

Monday 11 November 1918 Fighting ceased; Armistice signed
Seton sent a wire to his squadron asking for extension of leave. Then he and I set out for the Mall to see the 200 captive guns there. We heard that the Armistice had been signed so went on to St James and then thought Buckingham Palace would be the best place. On our way got NZ badges at

a shop in Victoria Street. The crowd was gathering fast outside the palace, all points of vantage taken. I asked a taxi man if I could stand on his spare wheel, which I did and paid 2/- for it. Seton stood on the bonnet of an RAF tender close by and we both had a splendid view of the proceedings. The crowd was beflagged all over and spent the waiting time singing snatches of songs. One ugly coster looking man sang 'All the lassies will be kissing all the laddies when the boys come home'.[5] A NZer with his flag was nearly up the top of the Queen Victoria memorial. Men were busily engaged in laying carpets and decorating the balcony of the palace, troops were moving into the courtyard and it was a long time before the Duke of Connaught came on and then he stood to attention and on walked the King, Queen, Princess Mary, then Pat Connaught.[6] The crowds waved and shrieked with every possible sign of intense loyalty. The Queen had no hat and looked very stately and sweet. She beat time to all the popular airs with her flag. The whole affair was simple and because of that had an earnestness and intensity of feeling. The band first played 'God save the King', then 'Home Sweet Home', 'Tipperary', 'Keep the Home Fires Burning' etc and a lot of national anthems to which the King and Duke stood at salute. It was a great sight to see the gathering sea of people. We slipped away quietly and managed to get a taxi home for a late lunch. Then later took a taxi with Wid for an hour and a half we drove through seething crowds in Strand, Piccadilly etc. It was just a huge carnival and sometimes we could not get along for the mass of people. Soldiers and girls jumped on the back of the taxi and waved flags to us. One man shook some fluffy stuff in my face and said, 'Hello Dolly', but everything was done in such a good-natured way. It was a great affair and Seton loved every minute.

We called at Selfridges and bought two flags, one New Zealand and one Aussie 6/- and we had them flying on our taxi. A New Zealander climbed onto the steps of our taxi; he was fairly 'blotto'. He confided to Seton that he and his friend had been with 'two young ladies of doubtful reputation who had left them and a very good thing, don't you think?' A NZ soldier rushed after our taxi and called out, 'Hello Mother, how are you …' and shook hands with me and I … gave him a hearty grip. Our taxi man was hungry so we had to let him go; he brought us back to '40'. Rita came by bubbling with joy. She said it was very sad at Southall [Hospital] when the guns fired they knew Armistice had been signed. The poor crippled boys put

5 Annie is probably misquoting lines from the song performed by famous Scottish entertainer Harry Lauder (1870–1950), 'The Lads Who Fought and Won': 'Oh, the lassies will be loving o'er the laddies/ The laddies who fought and won'. Lauder lost his only son, John, in the war.

6 Prince Arthur, the Duke of Connaught and Strathearn, was the third son of Queen Victoria. Pat Connaught was his youngest daughter, Princess Patricia.

their heads down and wept. They all felt their limitations and realised they were handicapped. While they are together they don't feel it so much but when they are returned to their civilian status it is going to be rottenly hard. They have always been so brave and cheery too.

We celebrated at dinner with champagne, drank first to the rotten colonials, then to Australia and New Zealand. After dinner Seton got another taxi and we went for another spin around the city. It was a weird experience and we saw all sorts of antics that were a source of amusement to Seton who could have gone on indefinitely. He was very grieved he had no mate to fly round with him. When we got back we all had a supper of coffee and cake and a nightcap and so ended our day of rejoicing.

Tuesday 12 November 1918

After breakfast Seton and I decided to go to the high commissioner's on the Strand and see the King and Queen drive past on their way to St Paul's. Later went to the Dugout in Regent Street and had tea in a window seat from which we had splendid views of the traffic. Then after some trouble we got a taxi in front of the Piccadilly Hotel and did another trip round London – very interesting as the lights were going on as much as shortage and restrictions would allow. Regent Street was very fine. Seton got his leave extension after lunch. We went out again tonight but it was disappointing this time, rottenly common 'civvy' crowd and about one dozen hoodlums clambered onto our taxi. We got rid of them after a bit but we didn't enjoy their pleasantry.

Wednesday 13 November 1918

Letter from Os written on his birthday and he hadn't received a single thing. It wasn't nearly as bright as usual. After dinner went early to the Troc. A few Australian boys made things lively by selling papers! and dancing but otherwise it was very orderly. Then Seton went to get a taxi and it took him nearly an hour. He was nearly picked up about half a dozen times, but there wasn't very much to see. Seton went back to Spittlegate tonight, arriving midnight.

Thursday 14 November 1918

After breakfast set off for Victoria with Mrs Plant. I was to take her to the Anzac Buffet where Rita works and then shopping at Gorringe's.[7] An

7   The Anzac Buffet was a London club for soldiers funded by expatriate Australians. It offered free meals and entertainment.

Aussie showed us the way. When we got there we found they were having a
hectic time with five helpers away and men pouring in so Mrs Harris commandeered us to give a hand. My task was to spread dripping on slices of
bread ready for sandwiches when required. I stuck at it until 1o/c and then
came home to lunch. Before dinner came downstairs saw an RAF cap hanging up and it was Seton back again, much to our surprise and delight. When
he went to see about flying this morning he was told he had to see the MO
[medical officer] first, who said he couldn't fly again for the next seven days
and then see him. He still has effects of the flu hanging about him.

Saturday 16 November 1918

Seton found a wire in the [letter] rack recalling him to Spittlegate. His friend
Colin Fyffe has his leave stopped too, so think the internal unrest here may
have something to do with it: the Red Revolution.[8] After dinner Wid came
with us to see the fireworks display on the Serpentine Bridge. There was
quite a brilliant blaze at the time but it was biting cold and we came away
early. This afternoon Rita told us about some people here who evidently
pitied her for being a colonial, asking her if she couldn't get naturalised. Mrs
Plant told us how her mother had written to Mrs Cadbury [of the chocolate
manufacturing family] to tell her she was coming over here and she got
a typewritten letter! from her saying she would put her in touch with the
'Women's National League' or some such thing – English hospitality?

Sunday 17 November 1918

Seton went off on the 11.40 a.m. train, however much to our surprise he
turned up again at 10.30 p.m. He was recalled because London has been put
out of bounds for khaki, but he managed to evade the law by taking his pass
for Hornchurch. So now it's a case of evading the Military Police.

Tuesday 19 November 1918

Got a letter from the War Office acknowledging the offer of my services
and saying that no further action was necessary on my part until I receive a
communication from that office. So that's that. Seton and I went to Oxford
Street on the top of a bus. It was a dense fog and it was a queer sensation
to see motors and other vehicles with lights going at midday materialising
a few yards away. The houses on each side were obliterated, just a few dim

---

8 Annie's rather apocalyptic and conservative reading of the industrial unrest that marked the last two years of the war and its aftermath, as workers struck in the face of food shortages and difficult living conditions.

twinkling lights shining through from their windows. Seton was quite satisfied with its density; he wanted to see a real dinkum black fog when you can't see your own hand when you hold it up. Have a tendency to nose bleeding today and a nasty pain in my head. Got three letters from Os in the evening post. One letter had a mummy charm for Al in it which he must have bought in Cairo. He wrote one letter from the Shepheard's Hotel;[9] he must have been on the move but doesn't give an inkling as to where. Went down to dining room and got teaspoon of salt and made a douche and used it and feel my head is a bit clearer.

9 Shepheard's Hotel in Cairo was one of the best known in the world from the mid-nineteenth century until it was destroyed by fire in 1952.

Seton, diary, 19 November 1918
Met McLachlan, my old observer, at the RAC, and went to Fuller's. We then went to the Russell Hotel and had dinner and a long chat until he caught the midnight train for Reading.

Letter from Seton, 21 November 1918
Spittlegate

I am not to fly for three days and I am going back to the MO, and as for the other business, people don't think I have any hope of getting to France, but there is nothing like trying. I have heard from a reliable source that this and the next 'drome are going to shut down as soon as possible. We don't get any leave warrants and we are supposed to attend church on Sunday. Have run out of rumours.

Saturday 23 November 1918
Thirteen aeroplanes flying in formation and sending off star shells as signals to turn round were very busy over the city this afternoon. This evening Rita told us how she was out at a supper party at Colonel C's flat and a subaltern discussing the war and he said, 'The Colonials were always given the "showy parts" and the English never liked boasting about what they did. It was their characteristic.' Cheek. All the times they have let our men down when doing their 'showy' bits. One of Rita's stories [from men in the buffet] was about the retreat in March.[10] The colonials noticed some Mons ribbon men in retreat and asked them if they expected a bar for this one. They call the Mons ribbon the 'running ribbon'. They say the men were pushing forward and saying to others to get out of the road and let the ones that could run do it.

10 The fighting British retreat ordered in March 1918 at the beginning of the German Spring Offensive.

Letter from Seton, 23 November 1918

I saw the CO and he was not at all favourable but I am not done yet. If I do have to work they will have to drive me to do it and it will be precious little I will do.

Seton, diary, 24 November 1918

Walked to Belton Park Hospital and saw [Bert] Reid. He was very well [recovering from influenza]. Called on NZMGC [New Zealand Machine Gun Corps] and saw several people I had met. Had tea there and met Major Chaytor,[11] who was on Gallipoli with Willie Montgomerie.

Letter from Roger to Annie, 25 November 1918

I am seriously thinking of leaving for NZ before next winter and will do so if there is a chance of getting a good ship to sail in, so you will have to wake up and see what you are going to do before leaving this country. Finances from NZ will be much smaller than you imagine I am sure and shipping for our produce will be scarce for a number of years. If 'Taukoro' is going to produce what you think we can return again by ourselves for a few months later on.

Wednesday 27 November 1918

It is the Victory Ball tonight and Rita got the tickets through the ANZAC Buffet people. Seton got some leave so he can attend and spent time trying to find a bed and simply can't find one so now he is going to catch a train and go back to Grantham. He set off with four charges, Rita Harris, Wid, Mrs Plant and Miss Bishop. Gave Wid 10/- for a ticket. I lent Mrs Plant my fur coat.

Thursday 28 November 1918

A guest at the hotel asked me to go to a Christian Science lecture at the Queen's Hall where a queue had started to grow even though it was such a wet night. It was a most interesting lecture and the speaker spoke very clearly on his points. His argument is that God is omnipotent and consequently evil cannot have any power, except we allow it.

Letter from Roger to Annie, 28 November 1918

I don't see the money is your hard earned income, if there is any hard

---

11 Lawrence Clervaux Chaytor (1892–1954), younger brother of Major-General Edward Walter Clervaux Chaytor (1868–1939), who commanded the New Zealand Mounted Rifles Brigade in the Sinai from 1916 to 1917 and in April 1917 became commander of the ANZAC Mounted Division.

earning it has been done by me. I think Xmas and New Year time there will be too much hustle and bustle for my liking and am not anxious to join the merry crowd.

Saturday 30 November 1918
In a letter from Os he mentions sending me a parcel from a firm in Port Said so that indicates he's moving somewhere across the Mediterranean, I do wish I knew but this letter had been opened by the censor. He is now full of ideas for peace pursuits again. Roger's letter mentions having seen in the papers that the English government will pay all our fares back if we apply before 31st January 1919. Seton inquired about his passage refund: they told him he was to apply to the English government when ready and they handed you on to our own people here and you got your passage. Dr Groves came to see Wid and said the little lump inside is some catgut and pain is caused by its pressure on a muscle. He congratulated Wid on having the operation, says that 30% of troubles in her life are over and that stairs do not cause adhesions. He set our minds at rest completely.

Sunday 1 December 1918
Seton and I had a great old castle building talk. We were planning to get a car when the boys are released and motor in France, also England and Scotland. Wid was throwing cold water on our dreams but as I said we had carried through a much bigger thing than that and there is no such word as can't. She has been very nervy but is so much brighter since the doctor reassured her about herself. Cyril came for lunch then both boys went to see Marshall Foch and Clemenceau,[12] who are having a public reception today. It has been wet all morning and I am not fond of crowds so didn't think of going. The boys and Colin Fyffe came back and we ordered tea in the smoking room but the waiter, who is a Dane, wouldn't let us have buttered toast so Rita and I came up to my room and made some. We get a butter parcel from Devon and I gave Rita Harris half. There were six of us and we had a party together and ate some of Rita's Aussie cake.

Seton, diary, 1 December 1918
Raining in the morning. McLeod and I went and saw Marshall Foch arrive in the afternoon and got a splendid view of him.

12 Georges Clemenceau (1841–1929) was Prime Minister of France from 1917 to 1920. As one of the main participants in drawing up the Treaty of Versailles in 1919, his attitude towards the Germans was particularly punitive.

Monday 2 December 1918

Seton went back to Spittlegate. Visited Mrs Glenn and heard some news of Wanganui people. She told us Bob Earle is a prisoner in Germany and also Walter Fernie wrote a letter to his colonel asking him if he got wounded and sent back to England would he see that he got some extra leave as he wanted to go to Scotland and buy some sheep.[13] Also saw Malcolm Stewart. He says the whole army retreated in March but it only took a division! to stop the Germans. He says our boys are rebelling about going to Germany. They broke some of General Russell's windows and gave him 24 hours to get them out of it![14] Another story from Rita. An English working girl on a bus saw some Maoris standing on the street and said to a friend, 'I say, what's them?' The friend replied, 'Them's Australians.' 'My Gawd,' said the first. 'Give me an Englishman any day.'

Letter from Seton, 3 December 1918

Went to see the MO and I expect to get another two weeks without flying – he said we should not fly for six weeks after the flu. After having a few words with him he said, 'You are Montgomerie, aren't you? You come from NZ?' He had been to Wanganui College, Christ's [College in Christchurch] and Waitaki. He was at school when 'The Man' arrived. I don't think I should have any difficulty in obtaining leave whenever I desire it. Met a NZ cadet, his name is Tennent.[15] He was in the NZFA [New Zealand Field Artillery] and was sent back to NZ, and came back to fly as a civvie last Nov [1917]. His brother is a major in the RAF in Egypt. He went to Wango Collegiate and was at school with Dick and Roy.

Friday 6 December 1918

Seton turned up and later went to NZ Headquarters to see if he could get some half-fare vouchers from Major Watson. Major W. wasn't there but he got them without any trouble and came back jubilant with half a dozen. After dinner he took us to the Marble Arch Picture Pavilion. The German boats were surrendering and there was a war picture by Charlie Chaplin.[16] Seton and Wid just roared and I have not had such a good laugh for a long time; it was a very good show. Seton bought some Formalin lozenges to fortify us against influenza microbes.[17] Had a supper party later.

---

13 Robert Charles Earle, a former Wanganui Collegiate pupil, had been serving as a trooper with 1st King Edward's Horse (The King's Overseas Dominions Regiment). Walter Edward Fernie, 65523, who had fought with the Canterbury Infantry Regiment, had been a farmer before the war.

14 Annie is referring to the New Zealand Division sent to the Rhineland as part of the occupying force. They were not there long: their role ended on 25 March 1919.

15 William Cowper Tennent left New Zealand on 16 October 1914 with the New Zealand Field Artillery. He was a trumpeter.

16 Opened in 1914, the popular Marble Arch Pavilion in Oxford Street, complete with Corinthian columns, six private boxes, a pipe organ and a tearoom, was built and run by Israel Davis, who had other 'Pavilion' cinemas in and near London. It could seat 1200 patrons. Annie is referring to the 1918 Gaumont newsreel showing some 150 German submarines surrendering on the River Stour. The Chaplin film, silent of course, was *Shoulder Arms*, a comedy set in France during the war.

17 Such lozenges, containing the disinfectant and antiseptic paraformaldehyde, were widely used during the influenza pandemic.

Friday 13 December 1918

On the 9th had a cable from Os!!! saying 'Send no more mail' and I am jumping with excitement. It is six months last Monday since he went away. The parcels he sent from Port Said have arrived. Collected 11 returned letters from Cox's. In his last letter Os said he hadn't had any mail for seven weeks. We also went to the bank and I am £40 overdrawn at the moment so arranged for a cable for £500 more. Then Wid said I should have sent for a letter of credit instead of sending a cable so I went back to the bank and everything will be all right. Wid and Seton went to a show tonight. She wore her grey and pink Felicia frock and it looked so sweet. They enjoyed the show, I left the gas turned low and the kettle on the boil for them. One of those English people here was working off steam about the inconsiderateness! and unthankfulness! of the working class. She is one of the Free Traders lot and is getting excited about labour's growing strength.

Sunday 15 December 1918

At supper time I came in for universal condemnation because I can't see that the British Navy has done any great work in this war. Seton was very hurt and vexed about it because I said they were not holding the Germans until the Americans came in. I certainly never felt secure till then: leaky blockade, raids on east coast and Channel, raiders in the Atlantic and Pacific, submarines. It was a long nightmare and the Jutland mess to crown it.

Letter from Seton, 17 December 1918

I don't think anyone who matters knows about my weekend absences … Any prolongation of my present lazy life may mean [medical] board and I don't want that as it might end in my flying pay going west, and I won't risk that one. I am really quite fit to fly now … The gramophones are making such an infernal racket I shall leave off.

Wednesday 18 December 1918

Al came back; I met her at Waterloo. There was a wild crush of khaki on leave, going there the tube was simply packed. Was told the Exeter train came in on platform 13 but it was number 11. I ran in real panic, expecting to miss her altogether, but she was there all right. Saw the King and Princess Mary in the park as we came in a taxi.

Seton is passed fit for flying on 19 December and is quickly back in the air, though he finds his flying skills are a little rusty: 'that finesse!!! of touch and execution has to be cultivated.' Os writes to say he is in Marseilles and on his way home.

Wednesday 25 December 1918

Gave out several tips to the page, kitchen maids, waiter. Sat in the drawing room all morning. It was a very slow Christmas but we enjoyed turkey and Christmas pudding for dinner. This evening in the drawing room a guest blew off about the inconsiderateness of President Wilson coming on Boxing Day and spoiling the day for the King and Queen and for the bank holiday of the people!! So I told her there were more important matters to be considered than Christmas for the King or people and the whole world's Christmas would have been at stake but for him.

Thursday 26 December 1918

After breakfast made up our minds to go on the bus along the route of today's oration to President Wilson. I had a nasty attack of flatulence but wanted to go. After taking a bus to Piccadilly we walked through St James Street to the palace there. The bunting was a sight to behold so after lunch we went outside Buckingham Palace and saw the President with George and Mary on the balcony.[18] Mrs Wilson was waving a Union Jack about. I guess this is a red letter day in the history of the world. When out earlier when trying to get on a bus went through some awful streets and saw some truly awful people – poor, degraded, dirty, wolfish, unwholesome and perfectly horrible. It always makes my blood boil to see these slum people; it is an unthinkable crime to have such conditions.

Letter from Seton, 26 December 1918

We had a very good time yesterday and a splendid dinner – had small amount of 'fizz' and when that was finished had to fall back on ordinary beverages. Seeing that there was aviation this morning I retired about 10.30 but the others didn't. I was up solo this morning and the castor oil and perhaps last night aggravated it, it has gone to my head.

---

18 As the *Guardian* reported on the 27th, 'The expressive countenance of our streets was hidden under a brilliant mask of flags. There has not been such a show of colour or such genuine lightheartedness in the crowd since Coronation days in the world before the war.' Tens of thousands turned out to see the president make his 'wonderful progress' from Charing Cross to Buckingham Palace.

Saturday 28 and Sunday 29 December 1918

Sat in smoking room after dinner to hear what the English element would have to say about the results of the election. Old Asquith has been defeated and put out; his followers are very distressed.[19] One creature said that he wouldn't have blamed Asquith if he had made peace three years ago! He never expected we would win then and lots of other soldiers thought the same! This particular creature was an ASC [Army Service Corps] man so he should talk.[20] I still feel a bit off colour and have a pain in the appendicitis corner. On Sunday Seton and Al went for a walk and saw Sir Douglas Haig with his family.

Tuesday 31 December 1918

Had afternoon tea at Harrods. After dinner Miss Cowlishaw brought her cards and told our fortunes. Spent the rest of the evening doing card tricks until 12 o/c. Then we all went out on the street and listened to the 'All clear' and other sounds. It was bitterly cold so we ran upstairs and got our coats and walked to the end of the street. After a late supper we said 'Goodnight' or rather 'Good morning' at 1 o/c.

---

19 The Liberal leader and former prime minister lost his seat in the House of Commons.

20 Annie seems to be implying that because this man belonged to the ASC, responsible for supplying the army with food, equipment and ammunition, he was not a 'real' soldier.

CHAPTER TWELVE | 1919

Os is welcomed back and then begins the complicated process of finding the Montgomeries a place on a ship home. There were thousands of men to be repatriated, and the glacial rate at which this happened led to several riots in Sling and other camps. The last New Zealand troops would not reach home until May 1920.

Thursday 2 January 1919

A wire from Os to say he was at Southampton, so thank God he is safely back in England. After dinner dressed for Norfolk House At Home – was so thankful we had gloves, without we would have looked silly. We filed through from the drawing room to the ballroom and were introduced to Princess Marie Louise,[1] the Duchess of Norfolk and Lady Carmichael. Then we went to supper in the dining room and it was a fearful crush, but at last we managed to get some fruit salad, trifle and cake so everything was A1.

Sunday 5 January 1919

Oswald's lieutenancy was gazetted in the *Times* yesterday. Roger has arrived, so we all went to Norfolk House and entertained Miss Jill Crossley Batt for tea.[2] She is the girl who volunteered to get an aviation magazine for Seton because it has old 2nd Squadron aerodrome in it. Miss Batt kept us interested. She is the only lady correspondent of the *Times*. She is an Australian who came over here some time before the war to study at Oxford. She is a BA, BSC and OBE. She inspects factories and is interested in all sorts of things. She sent a wonderful plan for catching submarines to the authorities but she never received any reward.

Monday 6 January 1919

Os is at Arundel, Sussex and hopes to be here later this week. Went to the bank for £20 for Scotland trip. Heard that a NZ boy who had been taken prisoner in Germany had told Mr Mills the whole battalion of 1000 men

---

1 Princess Marie Louise (1872–1956) was the daughter of Prince Christian of Schleswig-Holstein and a granddaughter of Queen Victoria.

2 Explorer, scientist and writer Dr Jill Crossley Batt would travel to Tibet in 1931 with her future husband, Dr Irvine Baird. They discovered a 'lost tribe' in the Himalayas.

had been taken prisoner. I refused to believe it as we heard NZers had only lost 371 taken in the whole war. We spoke to a NZ boy on the street and asked him about it. He said NZ had lost an entrenching battalion, which might be about 250 men, but that was the worst that had been taken.[3] Seton is very keen on the idea of himself and Dad going up to Scotland tomorrow night.

Tuesday 7 and Wednesday 8 January 1919
After lunch Roger and Seton went to see the aeroplane factory that Miss Batt gave them cards for. Later when we got home we found a wire from Os asking Seton to go down to him as 'leave impossible'. I did feel utterly unhappy about the way things have worked out.

Seton, diary entry 12 January 1919
Arrived London and after having breakfast I changed and caught the 1.36 to Littlehampton. Arrived there at 4 and Oswald turned up soon after. He is looking as well as ever and has had some very fine experiences.

On Saturday 11 January Annie takes Al to a doctor in Harley Street who says that she will 'grow out of her trouble, but at present her heart is decidedly out of place, also that she is anaemic'. Poor Al is in a bad way: 'The hairdresser says her hair is falling out because of high temperatures during the flu.' (Seton later has the same problem and is forced to seek treatment at the Aseptic Toilet Rooms in St James Street.) But Al is able to enjoy foxtrot classes with Madame Van Dyke in Regent Street, which are all the rage; Seton also attends when he is in London. On Wednesday Roger hears that Massey has arrived in London 'on a man o'war': he left New Zealand on 12 December 1918 to attend the Paris Peace Conference and sign the Treaty of Versailles on 28 June 1919.

Monday 20 January 1919
When we got back for lunch we found old Macaciac [presumably a nickname for Os] in smoking room. He is looking very well and is just the same old dear. After lunch we went out to post office and sent Cyril a wire, bought book about German fleet surrender 1/6 and looked at Egyptian photos and talked for rest of afternoon … Oswald has only got 12 days leave; he may get the other later on.

---

[3] Annie was almost correct: 414 New Zealand prisoners of war were repatriated at the end of the war. The capture of members of the 2nd New Zealand Entrenching Battalion at Meteren in France during the Battle of the Lys in April 1918 was the largest of New Zealand forces during the war. Units on either side withdrew without telling the battalion, which was then surrounded.

With Os home there is much talking and tea drinking and socialising and Annie continues to spend up large in London.

Letter from Seton, 21 January 1919
Will go to London for weekend leave but it all depends on the state of my pocket – seeing that I hope to leave with a tidy nest egg and don't want to spend half my pay on the Great Northern Railway. We have started a camp magazine and I spend a bit of time endeavouring to please the editor. It is my desire to attract ridicule on the head of my old instructor who I do not love. He lays himself open to it.

Wednesday 22 January 1919
Os was very pleased with his visit to Air Board. He is to have a [medical] board and if passed can take his 'wings' and then go out to NZ as Special Reserve. In which case he will have to fly a month every year for four years – and he thinks it carries a salary of £150 a year.

Friday 24 January 1919
No letters. I was down first to breakfast, then Os arrived, arrayed in mufti, and later on Wid came … Cyril came in to lunch with Os and afterwards they went out together to see the German aeroplanes [on display] in St James Park and have tea at Troc. Seton came soon after they had gone …
He is finished with his instructing now, as all flying has to cease on February 15th and it is no use going on. He has been flying 'joy rides' instead, and doing lots of stunting, which I do not like very much … Os has a cold so I opened the bottle of good old brandy that he brought me from France and made him have some – also some quinine.

Saturday 25 January 1919
Seton went along to the Air Board but couldn't see a satisfactory man … After lunch the boys all went out together again. They meant to go to the *Maskelyne Mysteries* and order horses at Marble Arch for tomorrow morning and Seton was to work in a trip to Major Watson but it all ended in them going to NZ Records and paying a visit to NZ Ordnance – where they found they could have been getting their things miles cheaper if they had only found out in time … After dinner we all went to Marble Arch pictures

– we were too late for the beginning of *Shoulder Arms*, which was a pity as Os hadn't seen it.

Tuesday 28 January 1919

Went in taxi to [?] House to see if they would take some of Oswald's negatives but napoo. But they sent him on to a printing house in Ludgate Circus as likely to use them, and they said if only he had come a month earlier they would have used several of them in the history of the war – hard luck … Freddie Thorpe called before dinner to say his wife has 'flu'. He is very worried.

Wednesday 29 January 1919

When we got down to dinner we found Seton and Cyril had returned [from Spittlegate]. They had a joy ride yesterday and Cyril nearly caused a disaster by turning off the engine when Seton called out to him to turn on the oil. However Seton noticed in time and saved the situation. After dinner sat in smoking room and then the young people had a hop [dance] in the drawing room. Os is as keen as Cyril now [on dancing]. He wanted to go to the Elysée in Queens Road this afternoon.

Thursday 30 January 1919

The boys had a foxtrot lesson before lunch and later went to a thé dansant [tea dance] at Madame Van Dyke's. Oswald is full of the idea of joining up with the army of occupation [in Europe] and today we have all been trying to argue him out of it and I hope we succeed.

Saturday 1 February 1919

Both boys have nasty colds and they have had to go out for a rum and whisky at the pub. It seems to ginger them up. It's rotten having to let them go out like that to get it [alcohol] but it's absolutely impossible to get it for oneself to have at home. Os goes back to Arundel tomorrow. Roger wrote a letter to say he is moving to Princetown Woods on Monday.

On Monday 3rd Annie notes that the 'tubes are not running, the big iron gates are closed and the men on strike'. There is industrial action in Belfast and Glasgow as well as London, where the railway workers go out in sympathy with the tube drivers. The workers in London are seeking a 40-hour week. By Tuesday she cannot 'get near a bus so had to get a taxi'. On Wednesday, the strike is 'still going strong and promises to be worse. It has been sleeting and snowing all day and making things doubly uncomfortable for the general public.' After talking to the postmaster on Thursday, who says there is 'a big possibility' of a postal strike, Annie writes letters and sends off parcels. 'At 6 o/c we waited to see if the electric lights would be cut off as the strikers threatened, but they didn't. Rumour says it has been deferred till tomorrow.' On a happier note Annie also reports on a conversation with a fellow guest who had worked in a Bournemouth canteen: 'she says the NZers are the nicest men she has ever known.'

Friday 7 February 1919

Before lunch Os turned up: he was sent on duty to bring a party of men to London. He was very cold, having had a freezing trip from the station on the top of the bus. He has a room at the Officers' Club in Hereford Gardens. Os was head of operations to melt the solder on a tin of food sent by Mrs Barron.[4] We used the drawing room poker and heated it on the gas stove.

Letter from Seton, 7 February 1919

I don't think you need to worry about postal strikes as the government has said it intends to keep such services going. We could quite easily render aeroplane relief to the hungry citizens as you suggest. I am due to leave any day now to relieve the war heroes in France. Quite pleased really as shall have opportunity of seeing France, Belgium and possibly Germany. I do intend to do my utmost to get to No. 2 [Squadron]. You need not worry about me staying two years as I intend to swing it after about three months and come home.

Saturday 8 February 1919

Os had to bustle off to catch the 3.30 train, but he rang from London Bridge Station to say he'd missed the train and was catching the train an hour later. He had missed the train by four minutes; the congested traffic caused by the strikes delayed him. Had a letter from Seton saying he expects to be sent back to France any day to relieve the men out there. He is quite pleased, but I am sorry as I shall be glad for him to get out of khaki.

4   Tins of food sent from New Zealand were soldered shut to prevent contamination.

On 10 February Roger reports that he has turned down an offer to manage the wood where he is working: 'The best thing is for us to get to "Taukoro" as soon as possible.' A couple of days later Annie is stopped in Oxford Circus by a gypsy woman wanting to tell her fortune: 'said I had a kind face and smile and that I had good luck in front of me, that I am unsettled in the place where I am, have a lot of roving to do and have a big journey in front of me. I am lucky, and I loved and was loved.'

Sunday 16 February 1919

After lunch sat in drawing room and had a talk with Mrs Abraham. She tries to make out that we shouldn't discuss anything that is past about England's errors – pretty good, that. While the war was on she argued that we shouldn't say anything as that would hamper her, and now it's over we shouldn't go back! The Jutland Battle was one of the topics specified. A newsboy went down the street yelling something which sounded like more trouble and sure enough the Germans had broken the Armistice and are fighting Poland.[5] It made me feel all stirred up again. I hope Foch can pull them up with a jerk, but it means more of the old anxieties.

Monday 17 February 1919

Os went to the Air Ministry … He can't go against existing orders, which means he can't go on with his flying and now he is keen to get back to NZ as soon as possible. He is very disappointed. That means a complete change in our outlook. I don't like him going on his own but still I know it's wisest from his point of view but I feel there is always a destiny shaping our ends, something guiding us in our blunderings.

Wednesday 19 and Thursday 20 February 1919

Noticed an appeal from a lonely colonial in personal [column] so wrote him a note. Thursday a letter came from Seton he says he has chosen to be discharged. I am glad. It makes one feel our faces can really be turning homeward.

Saturday 22 February 1919

Mrs Wright told us this morning how she makes a chocolate cream pudding. Allow one egg and one tablesp sugar with each thick bar of chocolate. Pour boiling water over the chocolate which should be placed in a pie dish

---

5 The Greater Poland Uprising, which began on 27 December 1918, sought emancipation from the German rule that much of the country was still under at the end of the war. Fighting between Germans and Poles began at the end of December and continued until a ceasefire in mid-February.

or some such thing. When soft pour off water. Beat the yolks of eggs with sugar. Add choc and then stir in the well beaten whites, put in glass dish and put in freezing box. Nicer if half plain and half sweetened choc is used. Serve plain biscuits with it.

Sunday 23 February 1919
Wid has had a phone call to say that the colonial governments are not paying anyone's passage after May so that means we must look into things pretty quickly. We heard about some English people discussing Princess Pat's wedding and saying it could have been worse – it might have been a colonial!!! – and hoped Princess Mary wouldn't get any ideas from her.[6]

On the wedding day, Thursday 27th, Annie and her family walk to the Mall from Piccadilly: 'saw all the Royalties as they passed. Got a topping view of the bride who looked well powdered and, I thought, awfully sad. The Queen looked very nice and wasn't a scrap made up …' *On Saturday they watch the king take the salute at the Review of the Troops, then hurry to Hyde Park Corner to see the royals.* 'The two princes were very shy looking and flushed as they rode along, the two queens bowing like mandarins. There was a feeling of spring in the air.' *In January there had been only 11 hours of sunshine.*

Letter from Seton, 25 February 1919
Captain Dixon told me he had received word that there would be two regular squadrons in NZ and that they required instructional staff. He thinks it would be a good opportunity for me. I am not allowing anything like that to influence me, but such things should be kept in view so that when I have to choose what is best for myself I may pick something really good. This also gives Os the chance that he required … If I could secure a responsible position in commercial aviation from above I should be a fool not to take advantage of it … Taukoro is by far the best occupation for both of us, but we must not be blind to outside opportunities.

Letter from Seton, 27 February 1919
I am practically running the flight at present. Some of our machines are being sent away, and it is necessary that they should be fit to fly. We possess so few mechanics they are all engaged in that work and we are unable to fly.

---

6 Princess Patricia of Connaught (1886–1974) renounced her royal title when she married commoner, naval officer and future admiral Alexander Ramsay.

It is really annoying to have a nice fine day and walk into a shed and find all the machines locked up ... That expensive hair wash of mine has cured my hair right enough. I am becoming quite a masseuse.

Thursday 6 March 1919

My dear little precious sister [Jen] had an operation for appendicitis on 21st January. I would give anything to be near her and cheer her up. I have never felt so deeply the distance between us but I know God can bridge it and I'm sure he'll let my love reach across. Jack Fergusson says it's absolutely true some of our NZ boys have been put in clink in Germany for not saluting those insufferable Guards officers. He nearly got into trouble for not saluting Sir Charles Fergusson, but he and his mates buzzed off when the sergeant came after them. Guess Sir C would have had a nasty bump if he had caught his own cousin.[7]

Friday 7 March 1919

During breakfast I was just boiling over to hear the comments of all the different tables about a riot among the Canadians at Rhyl, the chorus how they were disgraceful, outrageous, reference to undisciplined etc. They can peck at the colonials at the slightest opening but there was never a cheep of praise out of any of them when these same troops were saving the situation in France. When their own men behaved so badly at Folkestone a few weeks back there was never a word about their disgraceful behaviour, also the troops in London who demonstrated at Whitehall because their leave was not forthcoming.[8] I expressed my feeling pretty plainly to Mrs Abraham and after breakfast didn't go into the lounge in case I raised a riot there, so I went upstairs and blew off steam in Cowlie's [Miss Cowlishaw's] room.

Saturday 8 March 1919

Os is on indefinite leave. This morning all the young people were busy in the drawing room getting it ready for a dance. After lunch I even tried a waltz, first with Os and simply couldn't manage a step, later with Seton and got on a wee scrap better. Then I strummed 'K-K-K-Katy' and the boys practised together.[9] The dance started at 3 o/c there were two men too many and at first Os didn't get many dances and he was rather fed up. There were 18 young ones altogether. Towards the end he enjoyed it better.

---

7 General Sir Charles Fergusson (1865–1951) had served with the Egyptian Army under Kitchener. During the war, he had commanded the 2nd and, later, the 17th Army Corps in France. He was Military Governor of Cologne from 1918 to 1920. On 13 December 1924 he would become New Zealand's third Governor-General, a role he held until early 1930.

8 Annie's slightly skewed view of two of several mutinies that took place in the winter of 1918–19. The discontent among the British armed forces had a number of origins, including bad conditions, the possibility of being dispatched to Russia to fight the Bolsheviks, and delay and confusion concerning demobilisation. There was a large mutiny on 3 January 1919 at Folkestone and on 8 February 3000 troops marched on Whitehall after refusing to return to France following leave.

9 Written by Geoffrey O'Hara in 1917 and published the following year, 'K-K-K-Katy' was advertised, on the cover of the sheet music, as 'The Sensational Stammering Song Success Sung by the Soldiers and Sailors'.

The Brazilian ambassador's daughter was here, also Trollope, the airman that shot down six Huns in a day. He has lost an arm and before dinner when washing hands in the telephone room he had to ask Cyril to help him.[10] It was really very successful. The young folks rolled back the carpet and had the room straightened up like magic before dinner. Later they all went off to Madame's for more dancing.

Sunday 9 March 1919

After breakfast had a great old argument with Mrs Abraham. She argues we should sink all our grievances and let the past go, but, as Seton told her, we want to have some wrongs righted first. She hasn't got the grip of our side of the question, in fact no English outlook can. Coming home from the Troc we saw some posters about the 'riot' in the Strand. It turned out to be some Canadian and American soldiers having a 'go' at civvy police: some more clumsy bossing of the colonials and they won't stand it.[11] Wid has gone to Hornchurch, Mahutonga Club, and she seems to like it.

Letter from Seton, 12 March 1919

I had quite an interesting journey up. At first I thought I had fallen among Bolsheviks, but they were harmless Norwegians. There were four of them and a Yank and I really thought they were socialists as they were going to Stockholm. They could all speak English, some quite well, and it seems they are pulp and paper merchants … The Yank talked about the internal conditions in America, and he said the position was as bad, if not worse than over here. He spoke of the Russian Jews in the ghetto of New York city. In his opinion they were quite a power for the Bolshies, so I hope you take note of this for the future reference.

Thursday 13 March 1919

We went to the high commissioner's and learned that Dad and I can go back first class, £50 for the two of us. Dad must apply to the Board of Trade. I certainly think Al should be included [in our passage], and that Wid's work should count for a concession especially as she broke down at Records. I spoke to an Australian soldier waiting at the Merc[antile] today but he was a fearful frost. He wasn't a 'pukka' Australian at all, just an English thing togged up and full of the English narrowness.

---

10 In fact RFC pilot Captain John Lightfoot Trollope shot down seven enemy aircraft on 24 March 1918. He was later captured by the Germans and so badly wounded that his left hand had to be amputated, and then the whole arm.

11 This riot was not quite as mild as Annie implies. The Battle of Bow Street, as it is known, began when two police officers encountered three American servicemen playing dice outside a YMCA recreation hut and told them this was illegal. The men protested, reminding the constables that they had fought for the empire in the war, whereupon they were arrested. A fight broke out in which some 50 police did battle with 2000 American, Australian and Canadian servicemen. The riot did not end until later that night.

Letter from Seton, 16 March 1919

I saw a fine sight today in the form of an aeroplane – I was going to say new but it was designed in '16 and first flown in Aug '17. It climbs to 2,000 feet in 30 seconds and 10,000 in 3½ minutes. Its speed near the ground is 150 mph. You will not be surprised it never went near France as it would have been too hard on the Huns. One can hardly believe one's eyes when it is performing. I heard of them first when I was at Winchester – it is a wonder we won this war.

Tuesday 18 March 1919

Went to Hornchurch to see Wid; she looked awfully well in her blue uniform. Four NZ officers came in to tea and we had some delicious NZ iced cake belonging to one of them. We had some great old arguments, and they are pretty good fighters even though they don't seem to have much grasp of the real state of things … Heard that in the trains lately people have been heard discussing the Canadians and they said 'the sooner they get rid of them the better'. They were finished with them and would only be too glad to get rid of them. That's exactly the attitude here to all colonials, also Americans. Miss Cowlishaw [was saying] to an English friend that she thought the Canadians had a big grievance in fact that they volunteered at the beginning of the war and should have been sent back before the Americans who came in so much later and the friend said, 'Yes, we are only too glad to get rid of them!!'

Sunday 23 March 1919

Heard from an Australian major that the English papers had circulated this story that the [rugby] match between NZ and Aussie had to be arranged to be played at Bradford because the two countries had such strong feelings towards each other that they were afraid they couldn't keep order among the troops if it were played in London. I want to know what propaganda game they are up to this time. I'm sick of double dealing and lies. Colin Fyffe came in and told me lots of people are indignant about the Guards being paraded yesterday. One Aussie standing by him remarked he didn't know what they had done to deserve it, that if it hadn't been for the colonial troops London would have some very different troops parading in it, which is the truth.

Annie has more to say in this vein the next day: 'The papers are busying themselves in a very patronising manner about having a march of the dominion troops and I do hope they refuse, and tell them they were never second to the Guards in France and won't be here either.' She notes, later in the week, that 'all the colonials, NZ, Aussie, Canadians and South Africans, protested at the War Office meeting about the untruthful insinuations of the press about the bad feeling existing between different colonies and the papers are taking a very different tune now'. In a rugby match at Twickenham on Saturday 29 March, which Seton attends, New Zealand triumphs over South Africa, 14–5. Jill Crossley Batt comes for lunch on Sunday – 'she has been writing up some new patent … which is to come out soon on some Canadian cars' – and then Annie and the boys travel through the snow to visit Wid and her friends at Hornchurch: 'Had afternoon tea with four NZ nurses and about half a dozen khaki men in our party.'

Letter from Seton, 25 March

Spoke to the major about leave to go to Edinburgh [for New Zealand–England rugby match] – he fell in with the idea. Quite often it is necessary to shout your wants about six times before his ears pick up your voice … If the RAF would give us something definite to do I would feel less restless.

On Monday 31 March Roger arrives, 'looking awfully well'. The next day he and Annie go to see The Law Divine, *but have less success on Wednesday when they try to go to the very popular Marble Arch Pavilion: 'couldn't even get standing room'. They return to the same venue on Friday after dinner to see what was presumably a film of the recent boxing match at Covent Garden between Welsh flyweight world champion Jimmy Wilde, known as the 'Mighty Atom', and American Joe Lynch: 'Judging by the photographs I should think Lynch won: he seemed to be punishing Wilde at the time.' In fact, Wilde won on points.*

Saturday 5 April 1919 NZ beat England 6 to 3 Hurrah!

Answer to the cable of 12 March: 'Montgomerie present debit £360 – Surplus stock unsold owing to unfavourable markets – Estimate account in credit £500 after sale. Can have overdraft of £1,000.' Roger said it was better than he expected but it is a bitter disappointment to me. We have to thank this rotten country for the unfavourable markets as she took our ships to suit herself and hasn't returned them yet. I saw 'red' tonight in the smoking room but managed to keep quiet as some of the English creatures were discussing double tax together. They said we had enjoyed the hospitality of England and should contribute to its upkeep. They have charged us to the full for the hospitality!! The grabbing wasters.

Wednesday 9 April 1919
Gerry Barton told me he has offered to go to Russia. I did my best to dissuade him and told him the NZers were too good for that kind of work: it is only policing and debt collecting and much more of the English line than ours. But he said he has to look for a job as soon as he gets out of khaki and he likes to put it off as long as possible.

Sunday 13 April 1919
The anniversary of Gran's death. I tried last night to feel a message from her, but none came. There must always be unfulfilled longing – Ah me.

Letter from Roger to Annie, 13 April 1919
Sent in my repatriation papers last Tuesday. Counted 17 rabbits out of my kitchen window just now. T'is a horrible day here. Made Al pancakes this afternoon. Two more horses came last night and we want several more at once. The aerial rope way is progressing slowly and will not be finished for several months yet the way things are going on. It seems as though they want the wood to rot … All the men had to walk home yesterday, some 14 miles as the car was in repairs at Tavistock and there was some swearing at the start as it was raining hard and blowing strong. Monday it rained and blew a hurricane last night. Only one load more. Don't think anything will be done today.

Monday 14 April 1919
Os tells me that his dysentery is troubling him and he might be sent to a hospital at Hampstead which would be kapai [good].

Letter from Seton, 13 April 1919
This prohibition stunt is quite startling, and I shall be very keen to see the result … For myself, which is selfish, I like the odd spot, but for the family and country in general things might be better without it …[12]

12 Seton is referring to the special nationwide licensing referendum held in New Zealand on 11 April 1919. Prohibition seemed certain to be brought in but the votes of 40,000 troops still overseas or on ships meant defeat for the temperance movement.

Wednesday 16 April 1919 NZ beat England at Twickenham

Went to the ticket office and got three seats for football match 15/-, our ones were just behind the Royal box. Prince Albert was there, also Mr Massey and Colonel Hall. The match was exciting and our boys kept the 'stepmother's land' pretty much in hand. They had a couple of good men though who made a couple of brilliant spurts. The people around us were calling out 'England, England' and one little pup in front of us was being very sarcastic about 'our play' and when we won he took his beating pretty badly. It was lovely to see thousands waving their hats and cheering.

Less encouraging is the news in a letter from Roger to Annie, written the same day, concerning his request to the Controller of Timber Supplies in London for repatriation to New Zealand for Annie, Roger, Wid and Al, travelling first class. The answer from the Labour Section in Exeter states: 'I am directed to inform you that as you were not engaged on the understanding that a free passage would be provided for you and your family it is regretted your request cannot be granted.' To add to Roger's woes, 'it has been bitterly cold and windy'.

On the morning of Saturday 19 April Seton pays a shilling to visit the RAF exhibition of coloured photographs called War in the Air at the Grafton Galleries; he buys two prints. In the afternoon the family attends the France–New Zealand rugby match at Twickenham; the Kiwis triumph. Annie describes the scene.

Saw the King and four princes shaking hands with our team and present the cup. Then the Frenchmen came on and looked very fresh and clean in their red, white and blue. They also looked very alert and were a fine-looking crowd. They could run and kick awfully well. The first half the score was even but the next half our boys played up and the Frenchies were overpowered. One man had his pants ripped off him but he managed to save the situation by wrapping his torn garment round him. Then a new garment was produced and the two teams made a ring round and he changed. Another Frenchie has his ones torn and he also had to change. We won quite easily. Sir Douglas Haig and Sir Henry Wilson were present and Seton had to salute Sir Douglas as we passed him.

Easter Sunday 20 April
The Addingtons astonished me today by going to church this morning and dancing foxtrots this afternoon. It's a funny mentality.

Monday 21 April 1919
Went up to Hampstead Heath and walked around the sights, which were anything but savoury. Such sordid men and women, and you could smell them just like a Maori pa,[13] and such dirty people at the food stalls. The only nice sight was some aeroplanes flying round. As we came away several lots of drunken girls and men were getting there, such horrid-looking creatures.

Letter from Seton, 23 April 1919
It was like the proverbial valley of death, not a soul to be seen anywhere when I returned [from London] yesterday. We are a very small party now.

Letter from Roger to Annie, 23 April 1919
Your letter came with a copy re repatriation. I could have said a good deal more to the authorities in London – may yet if they do not comply with my instructions. Our motor driver smashed up a motor [car] last Thursday after taking all the men away, waipiro [alcohol] was the cause. Last night a big Argyle car came to grief not far from here and two of our horses pulled it off the road, it also had waipiro trouble with officers in it.

Thursday 24 April 1919
Went to see the ANZAC procession with Mrs Stephens near the bank, hardly a cheer from any of the crowd, in fact no cheer except from a few children across the street who greeted them all as they came along. Such a frozen up, petrified, ungrateful crowd. I hope the colonies will let them do their own fighting next time and see where they land. I spoke to some NZ boys. They said they always went to Scotland for their leave: they got a welcome there and never felt like that in England. They also said that the 'Tommies' didn't like them but the Jocks would always say, 'Hello diggers' and they replied, 'Hello Jock.' Heard a story about an Englishwoman who invited some Aussie soldiers to tea. When they arrived she showed them all over the house, evidently under the impression they were used to such. When

---

13 It is interesting to contrast Annie's attitude here, not unusual in its day, with the family's easy use of such Maori terms as 'kapai' and 'waipiro' and the 'Kia ora' on top of the cake sent to Seton by his aunt.

showing them the dining room she said, 'This is where we dine.' Then she marched them to the kitchen to make their tea and they declined it saying, 'If your housemaid had invited us we would have taken it with pleasure but when the mistress invites us we expect to have it where she does.'

At the end of April Annie is preparing a letter for the papers about 'wool, meat and shipping'; Mr Mills at the bank is not in favour, though he acknowledges 'it was correct what I said'. On 7 May she gives Os the letter to read 'and he is quite prepared to take it over and send it along in his name'. (The paper will not accept a letter from a woman.) It is posted on the 8th. The next day the Times *'contains news that sheep are selling for 4/- a head in NZ owing to congestion in freezing chambers: it is more than time my letter went to the press'. Then on 12 May: 'When I opened the* Daily Mail *our Magnus Opus was heading the paper column, quite a pleasant surprise.' Annie's letter also appears in the* British Australian *[newspaper] at the end of May, though she is not pleased as 'they have altered the sense of one of my points'.*

Saturday 3 May 1919
Went to see the Dominion Men's march.[14] We arranged to go to the Marble Arch cinema to get space on their balcony if we bought seats for the show – seats 14/-. We had a splendid view; it was an inspiring sight and all the men looked superb. For a wonder the crowd actually cheered. I waved my NZ flag to all the troops.

Seton, diary, 30 April 1919
All the colonials here not in the army of occupation received orders to go to repatriation camp at Harlaxton [in Lincolnshire]. The major heard rumours of them breaking things up and closed the bars and we think he ordered the power station to 'have trouble' so that the lights went out about 9.30. Feeling is pretty high about it.

Seton, diary, 1 May 1919
All colonials have moved to Harlaxton today. Civilian flying recommenced today.

Birthday card from Roger to Annie, 2 May 1919
Kia ora. Many happy returns of the day. RANGATIRA O TAUKORO

14 The Victory Parade of Dominion Troops, including New Zealanders, Australians and Canadians.

Letter from Roger to Annie, 6 May 1919

The meat ration is to be only 1/8 a week. The butchers are refusing to take only 40% finest meat and will not have any frozen unless they get 80% fresh down this way … Peace is a long time coming, isn't it? … I am quitting this job as soon as my correspondence is settled with the Board of Trade re repatriation … Am up every morning at 5 a.m., which is no good to me. I think the daylight bill is a rotten thing at any time and am sure that it will have a very deteriorating effect on the young people and children going to school. With twilight the days in this country are quite long enough … Don't know where to kill time until we go back but am thinking of going up north somewhere in Scotland. The Dartmeet is supposed to be very very pretty[15] … if only they could see the river in front of Taukoro house they would think nothing of this, it would knock the conceit out of them.

Letter from Seton, 7 May 1919

I expect you will be very annoyed over the little bit of news that follows. Just go eating that breakfast of yours and don't let the whole house know I have fallen victim to appendicitis. I had intended telling you before but they are operating sooner than I expected. This way will save you all the worry. I came here yesterday and the surgeon said he will operate tomorrow. He is one of the best surgeons in the country and makes a very small incision. Belton Park Hospital, Grantham will find me … Don't run away with the idea that I am bad because I have no pain at all, I have had it several months … I shall send a wire after the operation but you can be assured I will be all right.

Thursday 8 May 1919

After lunch a telegram arrived from Seton to say 'Operation successful, feeling fine'. I felt quite stunned and then Os told me that Seton had appendicitis hanging over him for several months and didn't want me to get worried so hadn't said anything. He had been keeping on going so as to secure his gratuity etc. After dinner got a letter from Seton that he meant me to get this morning.

Saturday 10 May 1919

Letter from Seton, written in pencil. He wasn't too bright but hoped another

---

15 Dartmeet, in the centre of Dartmoor, is a celebrated British beauty spot where the east and west tributaries of the Dart River meet.

24 hours would make an improvement. It was such a comfort to get it but it must have cost an effort to write it.

Letter from Roger to Annie, 11 May 1919

When you think about what Germany held before the war the peace terms seems pretty drastic. It is not dictating terms if they [Germans] are allowed a few days to consider them ... NZ will be in a terrible plight if the freezing works are not operating. Yet there seem to be a lot of boats going out which ought to relieve the congestion a little. The *Fifeshire* came from NZ with £67,000 worth of butter and cheese lately. Have had about two mouthfuls of cheese since coming to Brimpts [in Dartmoor] ... You might see Cecil Wray at the high commissioner's about it [repatriation]. He should be able to tell you if there is any chance ... Should we have to go on our own we should get away as soon as possible. It is in my mind we could get much cheaper lodgings down this way or in Scotland ... Taukoro is the place for me, not old England, Blighty.

Seton is hard on his mother immediately after his appendectomy. In a letter written on the 13th he berates her for sending grapes: 'If you waste any more money on them I will cease all diplomatic relations immediately. They might be useful when one is unable to eat anything else but I have no use for them ... No space for any more Aucklands [papers]: I possess two tiny shelves for my present daily use. I think you and I had better write every two days now. I am not dying or anything like that so I see no necessity for wasting energy at all.' But his mood is probably a result of the infection — what he calls 'puss' — he has developed, which requires further operations on the 15th and again on the 17th. By the 18th he is much better — 'After the first operation I never felt right and put it down to the nervous state I had been reduced to' — and on the 19th he can report that he is 'feeling very fit' and 'getting over that bad weariness'. Os visits on the 25th and by the 28th Seton is able to spend the afternoon 'out in the shade of the trees. They took me out in a wheeled conveyance and I sat in a big armchair with my feet propped up. There was a beautiful cool breeze blowing.'

On 10 June he writes: 'I have been walking around a bit, but they won't let me loose at all until the wound has healed up. Under the impression that the hip is weak I have to wear an enormous flannel bandage round my stomach and hip to give it support.' Four days later: 'I am allowed to walk a little more now, but I can't stand long without my nerves starting to shake. Sometimes I find it impossible to write as my hand refuses to act in a reasonable manner. My nerves were nothing to write home about before I came in, but the puss has taken them lower so that when they do get fit my arms are useless for writing. It shows I will have to pull myself together.' By the 18th he is feeling 'quite strong'. At his medical board on the 24th he is granted a month's leave.

Sunday 18 May 1919

Wid has a new friend, a Canadian. He is a nice boy of 21 and has been in France three years without a wound but his nerves are quite shaky, poor kid.

Monday 19 May 1919

Miss Cowlishaw gave me the last *British Australian* to look at as it has a leader in answer to my press letter. Found their shop near Chancery Lane and got four copies 4/-.

Tuesday 20 May 1919

Sat in smoking room and heard the verdict about Hawker's attempt to cross the Atlantic.[16] They think it is foolhardiness and can never be done – and shouldn't be allowed. If it had been successful I can imagine how they would have been holding forth about British pluck.

Thursday 22 May 1919

Os arrived about 11 and went off for NZHQ. He has been refused his 'flying' and now all his energies are directed towards repatriation. He also mentioned Dad's application, which they say has never arrived yet. Anyhow it doesn't seem altogether certain we can get it [a passage home] through Dad, so that means more fighting to be done. The heat has been intolerable and I can hardly crawl along; I am feeling very off colour the last few days. Os is appearing in mufti.

Letter from Roger to Annie, 23 May 1919

I am posting this with a repatriation paper from Plymouth Labour Exchange which they have asked me to fill in and return immediately. They may be asking too much so I am sending it along for you and Wid to ponder over and advise me what to do.

---

16 Harry George Hawker (1889–1921) was an Australian aviator who, in May 1919, attempted, with a co-pilot, Kenneth Grieve, to win the *Daily Mail* £10,000 prize for the first successful trans-Atlantic crossing. After many hours' flying the plane's engine overheated and the pair were forced to abandon their flight. A Danish freighter picked them up. The vessel had no radio so the pilots were feared lost until they arrived in Scotland. The *Daily Mail* awarded Hawker and Grieve a consolation prize of £5000. Hawker died in 1921 while practising for an airshow at Hendon. Seton also mentions Hawker's exploits in his letters.

Saturday 24 May 1919 Wid's birthday Went to sports at Walton
Letter from Seton, which sounds quite cheerful. He expects to be in bed at least another week, but the wound is not sore now. There has been a service in memory of the colonials who fell in the war. After lunch we set off for Waterloo to go to Walton for the sports. I lost my new veil on the way, which is most upsetting as it cost 25/-. We went into a tea shop, when the Masseys came Miss Massey came to sit with our crowd. Mrs [Christina] Massey was as nice as ever. Altogether it was quite a nice gathering of NZers. Felt very off colour all day.

Sunday 25 May 1919
Os was up early this morning, he has gone off to Grantham to see Seton. I stayed in bed all day to see if bed will pick me up, I seem to have caught a chill. Heard the good news that Hawker has been saved. We were very excited and joyful to hear it. Os got back about 11 p.m. He brought quite a good report of Seton even though it will be another month before he can get away from Belton Park Hospital. Os says the appendix looks a real monster.

Tuesday 27 May 1919
I spent the third day in bed but Cowlie went along to see the crowd welcoming Hawker. They mobbed him so much that a policeman had to take him up behind him on horseback and later gave up his horse to him. Cowlie said he looked like he had more than enough of 'worship'.

Wednesday 28 May 1919
Feel throaty and achy yet, but want to be doing things. Sat on balcony with Cowlie for a while before lunch. Every person would say, 'And are you better?' to which I invariably replied, 'Oh, yes thank you' and all the time I felt giddy and weak. These solicitations always annoy me. Wid got me some tonic at Atkins; I hope it pulls me together.

Annie continues to be unwell – 'weak and miserable' on Thursday and 'queer and ill' on her way to the bank on Saturday. Then it is Os's turn. After 'looking wretched' on Friday he comes down with a malarial attack on Sunday; 'gave him quinine, hot water bags and rugs and sent for Dr Groves. The doctor has ordered a restful day and gave him a month's course of treatment which he says will cure the malaria. The quinine is making him heavy headed.'

Friday 6 June 1919
This morning's mail has a cable from NZ to say this government here is trying to make arrangements with NZ about meat so that they can combat the American trusts and prevent them from lowering! the prices – I nearly exploded. America can never lower our prices like England has or exploit us. England has and there has been no trust of any kind in this war or otherwise to equal England's corner of our meat and wool. She is crafty and grabbing, but I do hope our NZers won't be such fools to be taken in by her. Have talked to people about the English government exploitation of the colonies.

Saturday 7 June 1919
Wid went to a dance at the Huttons [among a number of balls she attends] and didn't get back till until 1.30 this morning. I was getting very alarmed. Went to the bank, met Miss Massey: she says they are going home next week. Mr Mills gave me a great fright by saying I was £700 overdrawn. It turned out the letter of credit sent last December was not cabled for; I signed the papers today. I am fearfully worried because that means we will be that much shorter.

Wednesday 11 June 1919
Letter from Seton, he talks about getting dressed so he is getting on. Found that Wid had a horrid time at the dentist and two wisdom teeth extracted; she was pretty shaken up. After dinner packed till 2 a.m. ready to go to Devon.

Thursday 12 June 1919
After arriving at Tavistock did some shopping, Mrs Truscott got us a victoria as all the taxis were away at the Truro show. The temperature here is absolutely cold, yet it was frizzlingly hot when we left London. Tavistock looked very pretty and the country as restful and peaceful as ever. Everywhere we went this afternoon we were welcomed; it was a very nice feeling after the casualness of London.

Friday 13 June 1919

Wid's face is still swollen and it is very cold here. After breakfast mended all day, I feel restless and unhappy. I always feel I have dropped out of the world when I come down here and this time I am anxious to hear about Os so I have stuck doggedly at my mending and tried to work off the blue devils.

Saturday 14 June 1919

No word from Os, which worried me very much. We went down to Mrs Doidge's to see if we could get her jingle as this one is out of repair and the pony in use. The poor old thing was cleaning her stove but she insisted on us going in and gave us every detail of her son's illness and Charlie's death. It was perfectly tragic to hear it all, and she was very broken about it. Dad arrived about 3 o/c, had a bath and got changed, we got the jingle and went into town. It is the first time Dad has been away from Brimpts since he was in London and has £22 saved up. He is looking very brown and healthy but is thinner. When we got back we found a letter from Os to say he is feeling much better, but doesn't expect to manage his sick leave.

Thursday 19 June 1919

In Oswald's letter he does away with his idea of going back to NZ very soon as he is being treated with injections which are supposed to cure malaria. It means another couple of months anyhow over here. He had the first injection last Monday and it brought on an attack of fever so he had to stay in hospital that night. He is to come to London every Monday for an injection.

Saturday 21 June 1919

A wire came from Os: 'Going to a repatriation camp at Uxbridge on Monday.' I don't quite understand the wire. I sincerely hope he won't be going away soon. I thought he was safe for a couple of months while undergoing his malaria treatment. Seton's letter says he expects to get to London this week.

Sunday 22 June 1919 Wid and I went to Brimpts with Dad

Dad's little wooden hut is very primitive and comfortless, but it has many little fixings in it that show Dad's presence there. The foxgloves were ablaze in the fields nearby in pretty surroundings. We walked up to the mill, which is quite a big affair, and from there past Brimpts farm, crowds of rabbits were hopping round in the fields. Roger decided he would come back with us, so we went to Dartmeet first and called at Two Bridges Hotel on the way and had tea.

On Tuesday 24 June Annie notes that 'Mrs Reddicliffe says all their hearts warm to us and they will be sorry when we leave England'. The same day she receives a letter from fellow 40 Inverness Terrace resident Miss Cowlishaw, to whom she had sent a photo: 'It will always remind me of our little time together and the big heart of the Little Mother of New Zealand who helped so many over their hard places.' This is not the full extent of Miss Cowlishaw's admiration. On 1 July she writes to 'dear little Mummie: This is just to say how much I am missing you. I am upstairs and do miss your pretty little head popping round the door and your hands full of dainties! When the Great War called you out of your cocoon you spread your wings and came …'

Seton, diary, 25 June 1919 21st BIRTHDAY
Captain Alexander died this morning about 7.30. This was a cheerful start to my 21st birthday. I got my warrant and caught the 9.50 to London. Went to Cox's in the afternoon. Os came about 8.30 and had dinner with me at '40'. I went for a walk in Kensington Gardens and then went to bed.

Thursday 26 June 1919
The boys arrived a little after 7.30. If anything Seton looks brighter than Os. Os was very hungry so we got supper together as quickly as possible. It's lovely to have both boys here together.

Friday 27 June 1919
It was rainy and dull in the morning but cleared off later. A wire came from Miss Fearon to say Al was coming by the 6.30 train, so we got the four-cylinder Studebaker car from Truscotts and brought Al safely home. The boys were very interested in the car and gave it a good overhaul when we got out. Al's arrival gave universal pleasure. Had a supper of fried fish and strawberries and cream and then went for a walk up Pew Tor. Seton stood the walk into town quite wonderfully. It has been a great surprise the way he can get about, and to think that only a few weeks back they wanted to put

him on the DI [dangerously ill] list but the head sister wouldn't hear of it because it meant sending for the relations and getting the padre to call.

Saturday 28 June 1919
Poor old Seton had a very bad night and was sick at 4 o/c. He thinks the rich cream upset him. He has been very weak and out of sorts all day. The farm shearing was on today, we all went up to see it. The boys were almost exploding over the exhibition of shearing. The sheep were penned in one end of the barn by two long feed boxes, which they moved about as they wanted sheep, and the shorn sheep were pushed back there again. Jack Reddicliffe was just quite at home and making a manful effort but the other two were pitiful. Reggie was just too funny clipping away at a lamb … The flags have been flying in Tavistock for the signing of the peace [at Versailles that afternoon]. Seton has been feeling the cold so we gathered some sticks and had a fire this evening. The shearers were having some rackety revels in the kitchen and quite enjoying themselves. Roger came from Brimpts about 3 o/c and we were a complete family, with my old heart at rest for one night anyhow. Roger and Os shared a room and Seton had Al's bed as he needed a bed to rest himself properly.

Sunday 29 June 1919
Seton is much better but still rather weak, making him take phosferine and port wine. After dinner the car came and we set off again for Brimpts. We had to go to Tavistock for the dickey seats of the car, which young Truscott had forgotten to put in. The boys took some photos of Dad's hut and the woods, then we went to Dartmeet. A charabanc full of people started up Dartmoor hill just as we left, it was belching out smoke at a great rate, we left Dad at his gateway and came home via Two Bridges hotel, where we had tea … Os going back to London on Tuesday.

Thursday 3 July 1919
Walked up the Tor where we talked to Miss Watson and her friend. The friend is a very plain English lady who has a very poor opinion of NZ because a cousin of hers had gone out there and found it so hard to get servants and had to receive their bishop 'almost over a wash tub'. This old girl had sent a maid out and she had been married in two months! In the

end her cousin came back to England a perfect wreck. This evening letter came for Dad from the Ministry of Labour saying his application has been approved so now we are in a twitter of excitement. We had some <u>real</u> lamb for dinner today and enjoyed it very much.

Tuesday 8 July 1919
Seton found a car in yesterday's news and it was in again today so he determined to have a try for it. He managed to get the jingle and he and Wid drove into town and sent a wire asking if it was still for sale, and if so would call and give it a trial. A wire came in reply so tomorrow he is off to St Ives to see it. Sewing all day, it was Gladys' birthday and we gave her 5/- from us all. There has been a 'hay sweeting' epidemic this afternoon.[17] After supper the boys came into the passage and invited Wid to go to be hay sweeted. Edie called out, 'Miss Montgomerie, young John wants to hay sweet 'ee.' They call hay making Saving the Hay.

Wednesday 9 July 1919
A letter for Dad from the Shipping Authorities granting himself, wife and youngest daughter repatriation but refusing Wid as she is over 18. Seton went off early to catch the train to Hayle. He can't have found the car any good as no wire has arrived tonight about it. Mrs Hutton [from London] arrived and went up Pew Tor with us. Mrs H. tried very hard to get in here but couldn't succeed. She asked for Doidges' jingle to go back with and went off without paying – she is an absolute pusher, the less I see of her the better I will be pleased.

Thursday 10 July 1919
A letter came about a Broadwood baby grand [piano] which I have been inquiring about. It is £60: a bit more than I want to give. A wire came from Seton saying he would arrive on the 8.15 train. I drove the jingle and made Spider step it out. Seton enjoyed his trip immensely.

Friday 11 July 1919
Got a bombshell in the post, a letter from Os saying he will be sailing for NZ next Wednesday the 16th on the *Cape Verde*. It is an Australian transport the size of the *Remuera*. His letter also mentions that those blighters

17 Hay sweeting consists of doing one's utmost to kiss and rub hay in the faces of a member of the opposite sex.

have only granted us third class passages and that means more worrying and battling. I am feeling blue and worried. I do hope he can come and see us before he goes.

Monday 14 July 1919

Three letters from Os. There is just a chance the boat will be delayed until the end of the month. He seems to be bustling around at a great rate.

Thursday 17 July 1919

The Huttons landed on us again. They shared a horse between them, taking turn about. What Mrs H. looked like history doesn't relate. They are staying at a farm quite close to Tavistock. Found a four-leafed clover when I was walking down the drive with Mrs Hutton.

Saturday 19 July 1919 Beacons of peace lit

It has been a pouring wet day and I guess the procession in London will have its ardour cooled. I don't like these official demonstrations a bit and it seems to me fitting for nature to weep over the day and the dead than all their pomp and horse play.[18] At 10.30 we all went up Pew Tor to see all the beacons, Seton had his camera and took several snaps of the lights, Plymouth was sending up rockets and searchlights and the chain of beacons stretching along the hilltops of Devon and Cornwall was a thrilling sight. If only one could really believe they meant Beacons of Peace. It was very cold and we snuggled in behind a rock and sat there some time. I thought of London and its revels and I was glad to be on old Pew Tor with the great silent moors around me while I watched those lights and thought of the great price that has been paid for them. Then we stumbled down, Seton lighting us with his torch.

Sunday 20 July and Monday 21 July 1919 Farewell Devon

Packed up till dinnertime. After supper went up dear old Pew Tor to see the sun set and say 'Goodbye' to our beloved landscape. The sun was beautiful as it sank; we pictured it shining on Taukoro. Then we went up the tor and gazed on the sweet chessboard fields, all red, green, brown and yellow. It is a bonny landscape full of quiet peaceful beauty … When it came to saying 'Goodbye' Mrs Reddicliffe broke down completely, also Mrs Jeffrey, Goldie

18 Official peace celebrations were held in New Zealand at the same time. The Treaty of Versailles, ending the state of war between Germany and the Allies, had been signed on 28 June.

and Gladys joined in. So we left with the feeling we were really to be missed and they were genuinely sorry to lose us. Mrs R. is always bright and sunny and it seemed so strange to see her otherwise. We had a great load in the car but it managed it. No dining car on the train and precious little of anything to be got.

Tuesday 22 July 1919
It has been a shockingly disappointing day. Mr Mills and the cashier were absent on holiday and so it wasn't so nice at the bank, the shipping berths have been messed about and Os didn't come as planned.

Wednesday 23 July 1919
Seton had a satisfactory meeting with the shipping authorities. He has been sent to our NZ Commissioner and now we are under our own 'flag' again, which is good news indeed. Os arrived and Al arrived from Southlands. Dad filled in the HC papers about our passages and we made a good clearance of bundles into cupboard etc. Os seems brighter today. It has been a tiring day but a happy one. Al is looking much thinner but bonny.

CHAPTER THIRTEEN | LAST DAYS

After a trip to what Annie describes as 'Scotland, land of my dreams', to see the places her ancestors came from, the family returns to an extremely hot London on Saturday 16 August. 'The heat is very trying and Roger is very crotchety. He is always cursing his "B" stiff collars and pressed trousers. He is quite childish on the point.' On Tuesday the family learns that 'there is little chance of us getting away before Jan or Feb, but the boys have every chance and there is quite a chance for Roger too but not us feminines'. By Wednesday Roger is still 'fearfully crabby' about his collars and breakfast is 'very cool': 'I'm hanged if I can see why he should be such a trial. He's got a kink for sure.' Annie does 'a lot a lot of shopping' and takes in her stole and musquash to be 'beaten up'.

Tuesday 2 September 1919
It's the limit to think what a nightmare this business of repatriation is. They were nimble enough in bringing our boys over but now they have to take any chance to get back. Os has the chance to go via San Francisco but he would have to pay £45 on the last part of the journey.

Tuesday 9 September 1919
Went to the high commissioner's, heard a story about a naval fellow who was certain that the war was a glorious thing for England, she was making so much out of it. Spoke to a Mr Cameron; he is English and so biased. I told him when the English government asks any further favours from NZ it won't be my fault if they don't get a nasty rebuff.

Friday 12 September 1919
Woke Os early, he was having breakfast when I got down. There was only one letter addressed to me – from the bank. When I opened it I found it was a cable with the terrible news that Archie [Annie's brother] was killed when riding. His horse fell. It was too shocking to grasp at first. Even now it seems

like an awful nightmare. Os had to rush off to catch his train to Winchester and I came straight upstairs; I couldn't face breakfast. Everyone was upset and shocked, but whatever will poor Aunt Ethel and the boys do? All our thoughts went out to them. Later Wid and I went out and sent a cable to Ethel. I did some mending. I couldn't write today.

Tuesday 16 September 1919

Had a rest after lunch as I was feeling absolutely washed out, ordered tonic and byne hypophosphite.[1] Finished up letter on government profiteering.

Friday 19 September 1919

Al and I went to South Kensington to see the washing up machines. Roger wouldn't come. We were very satisfied with the demonstration; they seem to be a very good proposition.

Wednesday 24 September 1919

Went looking for costumes [suits]. In one little shop there was one for 35 guineas, fur cuffs and collar! We will hunt up ideas on styles and see Mrs Thomassett's tailor to make up. One guest here, Commander Underwood, was away from England for some time and now feels a stranger and disgusted with what is going on … A big railway strike is brewing.[2]

Friday 26 September 1919

We hear the strike is arranged for midnight tonight. Oh dear, this is a good country to get out of. Dad and Seton went to the HC today and he thought there is a possibility of our getting away in November. Hope on, hope ever.

Saturday 27 September 1919 Railway strike

Papers were full of railway strike, which has reached a very sudden crisis. Seton and I decided to go the bank. We got on a 20 bus to Marble Arch, walked to Bond St and caught another bus from there. Caught an Army Lorry no. 17 back home.

Sunday 28 September 1919

Went to Met station for my papers, no further developments of the strike. Spent the morning arguing unsatisfactorily with Roger about the poor

---

1 Byne is another word for malt so Annie seems to have bought a malt extract.

2 Railway workers throughout Britain struck from 26 September to 5 October over an agreement to standardise wages that would mean wage cuts for some. The railway companies and the government backed down.

wretched strikers' point of view and their rights as human beings. Made arrangements with Mrs Fraser to meet to go the Albert Hall to hear Melba.[3] We joined a queue waiting to get in. Some of Melba's notes beautiful but I don't really like her. She sang 'Mary of Argyle' and murdered it. The tenor was good and the pianiste. The hall itself is a great sight with its rows and rows of humanity. Mrs Fraser came back for dinner. She and Commander Underwood had a pretty hot argument about the strikers and their pay. He got quite hot and was rather rude, saying people from other countries were too fond of coming here and criticising their affairs. I found lots of amusement listening to some women in the queue discussing Clara Butt;[4] they said she was of 'no origin'.

Monday 29 September 1919

Went to Piccadilly Circus by bus. The manner and tone of the bus conductor didn't bode well for the public at large and I expect no buses tomorrow. Coming past Hyde Park today a woman remarked to me that it looked like war again, and I said, 'It is war.' She was very bitter about the workers, said the British workman was the curse of England and the leaders should all be shot! I didn't say what I thought, just 'boiled up inside'. These rotten smug creatures who have sweated the souls and bodies out of British workmen all these generations until the poor devils are hardly human. Commander Underwood asked Al if he had offended me. I'm glad his conscience pricks him.

Wednesday 1 October 1919

Seton wrote to the *Times* suggesting that Geddes should be asked to disappear from the political horizon and then things might straighten out.[5] At afternoon tea Commander Underwood came and sat beside us and asked if he had done anything to drive me from the smoking room – I seldom use the room at all. I couldn't say what I wanted with all the old tabbies listening. So he chatted away the same as usual. The news today is very serious as they are debating a general strike. The commander is of the same mind as ourselves about Geddes, says he can't understand why they don't see for themselves they ought to resign.

---

3 Dame Nellie Melba (1861–1931), the famous Australian soprano.

4 English contralto Clara Butt (1872–1936), who received a DBE in 1920, two years after Melba. Both women were honoured for their war work.

5 Sir Eric Campbell Geddes (1875–1937), a former First Lord of the Admiralty and Britain's much-criticised inaugural Minister of Transport from May 1919 until his resignation in 1921.

Thursday 2 October 1919

There seems to be a possibility of the strike being tided over if Lloyd George doesn't try to cover over his responsibilities too much; he hasn't made a very sensible beginning. These people here are crowing already about the strikers having to climb down. I think they are a bit previous.

Friday 3 October 1919

I tried to draft a letter for the press to show up the government's case against the strikers. The papers today are very serious as negotiations have failed, or rather reached a deadlock. No wonder, these people here are not very smart. President Wilson is very ill, so that means one of the strongest influences for good in this world is tottering.

Saturday 4 October 1919

News in paper very serious this morning. The strike negotiations have failed; the Geddes crowd are determined to save their face at the expense of the country's safety. The ASE men who behaved so disgracefully in the war, refusing to be conscripted like other trades, are helping Lloyd George, who saved them from France. I've no doubt his conscientious objector friends are also doing noble work for him! There is a flavour about some of the volunteer workers, rotten brutes that wouldn't lift a finger to fight for their country while the railway men did their bit.

Sunday 4 October 1919

Had a talk with Ettie, the maid, after breakfast. She told me of many wrongs the workers have to endure. There is very bitter feeling among the working classes, and no wonder. The papers are full of the strike and some of the articles are shockingly twisted and misrepresented. These smug people make me want to hit them. At dinner time people here came home with the news of the strike being ended, but no word as to what solution has been found. These smug creatures have been enjoying themselves picturing the strikers' discomfort and the expression on their faces. They return to work tomorrow. I hope the morning news will give them a bump the other way.

Monday 6 October 1919

Roger and I went to the high commissioner to see about the repatriation passages. We had a real go at the staff and I managed to let them have the benefit of most of my opinions about the English government and I told them it would be to their own good to get us away as we are only getting more and more discontented the longer we stay. They promised faithfully to try to put us on the *Kigoma* next month. I told Mr Balfour I would trust him as he is a Scotsman. The strike news did give those smug ones a bump: it is a compromise with the honours in favour of the strikers. The government overreacted itself with all its preparations and propaganda.

Monday 13 October 1919 Oswald's 23rd birthday
The little tailor that Mrs Fraser recommended is quite a genius at cutting out. He never measured us but just glanced at us and set to work with chalk and scissors and by the time he had cut out both he was ready to fit the first one.

Tuesday 14 October 1919
Paid Mrs Underwood's hairdresser a visit, had an electric hair massage; I am taking a course of them three times a week. Bought some hair-waving irons. Met a guest who told us her husband is a drug taker and a drinker and they live apart. We were very sorry but we decided that women must demand a higher standard from men and that they should have a say in the making of laws, which at present are so unfair to them.

Wednesday 15 October 1919
Called to see the tailor and had a fitting. Next Roger and I went to HC's and were told to come back on Friday for definite news. The *Kigoma* sails on November 15th.

Friday 17 October 1919
Went to see the high commissioner. We were met with very cold comfort. He practically held no definite hope so I blazed up and we had a go with the foils off. I told him if we had not been depending on him we could have paid our complete fare with what we had to spend on board here. Then he protested about the shipping shortage and I told him plainly that was only a bluff or why were the English authorities selling ships to Italy? I said in the next war we would see things were different and in any case they wouldn't

have the chance to hold us up because none of us would bother to help again. Later went to the little tailor's and had another big disappointment there; my costume is a frost [failure], Al's is pretty fair. Found a letter from sister Jen giving sad details of Archie's death. After dinner just sat too tired and unhappy to do anything when Roger came upstairs with a telegram from the HC saying they may be able to place us on the *Ruahine* on 31st October, if we call in the morning. We were all very pleased, happy and glad, our hopes are rising again.

Saturday 18 October 1919

Had a short treatment for my hair and then hurried off to the HC. Roger got there first and saw Dr Innes, who is booked for the *Ruahine*. We had a long wait, then were told we have two two-berth cabins in the second class part of the ship. We couldn't risk being hung up here indefinitely. It was impressed upon me the difficulty of making the Ministry of Shipping realise the existence of such small specks on the map as NZ and other colonies. I said, 'Oh indeed. They didn't find them too small specks on the battlefield', and we had another round with the foils off. Roger wrote a cheque for £194. Wid's is a first class fare for second class accommodation.

Sunday 19 October 1919

Oswald has to go into hospital with dysentery. He has been troubled with it … he doesn't look well at all. He has to report sick at Hampstead. He expects to be there about a month, which washes out hopes of him getting on our boat.

Wednesday 29 October 1919

Our sailing orders came. Seton has been put on the roll for the *Bremen*, and made arrangements for Os too. I feel it's the best plan for the boys to travel together, but I would give a lot to have them both on our boat.

Friday 31 October 1919

Closed accounts at bank. Roger drew £100 and sent £50 to Auckland and I drew £20 and sent £150 to Wanganui. Cowlie put on a dinner party for us at Les Gobelins; Dad wouldn't come. We had a nice dinner and then went to see Leslie Henson and Phyllis Dare in *Kissing Time*.[6]

6   Leslie Henson (1891–1957) was an English comedian, actor producer and director. *Kissing Time* marked his return to the West End after helping to run a concert party during the war. Phyllis Dare (1890–1975) was an English singer and actress who first appeared on stage at the age of nine.

Saturday 1 November 1919

Roger got a note from [Thomas] Cook saying he could get third class railway fares from Auckland to Wanganui. After lunch we took the bus to the Gaiety Theatre. We had several stoppages on the way – the first bus broke down and the next bus was off its usual route because the Shah of Persia was tripping round in London. The Tilleys were at Buckingham Palace last night in his honour.

Sunday 2 November 1919 Left London

After breakfast got to work on the last awful bit of packing. To everyone's surprise we got through in time to have a wee stroll to the Round Pond before lunch. Os arrived about 11 o/c so he and Seton, with Dad's help, got straps round the luggage, ropes tied and boxes labelled in A1 style. Our luggage made a goodly pile in the hall. After lunch the van arrived and both boys went with it to the station. We had quite a crowd to farewell us. We couldn't get third class seats so took first. There were a lot of NZers we knew on the station. Os was looking much brighter, assured me he was feeling jake [fine], but I hate to come away without him. The guard made a fuss of us travelling first but calmed down later on. Didn't read at all on the train, felt too 'mopey'. We were late getting to Torquay but Seton got us a cab and we went to the Torquay Hotel.

Monday 3 November 1919 Sailed from Torquay – England's last freeze-out

The hotel conveyance took our luggage and we walked to the jetty. Torquay must be very bonny in the sunshine but we unfortunately only saw it under wet conditions. The jetty was crowded with English mob onlookers who just got in the way and added to the general muddle. And it was a muddle. We were kept standing in the drizzle from 10 o/c until 12 o/c before we got on the tender which rejoiced in the name *Sir Walter Raleigh* – looked like some ancient galley and rolled like nothing on earth. The diggers worked like busy ants and got all the piles of luggage on board, and off we went.[7] Seton managed to get on too. He had lunch with us and looked over the ship. We had a long wait collecting our things as the diggers had a strike over their quarters and refused to go on with their work. About halfway through they slowed down: 'No lunch, no luggage'. In the end we got all our stuff safely

---

7   The New Zealand Shipping Company's *Ruahine* was carrying both passengers and returning troops to New Zealand.

on board. Seton and Dad collected all the cabin stuff. Seton was an absolute Godsend to us; we would have been lost without him. After tea Seton had to rush off, the tender was hooting vigorously. It was hard to see the beastly thing going away with him. It takes away all the joy of going back when I have to leave half my treasures behind me, but I am sure God will keep them safely for me. The *Ruahine* set sail and the sea was calm; she seems a good steady boat. I went down to bed and the others went on deck, feeling very 'mopey'. Roger's cabin is opposite ours and we can gaze at one another's. We were all glad that the last sight of England was dear old Devon.

CHAPTER FOURTEEN | GOING HOME

As the New Zealand newspapers report, the Ruahine *is carrying 382 troops, 46 civilians, 141 women and 41 children. The class divisions are soon all too evident.*

Tuesday 4 November 1919

Stewardess arrived at 6 a.m. with tea. It was a sunny morning with calm seas. Wid could watch a colour scheme in sky from her top berth and also see a big ship sailing by. We all got up for breakfast and later on established ourselves on deck. The diggers were grouped about in angry mood and some of them parading the first deck in angry defiance of barriers but after a while matters were patched up.[1] Mrs Innes sat beside us and we talked but before long the Bay of Biscay took effect and she had to retire. Very soon after the whole ship practically bowled over. Al and Dad lasted until after lunch and then had to give in. None of our lot got up to dinner. Stewardess brought us some fruit, which was all Wid and I had since breakfast barring tea, which only made us worse – ship's tea is always vile stuff. Some chaffinches are on the ship; Captain Greenstreet says they will hang on until we get to Tenerife.

Wednesday 5 November 1919

All up to breakfast and up on deck until lunchtime. Troops were paraded for fumigation and the CO addressed a group of privates along side of us. They were up against the [New Zealand] Shipping Co. and its treatment of them. In the end the CO dispersed them in peace. Dr Innes appeared this morning but not Mrs Innes. They have been allotted a crummy berth in 1st and also moved to the 1st dining saloon. The diggers and their wives and families have practically taken possession of the 2nd class deck besides calmly moving all over the ship. I can't take any interest in their wives although some may be quite nice. Al spent some time this morning trying to sketch the diggers etc. Nothing has settled down yet and every one is more or less

---

1 Because there were what the *Auckland Star* of 29 December would describe as 'a considerable number of first-class civilians and military passengers … on board what was supposed to be simply a troopship', they had been given the second-class accommodation, 'making it necessary for the warrant officers, sergeants and their wives and children to occupy third-class quarters'. And when the men saw the bad condition of their inferior quarters, they left the ship with their possessions and went to the commanding officer, 'with the object of securing the full use of the second-class accommodation, to which they were entitled, and for which they had paid on behalf of their wives'. Perhaps unsurprisingly, the top brass did not see things the same way, and there was much argument until 'After considerable demur they went on board, being given to understand that it was a case of "take it or leave it," and that if they did not take it they could be struck off the roll'.

discontented. None of us get the 11 o/c snack except the 1st saloon, which is grossly unfair seeing we have paid the same as them. The shipping control is reaping a big harvest out of us – more English exploitation.

Thursday 6 November 1919
A very rough night and morning. Even Al found it hard to get dressed. She was quite sick during process. Dad and Wid got up also but Al was the only one who could get down to breakfast. I stayed in bed all day. I managed to scribble a few lines to each boy and then found that the mail didn't close this evening after all. Had a bottle of soda water and some fruit for my dinner and we all had a glass of stout going to bed.

Friday 7 November 1919
Beautiful morning with calm sea and all of us managed to get up for breakfast. Stewardess brought Al some grapes this morning. Went on deck after breakfast and most of the passengers rolled up again ... At 11 o/c the colonel who travelled down with us got soup for his mother and Miss Russell but the latter wouldn't have it and he asked me to which I did. Then Dr Innes got some for his wife and Wid, and Dad, after interviewing the steward, managed to get some for himself and Al. They don't seem to think we in 2nd saloon need it but we will have to let them know plainly that we intend to have it ... After lunch rested until tea time. It was a glorious moonlight night with masses of white clouds. The diggers had a concert and dance among themselves.

Saturday 8 November Tenerife
All up to breakfast, a hot sunny day with smooth, oily sea. Sat on deck for a little and then posted my letters and spent rest of morning in cabin putting away warm things etc. Just before lunch we saw an island in the distance and before tea we could see one of the Canaries ... After tea we had boat drill: we all had to put on our lifebelts and answer the roll at our appointed boat. The sun was pouring its rays on us and people were getting very sun burned. The 11 o/c trouble is settled very satisfactorily and we go along to 1st and get it. The island in sight was Tenerife. Its highest point stands out like Mt Egmont and is about the height of Mt Cook. We stood about after tea watching it grow nearer and after dinner

we were quite close to its rocky looking hills and we could see the lights of town twinkling and blinking to us. We didn't go ashore but the natives came out to us in boats and swarmed round the ship. Such a Babel it was for each boatload wanted to sell its wares … The troops were ready buyers but the Taukoros only got 1/- bananas and some boxes of cigars. Nothing was cheap and the lacework was on cotton. We dropped anchor about 9 o/c and left about 12 o/c. The mosquito fleet of bargainers rowed away in the moonlight, each boat with a lantern alight on board and soon Tenerife was just a fading picture of groups and lines of twinkling lights. Going in this evening the sunset had left a rosy glow in sky, which was very beautiful – we were all very sore about not being able to land and not to be able to see it in daylight. Now we are on our way to Cape Town.

The Ruahine *was to have sailed via Panama, but is diverted to Cape Town owing to a miners' strike in the United States and coaling problems.*

Monday 10 November 1919
It turned fearfully hot towards evening. After dinner the diggers gave a concert and most of us went. It was a very poor affair and the heat was appalling sitting on that side of the deck. The diggers' songs were decidedly common. Two English girls sang and they were painful specimens. A ship with lights glowing in the distance passed during the concert. Afterwards we Taukoros had a lemon squash and went to bed. A lot of English wives were camping on deck before we left. There seems to be a big margin of very ordinary men on board – and they have no end of assurance.

Tuesday 11 November 1919 Passed Cape Verde
Up early for bath; it was unpleasantly hot from earliest morning. After breakfast there didn't seem to be a cool spot on the ship … Major Brow sat and talked for a while and later on Roger joined us. Major B got pretty hot because Roger spoke rather bluntly about England's meat bluff. After lunch sat a while on deck and then came down and rested on Al's berth until tea time. Had a hot argument with the Scotch boy who sits beside me at table, about the Americans – he hates them. After tea stood on deck and watched Cape Verde – we were quite close to it … They are making a fuss about 'lavs' etc too – 150 women use the four 'lavs' next to us and they are

beginning to be offensive. A case of scarlet fever has broken out on board and there is general consternation for fear we shall not be able to call at Cape Town.

Wednesday 12 November 1919

The heat through the night was intense and today the sea is oily and the heat still unbearable. Just wore vest and pants and my frock; even then, I oozed at every pore … After dinner the deck was cleared for dancing between 1st and 2nd class but it wasn't a great success. They didn't fraternise very much. Both girls danced but they found that their Madam Van Dyke style was ahead of most of their partners. The diggers danced Maxinas etc with great gusto – Dad didn't dance.

As the voyage continues Annie has plenty to say about shipboard behaviour. On 16 November she is most unimpressed when she attends the Sunday church service. 'We had a sing song and hymns and then it was given out that as Padre Ross was ill a sergeant would take the service and Colonel Williams got up and walked off. The sergeant spoke quite fluently – just a short discourse. I didn't hesitate to tell Colonel Pilkington that I thought it beastly bad form of Colonel Williams to deliberately walk off as he did during the service.' The next day there is a 'very good concert on deck' at which a digger plays a harp and another sings 'a song full of local hits at food, people etc. They're daredevil Dicks all right and slash at anything or any body.' Annie mentions, too, three subalterns on board, each with a wooden leg: 'They are not looking forward to reconstruction [surgery] when they get home. They feel their humiliations very keenly.'

Thursday 20 November 1919

Up first – a very rough sea which had some victims again … The troops are getting very indignant about their food: it is getting worse and worse. They have their case well worked up and intend to make a big fuss when they get home. After lunch Dad and I found office and sent a wireless message to the boys … After tea went up to boat deck with Roger and watched the ship dipping and rising on the waves. Then sat on deck until dressing time. After dinner there was a dance on deck … The boat was swaying a lot. Wrote a letter for magazine but don't expect to get it in – it's too hot.

Friday 21 November 1919

Wid and I and Mrs Salmond went down the hold to look at our boxes. It's a gruesome place and the boxes are getting mouldy on the outsides … The editor of the magazine did think my letter too hot. He says they must keep it just a pleasant souvenir of the voyage … After dinner the 1sts had a gramophone at our end of deck and the 2nds had the piano going, and each class tried to dance but it was rather a fiasco and the gramophone was pretty dead and the opposition music was not exactly helpful – one end playing a waltz and the other a fox trot. The whole thing was a huge blunder. The barriers should always be down for a dance.

Saturday 22 November 1919

After dinner there was a social and dance on deck. A boy named Mahoney sat and talked to me for a while. He is the last of the four sons and is 80% disabled.[2]

Sunday 23 November 1919

At dinner tonight … that horrid man Gore turned on free drinks at the bar, and it was poor Long Bob's [Annie's Scottish friend's] undoing. He was so ashamed about his fall from grace and so honest about it that one couldn't be angry with him but it was very sad to see his nice honest face coarsened and spoilt with the muck. He made everyone laugh because he couldn't get the potato on the spoon when helping himself and he exclaimed, 'Did you ever read about the Elusive Pimpernel? Well, this is the elusive pomme de terre.' After dinner Padre Ross took the evening service; we had hymn singing first. The rest of the evening was the quietest we've had on board. Hardly any of the usual men came around; I think many more than Long Bob slipped.

Monday 24 November 1919

Long Bob turned up for lunch but he is still feeling very sore about his slip. He even confessed it to his mother in his letter he is posting at the Cape but I told him he ought not to worry about it. His nature is perfectly clear and honest. It was very nice to see his nice look again today.

On Monday evening the Ruahine *sails into Cape Town Harbour and anchors there.*

---

2   This was Ernest Andrew Mahoney, the eldest of the four sons of Cornelius and Harriet Isabella Mahoney of Ruatoki and the only one to return to New Zealand. The youngest, Ulic James, was killed at Gallipoli on 8 June 1915 aged 20; the third son, 22-year-old Edmund Lancelot George (known as Lance) died in Egypt on 9 August 1916; and Brian Gerald, who was with the RAF, lost his life in a flying accident in Britain on 3 September 1918. He was 28. Ernest, who joined the British services, was a lieutenant in the Royal Inniskilling Fusiliers and, according to an article headed 'Fighting Families' in the *New Zealand Herald* of 19 November 1918, 'saw much action in France'.

Next morning everyone is up early ready to go ashore. While the Montgomeries are breakfasting Roger's brother Jack, looking 'much older' to Annie's eyes, arrives; the siblings have not seen each other for many years. The next two days are devoted to sightseeing, including the Cecil Rhodes monument ('solid and enduring like his own life's work') and the great man's house: 'The whole place is an atmosphere of good taste and culture carried out with greatest simplicity.' Annie enjoys it all but is 'very disappointed not getting any word from my boys'. By the time she returns to the Ruahine *on the evening of the 27th she is 'almost howling' with tiredness and the ship is 'a desolation of dirt and discomfort', the cabin 'like a furnace'. After they leave South Africa the weather is 'fearfully rough', with 'deckchairs and occupants flying across the deck, and suitcases and boxes doing ditto in cabin'. Annie feels 'very small and alone tossing about in this tempestuous sea. I would love to know where my boys are.'*

Sunday 30 November 1919

There was no church service this morning although the sea is a wee bit calmer but most of the people are still prostrate and I think the padre is ill too ... The CO's cabin was flooded and a lot of the 2nd class people were flooded out – also the military kitchen ... I read the sergeants' list of complaints and demands [about food, accommodation and mess arrangements] this morning. It is very plain and earnest and I hope they win ...[3] In course of conversation today with Captain Berridge and Mr Peacock they tell me that the NZ officers are not having a fair deal with gratuities or pensions, that the Tommy officers get better than they do.

By early December the sea is much calmer, and the temperatures much lower, but Annie is incensed, on the 5th, to learn that 'the troops are very disgusted over Miss Fitzherbert and Miss Batchelor dancing together last night with fur coats on and smoking cigarettes all the time. They are not much credit to little NZ anyhow.' During the rest of the voyage Annie continues to be very particular about the company she, and her daughters, keep: 'Out on deck Sergeant Sheiran came back to talk to us and plumped himself down again.[4] He is much too pushing and has a very bad style. He must get over these ideas of familiarity.' Then he annoys Annie 'fearfully by trying to bounce us into letting Al dance after church and my back stiffened completely'.

The troops have become increasingly indignant at the food they are served on

[3] In the words of the *Auckland Star* on 29 December, the complaints, about accommodation and food, were 'set out in detail in a report by the committee set up by the men on the transport'. This was given to the Auckland Returned Soldiers' Association, which would forward it to Wellington with a report. The committee felt there were 'good grounds for a legal action ... Several of the sergeants were interviewed on landing here, and they were bitter in their complaints of the treatment received.' Cabinet's solution, reported at the end of January, was to grant a rebate of £4 per man to those who travelled by the *Ruahine*, 'the amount being the difference between second, and third-class messing'.

[4] This was Australian-born Warrant Officer Alfred Francis Sheeran, a schoolteacher from the Waikato, who had left New Zealand with the Auckland Mounted Rifles in 1916.

the ship, and 'mean to ventilate their grievances when they get home'. Annie also finds reason to complain. As they near Tasmania she writes: 'The last couple of days we have been without fresh fruit and also without eggs, and at dinner tonight the chicken was prehistoric judging by the toughness.' Hobart is the Ruahine's last port of call before she sails for New Zealand.

Wednesday 24 December 1919

Dad called me at 4 o/c this morning to see North Cape but I couldn't work up enough energy to get up, but after bath, dressed early and went up for a peep at coast line of God's own country. There were some sweet hills popping out of the sea and in the dim haze some higher ones behind. The loveliest and loneliest Island of the Empire.[5] After breakfast we all went on deck and gazed and talked … Later on went down to cabin and worried through some more packing and when I finished I had a howl to think I was back and no Gran and Archie there. Roger came down to tell me Cape Brett was in sight and I went up to see it and left my library books in the saloon. Took Thursie for a walk …[6] After dinner the whole ship was on deck watching the lights of Auckland, with Rangitoto guarding them. At first the lights looked like a diamond coronet and as we drew nearer they spread out in long lines. Our pilot came on board and we were soon at anchor with the town quite close yet we couldn't get there … Little Auntie is in Auckland waiting for us and we are all too excited to do anything but stand and gaze at the lights and the ferry boats, which are very pretty passing across the harbour. Several … gave us a hearty cheer.

Thursday 25 December 1919 Landed at Auckland

Up early and busy until breakfast, tipped all the stewards etc £5–10. After breakfast had to go into aft lounge about passports. The man made a fuss about my not having one, but when Dad and Wid went along it was all settled up … We didn't get to the wharf until 9.30. All the waiting crowd was held back by policemen, I thought I could see Fred and Jen but I was wrong. Al was the first to discover Auntie Jen and I ran down the gangway and got to her. She had been waiting on wharf since 5 o/c this morning, all by herself. It was heavenly to see her after all these years.

As the Auckland Star *reported on the 27th, 'a large gathering of the public and*

---

5 Annie is clearly thinking of Rudyard Kipling's much quoted 1891 description of Auckland as 'last, loneliest, loveliest, exquisite apart'.

6 Thursie was Thursday, a tortoise acquired en route.

next-of-kin collected on the wharf, and as the trooper came slowly alongside, raised hearty cheers for the returning boys'. Music was provided by the 3rd Auckland Regimental Band and there was a 'goodly display of bunting' on the wharf sheds. According to the reporter, 'with the brilliant sunshine of a typical Auckland summer's day pouring down the sight was one both stirring and in keeping with the spirit of the time'.

Eventually, after farewells to fellow passengers and making their way safely through customs (with the tortoise), the Montgomeries have Christmas dinner with friends in Auckland, before getting a taxi to the station, 'in time to see the soldiers' train go out', and catch the 4 p.m. train to Frankton, where Jen's husband Fred meets them with the car.

The car was very sick for most of the journey, and we had numerous stoppages – Fred battled away with it and at last got it going all right and we reached Turipahou about midnight after an exciting and most tiring day. An unforgettable Christmas.

EPILOGUE

Oswald and Seton sailed home to New Zealand on the *Bremen*, which left Plymouth on 7 December 1919 and reached Wellington, after stopping in Hobart, on 28 January 1920. On board were more than 1000 people, including 600 returning troops and 137 children. Among those travelling with the Montgomerie boys were former Premier Richard Seddon's widow, Louisa, and one of her six daughters, and Mother Mary Joseph Aubert, of Wellington's Home of Compassion, who had worked with Maori on the Wanganui River for many years. After the *Bremen* arrived at her next port of call, Sydney, on 2 February, it was discovered that five crew members were suffering from influenza and the ship was quarantined.

Oswald and Seton both worked on the family farm but received no remuneration for the first two years as the finances were not in good shape. In the early days there was a war on wild pigs, which were numerous owing to the 3000 acres (1250 ha) of native bush behind the farm. In the 1930s some of the first electric fencing was tried to keep them out.

In 1922 Seton stood for Parliament as a late candidate for the Liberals in the Rangitikei electorate. His neighbour, W.S. (Bill) Glenn (see p. 38), stood for Reform, the party in power under Bill Massey. On election day, 7 December, Seton came last, but it was noted that he made a plucky effort. The Liberals and Labour made significant gains, greatly reducing Reform's majority. This was not the family's only foray into politics: in 1943 Os, who was a staunch member of the National Party, stood as candidate for the Waimarino electorate, but was unsuccessful.

Roger died, aged 71, on 26 October 1936, while working on the farm. Seton married Violet Rait in 1938 and the couple had two daughters, Susanna and Egidia. Two years later Os married Beryl Clark from Melbourne, a younger sister of Eirtle Charles Clark, with whom he had served in the RFC. They had four children, Beverley, John, Roger and Helen.

Both Seton and Os joined the local Home Guard at the start of the

Second World War. In October 1942 Seton left his young family and was posted to RNZAF No. 3 Squadron at Lauthala Bay in Fiji, and then on to Guadalcanal. He returned to New Zealand in October 1943 and later went into the RNZAF Reserve.

Seton and Os farmed Taukoro together until 1952, when the Montgomerie Bros partnership was dissolved and the property was split. Both farms were later sold.

Annie and Winifred, who never married, retired to Wanganui after the Second World War. Annie lived to be 91; she died on 15 August 1958. Os died in 1965 and Seton in August 1969, while on holiday in Scotland; he is buried at Fort William. Winifred, who became the expert on the family's history, died in 1970. Alex, who married Waverley farmer David Rayney Jackson, died in 1986.

INDEX

Roman numbers refer to pages of illustrations.

Addenbrooke, Hubert 39
Addenbrooke, Jack 37
Addenbrooke, Lionel (Leo) 34, 39, 83
air raids 49, 85, 89, 106, 109–10, 113–19, 128, 140, 150, 162, 166; and Montgomeries 30–31, 34–38, 40–42, 50, 85, 91–93, 98–101, 103, 109, 113–14, 132, 146–47, 151; by Zeppelins 27, 30–31, 34–38, 40–42, 49–50, 119, 162
Albert Hall 230
aliens 53, 60, 73, 100–02, 124, 147
Allport, Captain J.M. 152
American troops 163, 166, 171, 175, 180, 210–11; *see also* United States
American volunteers 74–75, 161
Anderson, Hugh v, 38, 43, 109, 124, 144, 159, 161, 175
Anzac Buffet 193–94, 196
Armistice Day xxix, 191–93
Armstrong Whitworth aircraft xxi, 115–18, 123, 126
Artists' Rifles 23, 29, 46
Asquith, Herbert 51–52, 201
Aubert, Mother Mary Joseph 245
Auckland, return via 242–43

Auckland Weekly News 38, 138, 181
Australian servicemen 62, 134, 135, 149, 193, 211–12, 215–16
Australians in war 81, 125, 139, 143, 158, 167; referendum on conscription 143
Austria-Hungary 190

Balfour, Arthur 51, 88
Ballarat 81
Bank of New Zealand 22, 31, 51, 227
Barford, Keith Purnell 159
Barron, Ernest and Mrs 10, 48, 109, 114, 120–21, 127, 136, 154, 157, 175, 178, 206
Barton, Gerry xvii, 23, 179, 182, 213
Batt, Jill Crossley 202–03
Battle Abbey 82–83
Belton Park Hospital xxx, 186, 190, 196, 217–20
Bernacchi family 35, 44, 55, 57, 62
Berridge, Captain 241
Bettie, Aunt *see* Montgomerie, Bettie
Bexhill 82–83
Binnie, Mrs (pilot's mother) 135, 139–40, 154

247

Bluett, C. 144
Boucicault, Dion 113
Brander, Mr (at NZ Loan and Mercantile Co.) 160, 175
Bremen 245
British Australian (newspaper) 216, 219
Broadbent, Captain Sydney 152
Brow, Major 238
Bulgaria 181–82
Butler, Lance-Corporal Ernest 119–20
Butler, Lex 56, 113, 119

Cadorna, General Luigi 122
Cambrai, Battle of 129, 141
Cambridge 50, 54, 62, 71
Canadians 57, 104, 120, 131, 142, 152, 158, 209, 210–12
Canterbury Mounted Rifles 170
Cape Town 238, 240–41
Carson, Sir Edward 143–44
Cecil, Lord Hugh 125
censorship 124–25, 147, 197
Chalfont Park Convalescent Hospital 165–66
Chaytor, Major Lawrence 196
Christian Science lecture 196
Christmas Days 56–57, 135, 200
Chu Chin Chow xvi, 56
cinemas *see* films and cinemas
Ciro's YMCA 85, 95
Clark, Beryl 245
Clark, Eirtle Charles 245
Clemenceau, Georges 197
Clere, Miss 14–15, 31, 34, 40
Collier, Arthur 88

Collins, Second Lieutenant R.S. 152
colonials 75–76, 87–88, 131, 154–55, 174, 193, 194, 195, 209, 210–12, 215, 216; as combatants 158, 159, 166, 220, 233
Compton, Fay 71
conscientious objectors 87, 125–26, 164, 231
conscription 46–47, 148, 231; in Australia 143
Cooper, Gladys 84
Cowlishaw, Miss 146, 209, 211, 219–20, 223, 233
Curtis, Captain Leslie 37

Dacre Fox, Nora 34
dancing 69, 85, 149, 157, 203, 205, 209–10, 221
Dartmoor xix, 94–95, 218, 224; *see also* Pew Tor
Devon 94–95, 104–05, 107–08, 169, 176–91, 221–27, 235
Du Maurier, Gerald 85
Duchess of Westminster's Hospital, Le Touquet 164

Earle, Bob 198
Eastbourne 96, 101–02
Empire: relationships within 9, 53, 83, 87–88, 158, 160, 169, 228; Victory Parade of Dominion Troops 216
Empson, Mrs 22, 24, 61
English soldiers 50, 158, 166, 174, 179, 195

Index

Fergusson, Jack 113, 127, 158, 160, 209
Fergusson, Robert Arthur (Fergie) v, 14–15, 23, 38, 58, 66–67, 71–72; posted to France and killed 70, 72, 80–81, 113, 120, 160
Fergusson, Sir Charles 209
Fergusson, Sir James 15
Fernie, Walter 198
Fifeshire 218
films and cinemas xv, 65, 82, 198, 204–05, 212
finances 59, 70–71, 93, 98, 106, 119–20, 136, 160, 167, 191, 196–97, 199, 212, 221, 233
Fisher, Lord 75
FitzHerbert, Lieutenant-Colonel Norman viii, 22–23, 26, 29, 39, 52, 61, 67, 90, 93, 131
Foch, General Ferdinand 122, 182, 197, 207
food 67, 92, 125, 175, 186, 197; *see also* rationing
Fyffe, Second Lieutenant Colin 175–76, 194, 197, 211

Gaiety Theatre 71, 234
Gallipoli 72
Gaza, Second Battle of 83
George V 192, 199, 200, 208, 214
German spies 35–36
German Spring Offensive and retreat (1918) 150–51, 156, 161, 163, 169, 182, 184–85
Glasgow, Mrs 146
Glenn, Lieutenant William 38
Glenn, Mrs 198

Globe Theatre 69
Greenstreet, Captain H.E. 13–15, 19–20, 236
Groves, Dr 102, 118, 123, 197, 220–21

Haig, Sir Douglas 111, 124, 163, 201, 214
Halifax, Nova Scotia 18–19
Hamlet 81
Hammond, Lieutenant A.W. 152, 168
Harris, Rita 124–25, 145–46, 154, 162, 168, 191–98
Harrison, Jack 37
Hawker, Harry 219–20
Heney, Lieutenant John 138, 139, 152
Hill, Les xvii, 91
Hiroti (perhaps Turu or Jack) 38
Homersham, Lieutenant Alfred 152
Homersham, Private Flacton 125
Hornchurch (New Zealand Convalescent Hospital) xxiii, 127, 210
Howie, Harold ('James') 61, 66
Hyde Park v, xxvii, xxviii, 32, 34, 40, 57

Ibbotson, Miss (landlady) 44–45, 56, 79, 154, 189
influenza pandemic 184
Innes, Dr 30, 233, 236–37
Innes, Mrs 40–41, 236–37
insurance policies vii, 93, 167
Irving, Henry xiv, 71, 81
Italy 120, 123–24

249

Jackson, David xxxi
Jackson, David Rayney 246
Jackson, Priscilla xxxi
Jamieson, W.G. 138
Janet/Jen, Auntie *see* Pemberton, Janet/Jen
Jenkinson, Lieutenant R.A. 155
Jerusalem 190
Jutland, Battle of 15–16, 199, 207

Kaiser's abdication 191
Kew Gardens 81, 83–84
Kitchener, Lord 72
Knowledge for War (officers' handbook) x

Lansdowne, Lord 131–32
Lethbridge, Gunner Harry Bruce 183
Lethbridge, Lance Corporal George 70, 119, 122
Lipton's tearooms 27–28, 30, 35–40, 42–43
Lloyd George, David 50–51, 125, 158, 231
lodgings in London 22, 31, 33, 71; move to 40 Inverness Terrace 41, 44, 46; *see also* Ibbotson, Miss (landlady)
London: arrival in 22; impressions of 23–24, 36–37, 46, 95, 193, 221; sightseeing in 32, 140–41
London Pride 85
Lord Mayor's Shows 47, 122, 191

Mackenzie, Sir Thomas xviii
MacNab, Captain 34, 38
Mahoney, Ernest Andrew 240

Mahutonga Club 127, 210
Maid of the Mountains 77
Marne, Second Battle of the 169
Mary, Queen 65, 192, 200, 208
Mason, Archibald 162, 228–29
Mason, Gran (Annie's mother) 98, 126, 137, 140, 142, 153, 162
Mason, Jessie 79, 126, 142, 152–53
Mason, Ruth 60
Mason, Sergeant Robert (Roy/Robin) 35–36, 126–27, 142, 152–53
Mason, Trooper Richard (Dick) 26, 29–30, 33–35, 51, 60
Mason family 9–10, 33
Massey, Christina 220
Massey, Miss 220–21
Massey, William 40, 67, 174, 175–76, 203, 220
Matthews family 99, 128, 135, 146, 149, 151, 154
McLachlan (Seton's observer) 157–58, 163–64, 195
McLeod, Cyril iv, 25, 88, 107–08, 118, 166, 191, 197, 204–05, 210
McLeod, Second Lieutenant Alan 142n4, 159
McNab, Moira 75
medals xiii
Medina 81
Melba, Dame Nellie 230
Meldrum, Alexander (Alick) 38
Meldrum, Nora 34, 37
Mercantile *see* New Zealand Loan and Mercantile Ltd
Mile End Military Hospital 160

Index

Mills, Mr (BNZ, London) 22, 41, 216, 221, 227

Milner, Frank 34, 37

Mons, Battle of 55–56, 195

Montgomerie, Alexandra (Al) ii, 13, 31, 79, 223, 236–37; illnesses 56, 63–64, 69, 72, 132–34, 184–85, 189, 203; in New Zealand xxxi, 10, 246; at school in England 36, 39, 55, 82, 89, 101, 129, 169, 180, 184, 190

Montgomerie, Annie i, v, xix, xxvii–xxviii; faith in God 86, 88, 106, 133–34, 136, 157, 178; family history 9–10; hatred of war 31, 42, 57, 65, 70, 72, 74, 80, 86, 91, 156–57; illnesses 76–77, 195, 220; letters to newspapers 138–39, 216, 219, 229, 231, 239–40; in New Zealand xxxi–xxxii, 9–10, 246; support of sons in England 9, 13, 86, 130; sympathy with strikers 229–32; talismans for and of sons xvii, xix, 79–80; views on British leaders' 'blundering' 42, 70, 72, 76, 80; views on English 'muddling' 53, 58, 60, 73, 75, 87–88, 92, 118, 126, 148, 169–70, 173, 234; views on English people 46, 50, 57, 72, 75, 80–81, 83, 86, 92, 95, 102–03, 105, 122, 140, 199–200, 213, 215; views on suffragettes and women's role 40, 66–67, 69, 232

Montgomerie, Bettie 24, 30, 45, 126, 158

Montgomerie, Beverley 245

Montgomerie, Egidia 245

Montgomerie, Hastings 76

Montgomerie, Helen 245

Montgomerie, Jack 68, 107, 241

Montgomerie, Jim 123, 140–41, 144

Montgomerie, John (grandson) 245

Montgomerie, Oswald (Os) 13; appendectomy 25–28, 30–32; enlistment 34, 37–39, 44, 49, 51, 53–55, 60; ill-health in 1917: 62, 85–86, 89, 96, 98, 104, 106, 108, 112, 115, 117–18, 121–27, 141; malarial attack in 1919: 220–22; military memorabilia x–xiii, xx; in New Zealand xxxi–xxxii, 10, 245–46; officer training ii, xiii, 57, 67, 70, 71, 78–79; posting to Middle East ix, xxviii, 167–68, 170–71, 173, 176–77, 179–83, 190, 195, 197, 199–200, 202–03; repatriation 222, 225–26, 228, 233–34, 245; in RFC xi, 80, 83, 137, 147, 149; service on return from Middle East 204–07, 213, 219; in uniform iv, v, xxi, xxiii, xxvii–xxviii

Montgomerie, Roger 13, 96–97, 133, 177–78, 180, 181, 212–13, 222–25, 228; in army iii, 37–38, 42–43, 50, 54, 57–61; family history 9–10;

251

horse fair visit 69; letter to Seton xxiv–xxv, 93; letters to Annie 89, 91, 93, 119–20, 196–97, 207, 216–19; in New Zealand xxxi–xxxii, 9–10, 245; seeks wartime work 68, 71–72; timber work xiv, 72–73, 76–77, 79, 86, 93–97, 111, 126–27, 167, 176, 182, 185, 189, 205, 207, 213, 215, 217; view of peace terms 218

Montgomerie, Roger (grandson) 245

Montgomerie, Seton 13, 213, 225, 234–35; active service in France 129–43, 145–46, 152–65; appendectomy xxx, 217–24; enlistment 23–26, 28; enlistment in RFC 45, 47–48, 86, 90, 96–97; as flying instructor 169–85; hospitalised with flu (Oct 1918) 185–90, 194, 198; hospitalised with mumps in France (Jan–Feb 1918) 147–52; in New Zealand xxxi, 9–10, 245–46; in Notts and Derby Regiment 84–93; officer training ii, iii, 29–34, 39–42, 44–48, 50–54, 58, 60, 62–66, 68–69, 73–74, 77–78, 82, 99, 101, 104; repatriation 233, 245; RFC training 104–28; in Second World War 245–46; service after Armistice 204–08, 211–12; in uniform iv, xiii, xxi, xxvii–xxviii; wounded in action (April 1918) xvii–xviii, 163–67

Montgomerie, Willie (Archibald William) 23–24, 49–52, 170, 196

Montgomerie, Winifred (Wid) ii, v, xvi, xxvi–xxvii, 49, 221–22; befriends young servicemen xvi, 26, 85–86, 89, 91, 119; illness, air raid nerves and appendicitis 72–73, 99–102, 109, 125, 151, 181–88, 197; insurance policy vii; in New Zealand xxxi–xxxii, 10, 246; war support work xxiii, 24, 34, 38, 61–62, 66–67, 92, 102, 118, 130–31, 134, 144, 147, 162, 210

Moortown House xx, 104

More, Colonel 92–93

Morgan, Charles viii

Narborough 114–15, 120

New Zealand Convalescent Hospital *see* Hornchurch

New Zealand High Commission xviii, 22, 34, 37, 48–49, 51, 121, 210, 227, 231–32

New Zealand identity and pride 23–24, 46, 84, 102, 107

New Zealand Loan and Mercantile Ltd 70, 160

New Zealand Ordnance (in London) 204

New Zealand Record Office viii, 22–23, 26, 36–38, 42–43, 123, 131; Wid working at 66–67, 102, 118, 210

New Zealand Shipping Co. 236

Index

New Zealand Soldiers' Club 31, 38, 69, 110, 119
New Zealand trade with Britain 160, 216, 221, 238
New Zealand troops 59, 80–81, 116, 155, 158, 160, 179, 202–03; 30th Reinforcements 148; after Armistice 198, 202, 209, 212, 215; on Armistice Day 192; NZ Field Artillery 198; NZ Machine Gun Corps 196; on voyage home 234–39, 241–43
New Zealand War Contingent Association 22, 24, 61, 67
New Zealander, The vi, 157
Norfolk House 144–45, 202
Northcliffe, Lord 124
Notts and Derby Regiment (Sherwood Foresters) xix, 84–93, 107

Oatlands Park 66
Otaki 74
Oxford 70–71

Palestine 126, 176, 181
Panama Canal 16–17
Pankhurst, Emmeline 40
parcels to New Zealand 44–45, 98
Parker, Tommie 141
Parkes, Lieutenant-Colonel William Henry 26
Parliament: Houses of 140; Opening of 64–65
Parr, Captain 60–61
Passchendaele 59, 98

Payling, Gunner Alan vii, 85–86, 89, 122–23
Peace Conference 203; *see also* Treaty of Versailles
Peg o' My Heart 69
Pemberton, Janet/Jen 26, 39, 44, 77, 98, 127, 153, 154, 209, 242–43
Pettigrew, Gordon 26, 39, 114, 126
Pew Tor, Dartmoor xix, 95, 223, 225–26
photographic exhibitions 50, 57, 156, 167, 214
Pilkington, Colonel 238
Plant, Mrs 193–94, 196
Poland 207
Portuguese troops 161
Potts, Leslie viii
Prince of Wales Hospital 89
prostitutes 69, 76, 138

Queen Alexandra's Hospital 141

Rait, Violet 245
rationing 150, 154, 156, 169, 217
Record Office *see* New Zealand Record Office
Reddicliffe, Mrs and family xx, 104, 107–08, 169, 180–81, 185, 223, 224, 226–27
Remuera, RMS xxxi, 13–21, 39, 104
repatriation 196–97, 207–08, 210, 213–15, 217, 219, 222, 225–29, 231–35; return voyage 236–43
Richtofen, Manfred von 163

253

Robertson, Sir William 150
Robey, George 157
Romania 51, 55–56
Rose, Major 68
Rotorua 74–75, 81
Royal Academy of Arts 83
Royal Air Force xii
Royal Flying Corps (RFC) 29, 33, 98; No. 2 Squadron (of RAF from April 1918) 130, 134, 152, 159, 166, 174, 177, 202, 206
Ruahine 233–43
rugby 58, 211–12, 214
Russia 59, 73, 110, 112, 121, 149, 169, 213

Salt, Joe 121, 136, 154
Scotland 215; family origins 9; visits to 126, 197, 202–03, 217, 228
Seddon, Louisa 245
Seton, Guy iv, 25, 35
shearing day in Devon 224
Sheeran, Warrant Officer Alfred 241
shopping 24, 29, 32, 39–45, 52, 59, 61, 65, 71, 89, 133, 204, 228–29; London shops 'a wonderland' and 'fascinating' 22–23; for NZ Christmas gifts 98, 100; pendants for sons 79–80; at Peter Robinsons 23, 25–26, 28, 34, 40, 43, 54–56
Sling Camp 25
Sloss, Second Lieutenant James 175

Somme, Battle of 21
South African servicemen 143, 212
Spence, Lieutenant Lyell xxii, 161, 165–66, 170
St Dunstan's Hostel for Blinded Soldiers 70
St Leonards-on-Sea 27, 39, 82
Stephens, Ina 14, 36–38, 41, 103–04, 215
Stewart, David 42
Stewart, Malcolm 52, 198
strikes and labour unrest 174, 194, 199, 205–06, 229–32
Stuart, Lieutenant (South African) 107–08
submarines 21, 39, 41, 64, 69, 74, 125, 199; fear on voyage to England 16, 19–20
Sunderland 88–89

Taukoro xxxi, 10, 127–28, 157, 196, 217, 245–46; *see also* Barron, Ernest; Watt, Jim
Taukoros (family in England) 56–58, 157
Tavistock xx, 94, 128, 177, 221, 224; Goose Fair 183
Temple Church 103
Tenerife 237–38
Tennent, William Cowper 198
theatres and concert halls xiv–xvi, 60, 84, 108, 115, 157, 191, 212, 233–34; amid air raids 113–14; Annie's favourites xiv, 69, 71–72, 81, 85, 112, 165; younger generation's visits 56, 71–72, 77, 79, 85, 119, 123, 167–68, 175–76

Thomassett, Mrs 35–37, 39, 111, 133
Thorne, William 67
Thorpe, Freddie 205
Tilley, John (Jack) vii, 28, 88–91, 96, 107–08, 115, 123, 234
Tilley, Mrs 55–57, 85, 95, 135
Timber Supplies Department (of War Office) xiv, 72
Torquay 234–35
Tower of London 32, 82, 84, 120
Trafalgar Square 47, 66–67
Treaty of Versailles 203, 224
Tripe, Alexander (Allie) 30–31, 41, 120, 123, 147
Trollope, Captain John Lightfoot 210
Turkey 129, 189

United States 59, 64–65, 74, 77, 131–32, 142, 149, 174; *see also* American troops

Vanbrugh, Irene 113
Vanity Fair 79
Victory Ball 196
victory parades 211, 216

Waitaki Boys' High School 9, 34
Waitakian 102, 151

War Office 37–38, 48, 58, 72, 76, 92–93, 212
Wardrope, Lieutenant W.H. xxii, 155
Watson, Major 38, 198
Watson, Mrs 29, 32, 39, 125
Watt, Jim 88, 121, 125, 127, 160
Watts, Cecil 153, 159, 165
Watts, Laurie 148, 151, 155
Watts, Mrs 74, 84, 134, 153, 154, 164, 165
weather 24, 34, 48, 50, 61, 64, 66–67, 93, 125, 127, 134, 208, 228, 234; in Devon 94, 96, 127, 213
Whiteman, Colonel 80
Whiteman, Mrs 23, 26, 66, 91
Williams, Colonel 238
Wilson, Sir Henry 122, 150, 214
Wilson, Woodrow 74, 200, 231
Women's Social and Political Union (WSPU) 36–37
Woodward, Sister Katherine 66
Wray, Cecil 22, 218
Wyborn, W.S. (pilot) xxii

Ypres, Third Battle of 98, 107

Zeppelin raids *see under* air raids